SAIL AND DELIVER!

SAIL AND DELIVER!

RONALD PREEDY

FOREWORD BY SIR ALEC ROSE

PARTRIDGE PRESS

LONDON · NEW YORK · TORONTO · SYDNEY · AUCKLAND

TRANSWORLD PUBLISHERS LTD
61–63 Uxbridge Road, London w5 5sa

TRANSWORLD PUBLISHERS (AUSTRALIA) PTY LTD
15–23 Helles Avenue, Moorebank NSW 2170

TRANSWORLD PUBLISHERS (NZ) LTD
Cnr Moselle and Waipareira Aves,
Henderson, Auckland

Published 1989 by Partridge Press
a division of Transworld Publishers Ltd
Copyright © Ronald Preedy 1989
Illustrations © Ronald Preedy 1989

British Library Cataloguing in Publication Data

Preedy, Ronald
Sail and deliver!
1. Voyages by yachts – Biographies
I. Title
910.4'5'0924

ISBN 1-85225-093-3

Printed in Great Britain by
Mackays of Chatham Plc, Chatham, Kent
Photoset by Rowland Phototypesetting Ltd
Bury St Edmunds, Suffolk

*To my wife Mary
with all my love.*

CONTENTS

Foreword by Sir Alec Rose KB   ix

                                                    Boat

1   Introduction   3
2   Falmouth to Corunna, Spain   Prout 37   17
                                            Catamaran
3   Florida to Norfolk, Virginia, to   Southerly 115   43
    the UK
4   Newton Ferrers to Troon, Scotland   Sweden 36   55
5   Barbados to Florida   45-ft Ketch   69
                                            'Windward'
6   Les Sables d'Olonne to Vilamoura   45-ft Ferro–   85
                                            Cement Ketch
7   Plymouth to Poole (with Memories)   Super Seal 26   99
                                            'Miss Fidget'
8   Clyde to Plymouth   Sadler 26   121
9   Martinique to Charleston, South   Sadler 26   133
    Carolina
10 Lymington to Gibraltar   Nicholson 55   143
11 Falmouth to Poole (with Memories)   Sadler 26   161
12 Falmouth to Cork   Cobra 28   171
13 Newhaven to Gibraltar   Sweden 36   183
14 Palm Beach to Norfolk, Virginia   Super Seal 26   197
                                            'Miss Fidget'
15 Vilamoura to Falmouth   Biscay 36   211
16 Falmouth to River Crouch   1924 24-ft Gaff   225
                                            Ketch
17 Conclusion   239

FOREWORD

I am more than happy to introduce and recommend Ronald Preedy's *Sail and Deliver!* to all lovers of small boat sailing and to everyone who simply enjoys a good read.

Ronald Preedy is a professional yacht delivery skipper and I have often admired the skill and adaptability required to sail a boat one has just viewed from the quayside, stepped aboard for the first time and set off in with gear and equipment of perhaps suspect quality.

In *Sail and Deliver!* Ronald Preedy describes a whole variety of his adventures – for make no mistake, whether sailing the different yachts or dealing with sometimes difficult owners, each trip is an adventure in itself. Indeed, it speaks well for Ronald Preedy's diplomacy that he invariably completes the delivery on good terms with the owner.

Pick the book up and start reading – you will soon find yourself hooked and will want to return to it time and time again.

Sir Alec Rose KB

SAIL AND DELIVER!

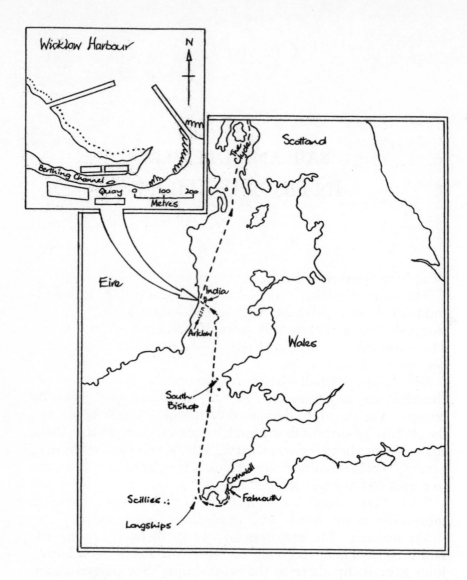

Wicklow Harbour – Halfway Up The Irish Sea

Chapter One

INTRODUCTION

'Will it be yourself with the engine trouble?'

The woman's voice came from directly above. It was well-modulated and pleasant, the accent unmistakably Irish. I stopped drying the cockpit seats of *Serenity* and looked up. There, on the edge of the granite quayside, stood a woman in her thirties, hands on hips.

She was quite small – barely five feet tall, I guessed – and her shapeless suit of greasy blue overalls made her look decidedly dumpy. Yet the close definition of her high cheek bones and the absence of surplus flesh beneath her chin caused me to think again. On her head she was wearing a dirty, woollen bobby-hat, beneath which strands of short black hair escaped here and there to curl about her ears and forehead.

'Yes, that's right,' I replied at last, the cloth hanging motionless in my hand. 'Fuel blockage.'

She nodded. 'Me man sent me down to have a look,' she said briskly. Then, receiving no reply, she added 'You know, John Moran, up there in the workshops.' She paused again. 'Sure and it was you that came up to see him a little while back, was it not?'

'Oh, er . . . yes, that's it, that was me all right,' I stammered, emerging at last from my trance. 'Sorry, I wasn't quite with you.'

'Could you grab hold of this?' she asked, picking up a black plastic bucket from the quayside.

I moved quickly along the side deck towards the decrepit-

3

looking ladder on the wall, my brain still trying to catch up with events. Come on, I told myself, pull yourself together. And try sitting hard on your prejudice while you're at it. Why shouldn't a woman be able to fix marine diesel engines? Reaching the bottom of the ladder, I stretched upwards for the bucket. It was heavy with tools and a torch and one or two small cardboard cartons were thrown in on top. Placing it on the cabin roof behind me, I turned back to hold the boat steady against the wall as the young woman descended the iron rungs with easy agility. Landing on the deck beside me, she wiped her right hand briefly on her overalls and then held it out to me with a grin.

'Kathleen Dunne,' she announced, her voice clear and firm.

I could see her face more clearly now. Her ruddy complexion spoke plainly of habitual exposure to sun and wind. It contrasted sharply with large, strikingly beautiful brown eyes, a tiny rosebud mouth and a snub nose. There was a smear of oil on her left cheek.

'Ron Preedy,' I replied, shaking her hand. 'Welcome aboard.'

'And welcome to Wicklow,' she rejoined with a laugh. 'John said you told him there wasn't much room around the engine. Is that the truth?'

'I'm afraid it is,' I replied, savouring as I did so the musical lilt in her voice. I made myself concentrate. 'I think it may be the fuel-lifting pump that's causing the trouble. That's down on the port side, right towards the back of the engine. The snag is that there's only about nine inches of clearance between the engine and the side bulkhead, and I simply can't get at it. Nor is there any way through the bulkhead from the cockpit locker. As it is, I can just about operate the priming lever on the pump, but as for taking it apart – well, it's hopeless.' I warmed to my theme. 'Some day I'm going to bring a yacht designer along as crew on one of these deliveries. One or two of them seem to think that as long as there's enough room for the engine itself, that's all that matters. Not a thought for any real working space around it.' I stopped, suddenly aware that I was sounding like a public meeting. 'Sorry,' I mumbled, a little embarrassed, 'it's a bit of a sore point with me.'

'Well now, isn't that why I'm here,' she replied brightly. 'Anyhow, why don't we go below and have a look?'

I felt suddenly like a little boy being soothed by his mother. Before I knew what was happening, she had picked up the bucket and was brushing past me.

'You should hear himself carry on about these small engine compartments,' she called back over her shoulder as she started down the companionway steps. 'Sure and isn't the air blue sometimes.'

I could imagine. The man I had spoken to earlier that afternoon had been well over six feet tall and built in proportion. If I found it difficult to get round some of these engines, he must have found it downright impossible.

'So he gets me to do it,' continued Kathleen dryly. 'Like I tell him, in the old days they used to send little boys up chimneys; now he's got me wriggling under engines. Honest to God, I sometimes think it's the only reason he keeps me around.'

I laughed, liking her more with every minute. She had already removed the companionway steps, leaving me temporarily stranded in the cockpit. Now she was unclipping the fasteners holding the large engine cover in place.

'Holy Mother of God!' she exclaimed, as she dragged the cover aside to expose the engine. 'I see what you mean. No wonder you couldn't fix it, especially out at sea.' She paused. 'Tell you what, I'll just have a little look for a bit.'

Kathleen was telling me nicely to keep out of the way. Nor was I sorry. For one thing, it was clear from her breezy, no-nonsense manner that she wouldn't hesitate to enlist my help if she needed it. For another, I was tired after more than 48 hours of single-handed sailing.

I had left Falmouth aboard the 26-foot Bermudan sloop *Serenity* soon after dawn on Tuesday, 24 April 1983, bound for the Clyde. Now it was Thursday afternoon. It had all been going too well, I reflected ruefully as I subsided onto the port cockpit seat. A brisk south-westerly had sent me romping through the inside passage between Land's End and the Longships lighthouse early on Tuesday afternoon. There followed an exhilarating 24 hours of broad reaching all the way up to the South Bishop light, just off the south-west corner of Wales. With relatively quiet seas and with the automatic steering system working with smooth efficiency, it had been easy going.

Then, slowly but inexorably, the breeze had died away with the onset of dusk. Well before midnight I had dropped the sails and started the engine.

For some hours after that the engine had chugged away as I concentrated on keeping clear of the shipping in the congested waters between Wales and Eire. Then, at 0400 hours precisely, it had suddenly petered out. I prefer to draw a veil over what followed. Suffice it to say that any serious attempt to sort out the fuel problem – for such it could only be – was wholly frustrated by the absurd confinement of the engine in its compartment. Mercifully, a faint air had come in with the dawn, again from the south-west. As though in response to my silent pleading, it had strengthened and persisted just enough to allow me to slip quietly between the Arklow and India banks during the late morning and so reach Wicklow harbour by early afternoon. I had been glad to get in.

Not that it was much to look at, I decided as I took in my surroundings. The sky had gradually become overcast during the afternoon, suggesting that rain was not far away. This, together with the drab grey warehouses on the opposite side of the berthing channel and the banks of black mud uncovering with the ebbing tide, combined to create a general air of dreariness. Yet had I been less tired, my senses less jaded, I might have noticed other things. I might have wondered at the softness of the light; acknowledged the harmony of muted colours in the harbour wall; felt the profound peace and quiet of the place. Right now, though, such subtleties were beyond me. Instead, I sustained myself with the awareness that this was one more harbour that I now knew at first hand; an important one, too, from a delivery point of view, given its location halfway up the Irish Sea. There was also the satisfying realization that I had finally managed to set foot in the Irish Republic – even if I hadn't meant to. The thought was at once wryly amusing and somehow faintly disturbing. . . .

'Damn it to hell!' swore Kathleen from below. There was a pause. 'Have you got a rag or something, Ron?'

I moved quickly to the hatchway and looked down into the cabin. I could only see the lower half of Kathleen's body. It was flat on the floor, the feet pointing upwards. The rest of her was hidden under the engine. Taking care where I was putting my feet, I scrambled down to tear a length of paper towelling from the roller above the sink. As I knelt down, an oily hand appeared from nowhere to take it from me.

'Thanks.' Another pause. 'Drop of oil in me eye. There, that's better.' I waited. 'Well now,' she announced, 'I think I can reach the pump. I'll have to dismantle it from underneath, but then you can't have everything.'

'Thank goodness for that,' I said, my spirits lifting. I tried to pin-point where the voice was coming from. 'I would have been absolutely stuck without you.'

'Could you pass me the torch?' she requested. 'And you'll find a small adjustable spanner in the bucket. I'll have that too, if I might.'

My eyes were becoming accustomed to the gloom, and I could see her more clearly now. She was actually lying to one side of the engine, her face almost immediately beneath the fuel-lifting pump. For a time she worked busily away, although it was impossible for me to see how she was getting on. Make yourself useful, I thought.

'Cup of tea?'

'Best offer I've had all day. Thanks very much.'

I filled the kettle and set it on the stove. How about this for role reversal, I thought, smiling to myself.

'Are you married?' she asked.

'Yes,' I replied. 'Twenty-three years next month. Yourself?'

'No such luck,' she sighed, leaving me unsure if she was joking or serious. 'Still, I'm working on him.'

In the companionable silence that followed I tried to think ahead a little. Once the pump was dismantled, the bits would have to be washed clean in something. A little ferreting around in the starboard cockpit locker soon disclosed what I had dimly remembered seeing earlier: a lemonade bottle full of paraffin with an old tin can beside it. It looked as if the owner had used it for a similar purpose before. I brought them back into the cabin.

'Did you say you deliver yachts?' she asked, as I poured paraffin into the can.

'That's right. This is the third one this year so far.'

'Been doing it long?'

'Since 1981,' I replied. 'I started soon after leaving the army.'

Whoops, I thought, mentally kicking myself; that wasn't

7

very clever. You really must be tired. Too late, I could see clearly now what had troubled me up in the cockpit about visiting the Irish Republic. Of course. Not that I could bring myself to believe that Kathleen would ever take advantage of knowing that I had served in the British Army. All the same, the remark would have been better left unsaid in this part of the world. Somewhat ashamed of my suspicion, I nevertheless waited to see if she would ask whether I had ever done a tour of duty in Northern Ireland.

'What made you pick yacht delivery?' The question came out just like the others before it.

So much for your suspicious mind, I thought, reflecting sadly on the power of the Northern Ireland tragedy to touch human relationships far beyond its borders. Rightly or wrongly, I resolved to ignore my misgivings. It was too late now anyway.

'Well, I managed to do quite a bit of sailing in the army and thoroughly enjoyed it. It's like they say,' I added flippantly, 'sailors take up mountain-climbing, soldiers take up sailing.' I thought for a moment. 'No, I suppose the real reason was that, for me at least, most civilian occupations lacked the physical challenges that I had become used to. Then again, maybe my wife Mary puts it best: she says I'm just addicted to risk-taking.'

Kathleen had evidently encountered a stubborn bolt, judging by the little gasps of effort she was making. Left alone with my thoughts, they drifted back to my sailing days in the army. It all started when I was selected to command a battery of 29th Commando Regiment, Royal Artillery. Although the regiment was based at the Royal Citadel in Plymouth, I was lucky enough to be given the naval gunfire support battery, permanently detached from the regiment at Poole in Dorset. A gunner throughout my army career, this posting opened up entirely new horizons for me. The battery's operational role was to land small clandestine parties on an enemy coastline in order to direct naval gunfire in support of Royal Marines amphibious operations. It followed that every member of the battery had first to win his green beret by passing the commando course at Lympstone in Devon, and then win his parachute wings by completing eight jumps at RAF Abingdon in Berkshire.

So began three very happy years at Hamworthy on the outskirts of Poole. As a family posting it was ideal. My wife,

8

small son and I enjoyed the luxury of married quarters within 100 yards of a little beach on the edge of Poole harbour. And it was there, in my fleeting moments of spare time, that the sailing bug bit me with a vengeance. Having cut my teeth, like so many thousands of others, on the Bosun dinghy, I managed eventually to consolidate this experience with a concentrated one-week sailing course run within the unit. For this, two Royal Marines sailing cruisers were made available, and it was aboard the smaller of these, a 22-foot Hurley-class sloop called *Normandy Maid* that, following the course, I really started to learn something about sailing. The Services have always rightly prided themselves on their sporting facilities. In this case it was open to any member of the unit to charter the boat for a nominal fee at weekends. Sometimes with the family, sometimes on my own, I made full use of this wonderful opportunity.

I caught the kettle right at the start of its whistle. 'Tea's up,' I announced.

'Now that's what I call perfect timing,' replied Kathleen. 'Could you cop hold of this lot?'

I reached down to take the bits of fuel pump, dropped them into the can of paraffin, and then turned back to help her out. To be honest, it was difficult to know which part of her to get hold of. Discretion suggested that it might be best to grab her ankles. But even as I did so. . .

'No, no, not there, put your hands under me thighs and just lift a little. It'll help keep me bum out of the bilges.'

I'm not sure how much I helped her. I was laughing too much.

Five minutes later, as I examined the contents of the can, I finally discovered what had brought me to Wicklow.

'There we are!' I held up the little pump diaphragm. 'That's the culprit.'

Kathleen was sitting on sheets of newspaper on the other settee, enjoying her cup of tea. 'Split in the diaphragm?' she ventured.

'Yes. It's not very big, but I wouldn't mind betting it's the cause of the trouble. The only question now is – have you got a replacement? As I told John Moran, I'm afraid there are no engine spares on the boat anywhere. I've already searched it from end to end.'

9

'Have a look in that blue carton in the bucket,' she said.

I did – and there it was. For the first time since arriving I felt really able to relax. I knew from previous experience that obtaining a particular make of engine spare could be a real headache in a small place like this. Granted, we still had to bleed the engine, but that should be fairly straightforward. As we finished our tea, Kathleen told me a little about herself. It was enough to confirm my impression that she was actually a qualified engineer in her own right. I was also able to form a mental picture of life in Wicklow that might easily have fitted more than one small harbour community near my home in Cornwall. I was just thinking how needless had been my earlier fears about disclosing my army background, when she spoke again.

'You'll be staying tonight?'

'Yes, I think I'll leave with the first of the light in the morning.'

She nodded. 'You won't mind then if I just say something?' Her voice had become quiet, suddenly serious. 'You know you were telling me about your time in the army. Well . . .,' she paused, 'it's just that if you were thinking of going for a drop of Irish this evening, it might be as well if you didn't mention. . . .'

'It's all right,' I broke in. 'I know what you're going to say.'

'Don't get me wrong,' she added. 'There's no one I can think of in Wicklow who would want to harm you. Perish the thought. But you never really know who's hanging around, if you get my meaning?'

'I do,' I replied, smiling gently at her. 'And thanks very much.'

'Well now,' she said with a smile, her voice brisk and businesslike once more, 'it's flat on me back again, I suppose.' She laughed. 'Sure and isn't that the story of me life.'

It took a few minutes for her to wriggle back under the engine, take the half-assembled pump from me and begin to install it. Then she spoke again.

'So what does Mary think about these yacht-delivery shenanigans, if you don't mind me asking? Doesn't she worry?'

Straight to the solar plexus. 'Well yes, she does,' I admitted. 'To be honest, I think she was hoping for a quiet life once we decided to leave the army and return to Cornwall. But I suppose on balance she would rather have me doing something I enjoyed than. . . .'

'Than being bloody miserable at home doing something you hated,' she supplied. 'Yes, I can see that. She must be quite a lady.' She paused for a moment, then added, 'By the way, I was thinking. Once I've got this on I'd better just check the stern gland while I'm here.' The stern gland is the watertight joint allowing the drive shaft to pass from the engine and gearbox through the bottom of the boat to the propeller outside. 'After all, you'll be in a bit of bother if it suddenly starts leaking, won't you?' 'Well no, it's not as bad as that,' I replied. 'There's an access panel in the floor of the cockpit. I had it off this morning at sea, hoping I could reach the fuel lifting pump from there. I couldn't, of course, but I did have a quick look at the stern gland while I was at it. It seems to be OK.'

It's strange how a particular word or phrase can trigger the memory. In this case it was the talk of a leaking stern gland that did it, carrying me suddenly back to July, 1977. By then, five years after leaving Poole, good fortune had given me command of 29th Commando Regiment, still based at the Royal Citadel in Plymouth. By then too, my simple enjoyment of sailing had developed into a passion. A year earlier I had acquired a second-hand sailing cruiser: a 24-foot Trident class Bermudan sloop called *Ahura*. Gradually the English Channel was becoming familiar territory, while my book shelves were filling with stories of long-distance voyages, especially single-handed ones. Yet fascinating though they were, these accounts served also to demonstrate that I was still only nibbling at the edges of sailing. And thus it would remain, I knew, until I took on something more ambitious.

So it was that, at dawn on the first morning of a two-week summer leave, I set off single-handed in *Ahura* from Millbay dock, bound for Vigo in Spain: a journey of some 550 nautical miles. Even now, six years later, I could feel again the sick apprehension lying like cold pudding in my stomach as I cleared Plymouth breakwater. Nor, surprisingly, did the settled July weather do anything to relieve it; quite the reverse, in fact. For despite all my earlier sailing trips, I had still not encountered a really hard blow at sea. I had always been close enough to land to be able to run for shelter. Did I but know it, what I really needed was a Force 8 gale – and quickly. Frightening and uncomfortable though it would have been, only such a stern test could have given me real confidence in boat and crew, dispelled some of my more lurid imaginings. As it was, I spent most of the first three days hovering anxiously in the cockpit, vaguely waiting for something nasty to happen. Meanwhile, the weather remained obstinately quiet, the light north-easterly wafting us gently past the island of Ushant off the north-west coast of France and out into the notorious Bay of Biscay. Try as I might, I could not shake off the feeling that I was being lured out into the middle of the bay where a terrible storm would be waiting to punish my temerity.

At last my morbid uneasiness was rewarded – though not by the weather. In the late afternoon of the third day I was standing up in my usual worrying position in the cockpit when I happened to look down into the cabin. It was six inches deep in water. For a moment I just stood there, refusing to believe the evidence of my eyes. Then I woke up. I don't remember going below, but suddenly I was there, the water washing coldly round my legs.

It was coming from the back of the boat; that much was clear from the direction of flow. Must be the stern gland, I decided. But any sense of relief I may have felt at diagnosing the source of the leak soon faded. The Volvo diesel engine effectively blocked any access from the cabin. The only route lay from above, by way of an inspection panel set into the cockpit floor. Then I remembered. One week before sailing I had secured the panel for sea with no less than 24 screws, each one set lovingly into a glutinous sealing compound.

Whatever the record was for undoing 24 screws, I am confident that I broke it. Tearing aside the panel at last, I stuck my head down through the hole. By now the propeller shaft was well under the water, but that didn't matter. If the leak was there, I would feel the pressure of the water flowing against my fingers. I reached down, found the shaft with my fingers, traced it back to the stern gland. Nothing.

Up to this point my feverish activity, together with my certainty as to the source of the leak, had managed to suppress the little flickerings of panic. But now the full realization of my situation began to sink in. The water in the cabin was noticeably deeper, lapping the top of the bottom step. I was well over 200 miles from land, there were no ships in sight and we were in imminent danger of sinking. I had a life-raft, of course, but . . . then I saw the spiral of panic for what it was. Concentrate, I told myself. Take it step by step. We hadn't hit anything so it had to be one of the openings in the hull. What about the bilge outlet? This is a hole in the side of the boat through which the bilge pump discharges waste water over the side. The outlet lay under the port cockpit seat, at the back of the locker. I flung back the lid, threw aside fenders, ropes, buckets . . . and there it was. The jubilee clip securing the outboard end of the bilge pipe to the side of the hull had somehow worked loose. This had allowed the pipe to come off its seating so that, with the boat heeled over on the port side, the sea was simply pouring in through the hole.

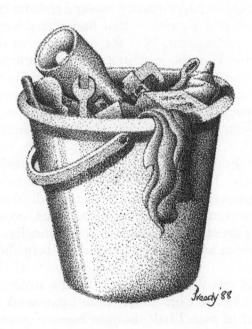

Five minutes later the crisis was over. Five days later I reached Vigo. On the way I had finally met up with my Force 8 gale off the north-west corner of Spain, only to be enveloped soon afterwards in a bank of fog between Cape Finisterre and the Vigo estuary. So, one way and another, it had been an eventful trip. Yet looking back on it six years later, what struck me most was not the evidence of my inexperience, plentiful though that was. It was more the realization that during the course of that traumatic week I had, slowly, imperceptibly, come to terms with the sea. By the time I entered the Vigo estuary, no longer did I feel out of tune with its moods, out of place in its vastness. The sea could still hurt me, I knew, and could do so with complete indifference. But now there was a quiet peace deep inside me; a realization that, for long periods of time out there in the middle, I had somehow managed to step outside myself, to become part of the sea and sky.

The Vigo exploit had virtually marked the end of my sailing in the army. It was a pastime that had afforded me contrast, challenge and excitement. Not for one moment did I suspect that it had also laid the essential groundwork for a second career.

'That's it,' called out Kathleen. 'Now then, you little scut, just behave yourself from now on.'

I realized with some relief that she was addressing the fuel pump.

It was one hour later. The bleeding operation had gone without a hitch. The cabin had been restored to order. I had even remembered to bury the old diaphragm deep in the rubbish bag; nothing is more useless, even dangerous, on a boat than a faulty engine part masquerading as a spare. Finally, I had settled up with Kathleen and thanked her for her help. Now she was ready to go.

'Well, I'll be away then,' she said with a smile, holding out her hand. 'It's taken a bit longer than I expected, but there it is. As a matter of fact, I half thought himself might have been down here by now to see what we were up to. No matter, I'll tell him I've had a strange man handling me person all afternoon. Sure and that might get him going.'

'Steady on,' I protested laughingly, as she turned to climb

the companionway steps. 'He'll kill me!' She laughed back at me over her shoulder.

In no time at all, it seemed, Kathleen had disappeared down the quay with her bucket, bending her head into the fine drizzle that had set in with early evening. I was sorry to see her go. Feeling decidedly flat, I started to prepare supper. I know what, I thought, I'll give Mary a ring later on. It was a warming prospect. I already knew how she would receive my call, my mood, the recital of my troubles. Not a hint that I had got what I'd asked for. Instead, she would just listen quietly and then proceed to restore both my spirits and my sense of proportion; and all before the pips went.

It had always been so, I reflected. Particularly with my very first yacht delivery.

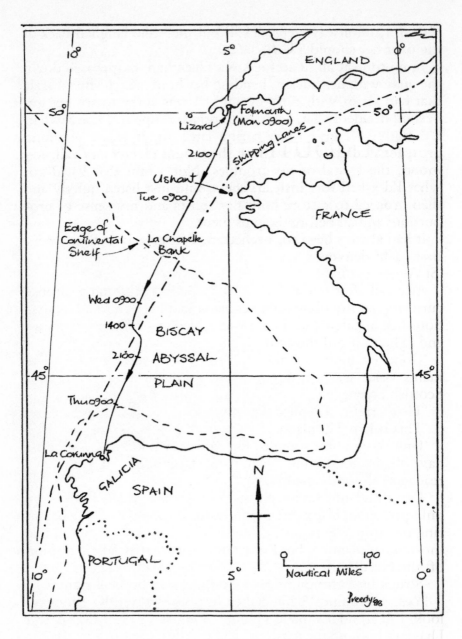

10°

5°

ENGLAND

50°   50°

Lizard   Falmouth
                      (Mon 0900)

2100

Shipping Lanes

Ushant

Tue 0900

FRANCE

Edge of
Continental
Shelf

La Chapelle
Bank

Wed 0900

1400   BISCAY

2100   ABYSSAL

45°   PLAIN   45°

Thu 0900

La Corunna

GALICIA

SPAIN

N

10°   5°   0°

100

PORTUGAL

Nautical Miles

Tveedy 88

*Track Of Allez Cat II From Falmouth To
Corunna*

Chapter Two

FALMOUTH TO CORUNNA, SPAIN

'St Agnes 3110?'

Any call after ten o'clock in the evening is bound to arouse curiosity, so my obligatory response had been more of a question than a statement. There was a bleeping noise at the other end. Then I heard the coins drop.

'Good evening, is this Mr Preedy I'm speaking to?' The man's voice was a little faint, but I still picked up the slight Scottish accent.

'That's right,' I replied, speaking up.

'This is Iain Thomson.'

'Iain! I thought it sounded like you. My goodness, you must have made good time.' Hang on, I thought, he can't have reached Falmouth already.

'I'm afraid not,' he replied. He sounded tired. 'Look, I've only got enough for three minutes, so I'd better be quick. I'm ringing from Weymouth. We started off from Lymington this morning as planned, but I'm afraid we were struck by lightning off the Needles.'

'Struck by lightning? Good God, are you both all right?'

'Yes, we're fine. A bit shaken but otherwise OK. Anyway, look, I'm afraid it's made a bit of a mess of the electronics. And I haven't been up the mast yet, so I just don't know what things are like up there. They don't look too bad from the deck, as a matter of fact, but I won't really know for sure until tomorrow morning. Now, I'm going to try to sort things out here tomorrow and then set off again, if I can, the morning after –

17

let's see, that'll be Saturday, won't it? So our ETA in Falmouth looks like sometime on Sunday morning. Is that all right?' he asked anxiously. 'Or will it throw your plans out?'

'No, of course not,' I assured him hastily. 'No problem whatsoever. In fact, why don't you stay another day in Weymouth? It might be as well in the circumstances.' I didn't like to mention that one of the circumstances was that neither of them was getting any younger; Iain was over 60, I knew. But that was what I was thinking. Quite apart from that, though, there was such a thing as delayed shock – I winced at the macabre pun – and after what they. . . .

'No, we'll press on, I think,' replied Iain. 'They're still talking about a high pressure next week with the winds in the north. I would hate to waste it.' His voice rose suddenly on an urgent note as the pips started. 'Anyway, I'll ring you from Falmouth when we get in, OK?'

The burring noise broke in before I could reply.

My thoughts were still racing as I replaced the receiver. A lightning strike: that was serious. Mind you, I thought, as I walked slowly back to the spare room to get on with packing my grip, it could have been even worse. It might easily have set the whole catamaran on fire and that didn't bear thinking about.

It was late May and I was at home in St Agnes, Cornwall. Eighteen months of concentrated sailing in my own Super Seal 26 had culminated in my fateful decision to take up yacht delivery as a second career. The die cast, I had promptly advertised in the yachting press, offering my services. As I waited at home for my first unsuspecting customer, I managed to conjure up all sorts of disturbing images. Storm force winds, bombastic owners, surly crews: in the face of these and other dire possibilities, the butterflies in my stomach were doing nicely. Then common sense would come to my rescue.

'Just relax,' I would tell myself. 'For all you know, the first delivery will involve nothing more than a stately progress up channel from Falmouth to Poole, gliding majestically before a gentle south-westerly breeze. Just the thing to get you started.'

Within two days of the advertisement being published I received my first call. It had been Iain. Understandably cautious, he was just wondering if I would consider skippering

18

his Prout 37 catamaran from Falmouth down to Corunna, Spain. He and his wife would be coming too. No less cautious, I had wanted to know more. By the time we had finished, I had undertaken to write to him with an offer and my terms of business.

In fact, I had already tried to set out on paper a business arrangement between the prospective customer and myself that would be fair to both parties. The result was hardly impressive, taking up barely half a page, but it seemed to fill the bill:

'1. The delivery is to be completed with all reasonable speed consistent with prevailing weather conditions and with the safety of boat and crew.'

I felt better for getting that one down on paper. Whilst not yet a victim myself, most of the sailing books I had read – and I had read quite a few by now – emphasised the dangers of trying to sail to a tight time schedule. Equally, however, this condition guarded against the owner who, coming along for the ride, saw the delivery in terms of a leisurely holiday, calling for frequent and prolonged stop-overs en route. Granted, there were obvious attractions to this approach but, for me at least, time would be money.

'2. The boat is to be insured by the owner against any loss – whether partial or complete – or damage occasioned during the delivery voyage; and for any loss, damage or injury involving a third party.'

The less said about that one the better.

'3. It is the responsibility of the skipper and crew to arrange personal insurance cover for the duration of the voyage.'

And that one.

'4. Neither the skipper nor the crew can be held responsible for loss or damage to the boat or its equipment unless occasioned by negligence.'

At first glance this seemed a little hard on the prospective customer. But a moment's thought about the inevitable wear and tear that is inseparable from sailing, particularly long-distance sailing, was enough to salve my conscience. That, and the certain knowledge that I would never knowingly abuse a boat; not so much because it was somebody else's valued possession – but because it was a boat.

'5. One third of the delivery fee is to be paid before the start of the voyage; the rest on completion.'

There was something unreal about this last one. I still couldn't bring myself to believe that someone was actually going to pay me for indulging what had long since become a passion.

Mary came home just as I was finishing the packing. In deliberate defiance of her painful osteo-arthritis, she had been attending a gardening club evening with her friend Nancy. She followed me back into the spare room. Small, dark, petite, she sat on the bed as I told her about the phone call. After nearly 25 years of marriage, she was well used to dramas of one kind or another. Even so, she was naturally concerned.

'No, it really sounds as though they're all right, love,' I reassured her. 'But it was certainly a lucky escape.'

'It must have been absolutely terrifying,' she agreed. Then, seeing that I was about to close the zip-fastener on the grip, she laid a tiny restraining hand on mine. 'Hold on, sailor, no good doing that up now – it will all get creased. Here, let me.' Practical-minded as always, she pulled the zip back again, started to unpack what she knew I had been trying to hide. 'I don't know,' she said, smiling indulgently, 'just look at your packing. Can't leave you alone for a moment, can I?' She was silent for a moment as she extracted a mangled-looking shirt and two pairs of socks from inside one of my sea boots. 'Anyway, when do you expect to go aboard the boat . . . what's the name again?'

'*Allez Cat II*,' I replied, inwardly acknowledging that the deliberate pun intended in the name was a lot better than my involuntary effort earlier. 'Well, not before Sunday morning at the earliest. In which case we'll probably leave for Spain on Monday. It all depends on how quickly Iain can sort out the damage to the electronics. It's. . . .' I stopped as a sudden thought struck me. The catamaran was literally stuffed full with electronics; Iain had told me so in his letter. 'Just a moment, love,' I said, 'I want to have a look at something.'

I returned to the sitting room to fish Iain's letter out of the file. Hurriedly, I skipped through the preamble. Then I found it:

'Our boat is a Prout 37 Snowgoose of which we took delivery in July last year. She is well-equipped with six-man life-raft, Tinker Tramp dinghy, roller reefing headsail, staysail, slab reefing mainsail, cruising chute plus the usual life-saving equipment. Main engine is a 30 HP Yanmar diesel with an 8 HP Bukh Saildrive as side engine. As recently retired from a senior position with' – here he named a well-known electronics firm – 'the boat is unusually well-fitted with electronics including radar, Decca, Loran C, ADF, Navtex, Nautech 6000 autopilot, a full suit of Brookes and Gatehouse wind instruments, VHF and MF/SSB radios and log and depth instruments.' My head was spinning, even though I was reading this for the second time. 'We can carry up to 50 gallons of fuel which gives at least 300 nautical miles' cruising range at 5 or 6 knots.'

I had first read this some two weeks before. Then, brought up as I was on nothing more than a sextant, a battery-powered radio direction finder, a chart and a compass, I had decided that it was the single most intimidating paragraph I had ever read in my life. The only consolation – unoriginal but savagely prophetic, as things had turned out – was that, with the exception of the radio direction finder, I could always depend on my equipment to work, no matter what.

But all that was beside the point right now. Clearly, Iain had a real job on his hands, sorting out the mess. In other circumstances, perhaps, he might have compromised, rectifying only those items that he considered essential and leaving the rest until later. But I already knew that the trip to Corunna was only the first lap of a much longer voyage. Thereafter, the Thomsons were planning to take the boat by stages down to the Mediterranean and then keep it there for at least a couple of years. It all had to be done now.

Ah well, I thought, I wish him luck tomorrow. He's certainly going to need it.

*   *   *

In the gathering dusk of Sunday evening I took a fresh grip on the top of *Allez Cat*'s mast as I waited for Iain to hoist the bucket from the deck below. My gaze wandered beyond the confines of Falmouth Marina to the other side of the Penryn river. There, where the incoming tide was about to cover the last of the mud, a chequer-board of black and white oyster-catchers prised open mussels with their red crow-bar bills. It would be their last chance until morning, just as it was our last chance now to sort out the masthead before leaving for Spain.

It had been a busy day. Just before eleven o'clock that morning Iain had telephoned to say that they had arrived. He had quickly added, the relief evident in his voice, that with the help of his old firm all damaged equipment, other than the masthead, had been either repaired or replaced. I was impressed. By the time I had driven to Falmouth Marina and found *Allez Cat*, Iain's wife Eileen had gone shopping. But Iain himself was there, working in the palatial stern cockpit.

He turned out to look a little different than I had imagined. Although not specially tall, his greying hair, blue-grey eyes and fair complexion suggested that he was of Nordic rather than native Scottish decent. He looked trim and fit for his age, but there were obvious signs of tiredness and strain around his eyes. Yet it was in the eyes themselves that I looked discreetly for evidence of his real state of mind. Years of living and working with men under stress had taught me that, while facial expressions often dissemble, the eyes themselves do not; not, at least, for long. What I saw suggested the presence of a quiet resolve, a resolve to press on regardless of age, lightning strikes or anything else. I felt reassured. The Bay of Biscay was no place for second thoughts.

As for Eileen, I'm not sure how I had pictured her beforehand. We hadn't spoken on the telephone, and the only clues I had were those Iain had dropped in his letter. From these I had gathered that she was a few years younger than Iain, fit, active and 'capable of standing a watch on her own at sea provided clearly understood criteria were laid down for calling for assist-ance.'

I didn't have long to wait to complete the picture. As we hurried up the pontoon to take her shopping bags, she didn't look to me as though – shopping bags apart – she needed much assistance in any department. It wasn't just the comfortable assurance of her matronly figure, emphasised incongruously by a dark green track-suit. Nor was it the impish grin on a face framed by short, greying, auburn hair as she extended her hand to me, nor even the attractive twinkle in her soft brown eyes. But perhaps, behind that twinkle, I sensed an inner serenity which, if it proved to be so, was all the more impressive for her recent ordeal.

Changing my cramped position in the bosun's chair, I heard Iain's exasperated voice floating up from the cabin below. 'I'm sure I put it in this one,' he was complaining.

There had been a great deal to do to prepare for our departure the next day. First, I had been winched up the mast to retrieve the blackened and twisted bracket on which the VHF radio aerial had been mounted. Iain already had a replacement aerial, but we had to take the bracket to a man in Penryn industrial estate who worked and welded stainless steel. Leaving it with him, we had returned to the boat for a quick snack lunch. Then, at last, came my long awaited opportunity to get to know *Allez Cat*. I made the most of it. As the afternoon flashed by, Iain and I covered the catamaran from stem to stern. She was certainly very nice. Still virtually new, it soon became clear to me that, once the VHF aerial had been remounted at the masthead, she would be ready in every respect for her Biscay crossing.

Inside, the boat was subdivided into three sections. The largest was the enormous central saloon from which steps led down on either side to the floats. The port-hand float comprised a sea toilet, bathroom and shower forward of the navigator's sanctum in which an array of electronic radio and navigational aids surrounded a large chart table. The starboard float contained a well-appointed galley amidships with sleeping berths fore and aft.

But it was the two enormous wooden cabinets, either side of the main hatchway leading out into the cockpit, that almost struck me dumb. The door of one was open, spilling out a billowing spaghetti of multi-coloured wires. Behind them, I could make out trays and trays of fuses, semi-conductors, printed circuits and other electrical gadgetry. It was time to come clean.

'Look, Iain,' I began, 'I'm a little ashamed to say so, but I ought to tell you that electronics and black boxes are not really my strong point. Don't worry,' I added hastily, 'I'm happy about using them – although the Navtex is new to me, I admit.' Not half, I thought. Unless I had seen it, I would have assumed it to be some sort of cleaning fluid for chart covers. 'But if any of it goes wrong. . . .' Then, to my enormous relief, I saw that Iain was already smiling.

'Don't worry about it for a moment, old chap,' he said, gripping my shoulder. 'You can safely leave any repairs to me. No, we want you for your sea-going experience. I'm quite sure you'll get us to the right place, with or without electronics.'

'Almost certainly without, if the last couple of days are anything to go by,' chipped in Eileen with a laugh.

I felt enormously relieved and not just because of the way my admission had been received. Eileen's remarks had confirmed my earlier impression that, in their book at least, the lightning strike had been firmly relegated to the status of a joke.

'OK, here it comes,' called up Iain from below.

My heart thumped as I suddenly realized where I was. Come on, I thought, no time for day-dreaming. There's work to do.

In fact, it took no more than fifteen minutes to drill two holes in the top of the mast with Iain's battery-powered drill and then rivet the mended bracket. All that remained was to fit the aerial and connect it up. Moments later I was back on deck.

We trooped back into the cabin to find Eileen once more in the galley. As she looked up, I noticed a crumb sticking to the corner of her mouth. That reminded me.

'Oh, there's just one thing before I go,' I said. 'With this northerly wind the sea will be pretty flat to start with tomorrow until we get some way beyond the Lizard. But once we clear the lee of the land, things could get a little lively on the way down to Ushant.' She might as well know now, I thought, looking at Eileen. She beamed back at me. 'Anyway,' I continued, starting to gabble, 'all I was going to say was that you obviously have your own ideas about pills and so on but it might be as well not to eat too much first thing in the morning. Just a thought.'

'And a timely one too,' said Iain. 'Thanks very much for

mentioning it.' He paused. 'Anyway, we'll see you just after eight in the morning, yes?'

'Yes, fine,' I replied, picking up my oilskin jacket. 'If we aim to leave just before nine o'clock that should give us the best of the ebb tide. It will also give you the chance of a lie-in – you certainly deserve one.'

As I walked wearily towards the marina office in the twilight, a pair of herring-gulls were quarrelling noisily over an apple core further up the pontoon. Time you were in bed, I told them. Examining my feelings now that I was alone, I realized that I was feeling surprisingly relaxed. At this stage of my very first yacht delivery, I had expected to be tense up to the eyeballs. As it was, I felt like whistling. Yet the reasons were really not hard to find, now that I thought about it. *Allez Cat* was a beautiful boat, and a manifestly strong one. My shortcomings as an electronics engineer had been noted, then dismissed. So, in the minds of my prospective shipmates, had the lightning strike.

There remained only one small, niggling worry at the back of my mind. It had to do with the crumb at the corner of Eileen's mouth.

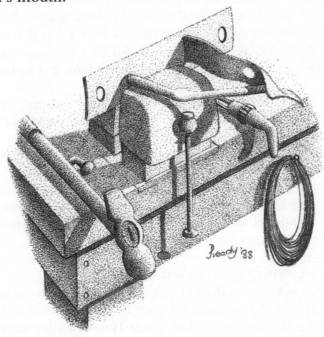

'It's almost time to go,' I said, looking at my watch. 'Happy?'

Iain took a deep breath. 'Yes, I think so. Just one thing: could you quickly recap on the overall sailing strategy so I've got it quite clear in my mind?'

'Of course.' I marshalled the factors in logical order. 'Stage one will be to make our course to a point about 20 miles due west of Ushant. That will keep us clear of the big ships coming down channel and going round the corner. Then, across the Bay of Biscay itself, we shall continue to stay about ten miles west of the shipping lanes. Admittedly, this will add a few more miles to our overall distance, but it's still worth doing, and for two reasons. First, it will keep us clear of the big ships at night or in fog. Second, and more important, it should ensure that, in the event of strong westerly gales, we will have plenty of sea room to play with. Boats still manage to get themselves embayed inside Biscay by strong westerlies, even today, and once you're in, it can be a real battle getting out again. All right so far?' Iain nodded.

'Finally, a point will obviously come when we will have to cross inside the lanes in order to reach Corunna. Now, other than saying that I will want to do this in daylight, I would prefer to leave the precise timing until we see what the weather is doing off the north-west tip of Spain.'

'Can that be a problem?' asked Iain, shooting a quick look at me.

'Well,' I replied, 'it certainly was last time for me. But I'm obviously not just going on that. If you listen regularly to the forecast for South Finisterre, you'll know that a north-easterly gale, or near gale, blows around the north-west corner of Spain for much of the year. Not that it would bother this boat,' I added hastily, noting Iain's serious expression. 'It's just that it would be nicer, if it comes, to run before it into Corunna rather than to try and sail across it from the west. So I'd like to leave that decision until we're within a 24-hour forecast of Corunna. OK by you?'

'I'm more than happy,' he replied.

'Right then, care to take her out?' Quite apart from deferring to ceremony, to the sentimental wish to let the owner start and, God willing, finish this voyage, I was aware that he knew how to handle *Allez Cat* at close quarters in a way that, at this stage, I could not.

An hour later, we were clearing Falmouth harbour, providing a welcome diversion for two shore anglers hunched at the foot of Pendennis Point. I went into the cabin to write up the log. Eileen was comfortably embedded in the large U-shaped settee surrounding the central table, reading a paperback. I was alarmed. Still, I thought grimly, she won't keep that up for long. The log completed, I returned to the cockpit. 'OK, Iain, my watch until 1300 hours,' I said, moving towards the wheel. He relinquished it to me with a smile, then settled himself comfortably on the port cockpit seat to enjoy the view.

I was glad. At this precise moment I didn't want to talk. I wanted to concentrate on what *Allez Cat* was trying to tell me, discover how to coax the best from her. We had killed the engine half an hour ago and now the boat was forging ahead goose-winged, the billowing cruising chute with its black cat's head poled out to starboard, the full mainsail out to port. Catamarans perform best running before the wind, and *Allez Cat* was showing off, the log reading 7 knots. For one used to monohull boats, her motion was decidedly strange at first. But that was something I had been prepared for. Moreover, now I was starting to realize that she was well-balanced for all that, answering surely, if not all that quickly, to the wheel.

I spent a few minutes mentally running through the practice drills for man overboard that we would perform later in the morning. Then Iain spoke for the first time in ten minutes.

'So let's see, I'm on watch again in three hours' time at 1300 hours, then you at 1600, me at 1900 – and from 2200 you're on right through to 0600 tomorrow morning. Is that right?'

'That's it,' I replied. 'Then you do four hours until 1000 hours while I get some sleep – after which we start all over again.' We had already discussed this yesterday, but I knew what he was going to say now.

'Are you quite certain about this, Ron?' he asked. 'It's a long time for you, right through the night.'

'No really, I'm quite happy,' I replied. 'Truly.'

'Well, if you're quite sure,' he said. 'I certainly won't argue with you.'

The very last sentence was the one that counted. It confirmed me in what I acknowledged to be an unusual split of watch-keeping duties. As I altered course to avoid yet another fishing float 50 yards ahead, I reviewed the reasons for my choice. First, I had excluded Eileen from formal watch-keeping, not because she wouldn't enjoy a spell of duty in the cockpit; she probably would. But I preferred to make that an informal arrangement, giving her the option to choose the time and place. Meanwhile, she had plenty to do with cooking and with keeping things shipshape inside. Always assuming, I added grimly, that she was in a condition to do anything at all, the way she was tempting fate.

As for Iain, his original letter had included two lines that I had been quick to read between. Although a competent navigator and watchkeeper, his night sailing experience was 'fairly limited'. He had also just been put through a four-day ordeal that would have exhausted someone half his age. No, there was no question about it: this particular watch-keeping schedule would be unlikely to catch on with other skippers but, right here and now, it fitted our situation like a kid glove.

Anyway, I thought as I engaged the automatic pilot on our course of 195° magnetic, never mind all that. A day such as this deserved more attention than I was giving it. Certainly, the great Monet, incomparable amongst the Impressionists for his living coastal scenes, would have picked up his brush like a shot. Animated by a fresh northerly breeze, Falmouth Bay was a thick scumble of brilliant white dragged lightly over a blue-green wash. White too, yet creamier in tone, a pair of saffron-headed gannets took off into the wind at our approach with a flurry of black-tipped wings. Calling out briefly to his mate following some 30 yards behind, the male turned to skim low across the water in the direction of the Helford Passage away to our right. And there, the wooded green slopes either side of the entrance were gradually unfolding as we headed southwards, opening up like giant petals to the morning sun-shine. It was quite a send-off.

Iain had been quiet for some time. Can't be queasiness, I thought. One glance across at him reassured me. He was studying a small plastic-covered card that I recognized immediately. In the difficult waiting period of the last couple of weeks I had, quite apart from framing my terms of business, occupied my mind in preparing what I had rather formally entitled 'Instructions to Watchkeepers'. After all, if things worked out, I would be faced with a succession of owners and crews, all of whom had a right to know clearly what was expected of them. I had given Iain the card yesterday, but I knew the rules by heart:

'Instructions to Watchkeepers'

'1. When on watch you are responsible, unless I have specifically taken over the boat, for:

a. The safety of boat and crew in all respects – navigationally, with regard to heavy weather, danger from other ships and craft, with regard to her handling and the use of fuels and gas.

b. Keeping an up-to-date position by dead reckoning and by use of the best fixing aids available.

c. Changing sails to suit the weather.

d. Ensuring the crew use such safety gear as is necessary to suit the conditions.

e. Frequently checking the condition of the boat and her equipment for chafe, wear, bilge water and safe stowage.'

'2. Please call the Skipper:

a. If ships or boats are going to pass within half a mile.

b. If the weather deteriorates or the visibility reduces to less than a mile.

c. If in any doubt about the navigation.

d. If not entirely happy about the boat and her company.'

It was the last one, together with the gradual increase in the boat's odd motion, that reminded me of something. Moving quietly to the hatchway to look into the cabin, I saw that I had been right in my earlier guess. Eileen had indeed stopped reading. Now she was knitting. The movement of her hands completely automatic, she raised her eyes above a tiny pair of half-glasses to give me another of her beaming smiles.

'Hullo, Ron,' she said. 'Something to eat?'

★   ★   ★

It was 2145 hours. Escaping with difficulty from my sleeping bag, I started to dress for the night watch. The sea was pretty lively, I realized, as I staggered suddenly backwards. Just after 1300 hours we had cleared the shipping in the lanes south of the Lizard, some heading east up the English Channel, others westward to America or up into the Irish Sea. Since then the motion had gradually increased to the point where, now, it was obvious that we had a really boisterous following sea on our hands.

Predictably, since going to my bunk at 2000 hours I had dozed rather than slept. As yet my brain was too active, my body too charged with energy, for proper sleep. But I expected to put that right tomorrow morning. I made a cup of coffee, then carried it carefully out into the cockpit. The brisk north-westerly – for such it had become since dusk – greeted me with a blast of cold air. Despite my oilskins and the several layers of clothing beneath, I found I was shivering.

'Manage to sleep?' asked Iain. He was hunched at the wheel, lit dimly by the light from the compass, watching the automatic pilot turn the wheel first one way, then the other.

'Yes, thanks, not bad at all,' I replied. I looked at the compass. It was swinging 15 degrees either side of 195° magnetic.

'Yes,' said Iain, noting where my attention lay. 'The boat's yawing rather a lot, isn't she?'

'No, not really,' I replied. 'It's this quartering sea that's doing it. To be honest, I'm surprised it's not yawing more – I'm fairly certain a monohull would in these conditions.' I looked up. Just before I had gone below we had shortened sail, taken down the cruising chute in favour of a reduced headsail and reefed the mainsail. Now, two hours later, *Allez Cat* still seemed quite happy with the way she was dressed. 'Barometer still seems pretty steady,' I said. 'It's dropped a couple of milli-bars since the wind shift, but that's nothing; especially with the night coming on. Anyway, time you were in bed.' Then, because twelve hours on a small boat at sea had quickly put us at ease with each other, I struck a comic pose, stood stiffly to attention. 'Pray may I trouble you for your report, Mr Christian?' I asked in my best plummy Charles Laughton voice.

Iain played readily along, rapping out his words staccato.

'Aye, aye, sir. Course 195° magnetic, wind nor'westerly 5 to 6, proceeding under reefed mainsail and headsail, no ships in sight – and all's well.' He saluted for luck.

My laugh got in the way of any answer as he clapped me on the shoulder and went down below to complete the log before going to bed. Left alone in the darkness, I handed my way to each side of the cockpit in turn to have a really good look around the horizon. As my night vision asserted itself, I realized that actually there were ships around, two of them. But the lights were far away, very faint and visible only for the briefest of moments as the passing waves obscured them from view. I returned to the wheel. It was a fine night but dark. It would be another four hours before the waning half moon cleared the line of clouds on the horizon. Still, at least a half moon meant slack tides, and I was glad of them. With the wind anywhere in the west, a spring tide ebbing down channel could kick up quite an opposing sea in the south-west approaches. We had quite enough to be going on with as it was.

I tried to gauge the sea state, never easy on a dark night. The serrated grey of the wave tops as they overhauled us on our starboard quarter suggested that the wind was nearer to Force 6 than 5. The resulting sea was inducing a corkscrew motion as *Allez Cat* ducked and weaved her way through the night. Despite the movement, I suddenly realized that I had lost the slight queasiness I had felt earlier on. Although supremely fortunate in never being actually sick at sea, it sometimes takes me a few hours to get my sea legs at the start of a voyage. In this case the combination of the lively sea and the catamaran's odd motion had rather taken the edge off the late afternoon and evening. Not that I had eaten anything so far, nor would I until tomorrow morning at the earliest. This was the inviolable personal rule that I had tried clumsily to pass on to the Thomsons yesterday evening. There was one other, of course. Whenever the sea is testing the stomach, one should either stay up in the cockpit in the fresh air, one eye on the horizon; or, better, lie down flat on a bunk inside the cabin where it is warm and comparatively comfortable. One thing is certain: to sit upright in the cabin is to ask for trouble, while to compound this with any sort of close work is to ask for a great deal more.

31

But all that was before Eileen. By now, of course, she had gone to bed in the forward bunk of the starboard float. But before doing so she had turned with relish to writing postcards, evidently her greatest pleasure. By the time I had gone below to seek my rest earlier in the evening, she had got through about a dozen and was just starting on the next.

'Oh, hullo, Ron,' she said, looking up, the pen for a rare moment idle in her hand. 'Now, are you quite sure you won't have something to eat?'

'No, not a thing, Eileen,' I replied, holding on tight as *Allez Cat* lurched suddenly to port.

'Ah, well,' she said with a comforting smile, 'perhaps tomorrow. I'll make you a nice breakfast. How's that?'

I was about to reply when I noticed that she was holding her right elbow forward slightly in front of her, the forearm flat on the table. Even allowing for the fact that we were now sliding downhill back to starboard, her position looked strangely uncomfortable. Then I saw it. Peeping out from behind her wrist was the corner of a brown bread sandwich.

*   *   *

By the time I came out into the cockpit at 1000 hours next morning, refreshed with sleep and a delicious breakfast, we were already some 20 miles past Ushant. Given our course, we were always going to be too far out to the west to see the island itself, but I had picked up the loom of the light just after 0200 hours the previous night. Half an hour after that we were close enough for me to confirm beyond question the two flashes every ten seconds. By then too, the first signs of the shipping in the lanes had appeared as an irregular line of faint pin-pricks of light stretching across the eastern horizon.

With the dawn the lights had faded, then disappeared, leaving us completely alone on the high sea. Now, sharply aware of our isolation and of what lay ahead, the focus of our thoughts and actions turned inwards to the boat itself. Leaving Iain operating with surgical precision on the multi-coloured intestines of one of his wooden cabinets, I carried out a thorough inspection of the boat. This had long since become an inflexible daily routine on my own boat, and it was even more important on a strange one. I was literally looking for trouble, particularly

32

for the slightest sign of weakness or insecurity in load-bearing components such as bottle-screws and shackles, for evidence of chafe on sails or rigging. This was followed by a quick look at engine oil and water levels after which, with Iain's concurrence, we ran the engine for an hour to top up batteries.

So the day wore on. By now I had come to terms with Eileen's eccentric behaviour and could even feel embarrassment at my earlier bland assumptions. Yet there was no need. If she had been aware of them, there was no sign of it in her bright, cheerful manner. Meanwhile, and despite her work in the galley, one paperback was replaced by another, the knitting grew longer, the postcards began to pile up.

By suppertime we were close to the edge of La Chapelle bank, 140 metres below our keel. This marked the edge of the continental shelf and by morning the bottom of the sea would have dropped sharply away to 4500 metres. During my first crossing of Biscay I had found this fact strangely daunting – as I suspected the Thomsons did now. But it was an irrational fear, at best. After all, it was just as easy to drown in 15 feet of water as in 15000. The idea was to stay on board.

Again, the wind changed in direction with the onset of dusk. It backed slightly to the west-north-west, now coming a little more on the beam. And with it had appeared a long, slow swell. But the barometer remained steady at 1021 millibars and, as the early night progressed, the wind showed no sign of increasing above its mean of 22 knots. It looked like being a reasonable night, I decided.

The wave hit us at precisely 0201 hours next morning. I know that was the time because I was in the act of filling in the log. To say that it struck without warning would be almost true, but not quite. As my pen travelled across the paper, I was aware of a sudden lull outside. Then there came a very slight hissing noise. The next moment something hit the starboard float with a force that almost loosened the fillings in my teeth. As my writing trailed wildly across the page, the whole of the starboard side of the boat reared up until it was high above me. I didn't have time to think about a capsize before it subsided once more. As it did so, there was the sound of plastic crockery bouncing about in the galley.

Without knowing how I got there, I found myself in the

cockpit, the noise of aerated foam loud in my ears as I looked over the side. A broad patch of white surrounded the starboard float. Now, by contrast with a few moments before, the sea had suddenly gone quiet, as though ashamed of what it had done. I turned to look up at the sails and rigging. At first glance all seemed well, but I knew I would have to take a closer look.

Iain's worried face peered at me from above the galley partition as I returned to the cabin to switch on the deck lights.

'What in God's name was that?' he asked in a croaky voice. He had obviously been fast asleep. For him, I guessed, it must have been a terrifying awakening.

'Rogue wave,' I said, bending down to switch on the deck lights. 'Ten to one it was a ship.'

'Goodness, he must have been close,' he gasped.

'No, there's nothing in sight at all,' I replied. I knew it was so because I had carefully scanned the horizon before coming below to write up the log. 'No, I had this twice on my last trip. Neither was anything like as bad as this one, but they were bad enough. The thing is, a ship's bow wave can travel literally for miles, from way over the horizon. And if it happens to coincide with a big natural wave at the wrong moment . . . well, you've just seen the result.' I made a move towards the hatchway. 'Anyway, I'd better have a good look all round the boat to make sure we've not sustained any damage. How's the galley area, by the way?'

'I can't see anything broken,' he said. 'I'll just tidy up a bit, I think – unless you want me in the cockpit?'

'No, don't worry, I'll be clipping on when I go up into the bow,' I replied. 'I'll yell if I need you.'

★   ★   ★

By 1030 hours next morning – Wednesday – it all seemed little more than a bad dream. For the time being that was how it would stay too, I resolved. As it was, my own strong conviction was that *Allez Cat*, decidedly no lightweight as felines went, had never even come close to a capsize; this despite having been caught almost broadside on. In the cold light of day, I estimated that she had been lifted some 30° above the horizontal. That was far enough, but still a long way from real danger. Yet despite this reassuring conclusion, I suspected that any attempt to pass it on to Iain would only beg in his mind the much debated question about the ultimate stability of catamarans, and for all practical purposes such a debate was irrelevant. Knowing Iain as I was beginning to, I was certain that he would already have faced, assessed and calmly accepted any risk. As for me, I already knew that, on the basis of this evidence, I would not be refusing catamaran deliveries in the future. I was sipping a cup of coffee in the cockpit, noting as I did so how the green water of the continental shelf had turned overnight into the deep ultramarine blue of the Biscay abyssal plain. The wind had veered to the north and had dropped quite a bit while I had been sleeping below. Now we were doing just over 4 knots. Well, I thought, stretching out on the warm cockpit seat, I'm certainly not going to complain about that. So far the engine had run for just two hours, and half of that had been in order to charge the batteries.

Eileen handed me her mug of coffee, then stepped out into the cockpit, almost for the first time since leaving Falmouth. She sat down beside me. 'Thanks, Ron,' she said with one of her smiles as I handed back the mug. She settled herself comfortably. 'What a lovely morning.'

'Gorgeous,' I agreed. 'Certainly an improvement on last night. Didn't you wonder what the crash was?'

'Oh, not really,' she replied, her smile unimpaired. 'It woke me up, of course . . . but it was soon over, wasn't it? I didn't really see any point in worrying about it.' A thought struck her. 'Now I come to think about it, I believe Iain did call out something to me, but I had nearly dropped off again by then.'

There you go again, I thought, wondering when I was ever going to stop underestimating this woman.

'Anyway, look,' she said, dropping her voice a little, 'I just popped out to say that Iain's feeling a bit off colour. He's gone to have a lie down for a bit. So if you want a break or anything, just give a shout, OK?'

'Yes, of course,' I said, concerned. 'Anyway,' I continued, 'there's really no problem. The automatic pilot is doing all the work and . . . oh, look at that, Eileen. Our first bit of Spain.'

Eileen looked at me, puzzled, then turned to follow my pointing finger. But it wasn't land we were looking at; it was much too soon for that. There, a mile away, a Spanish fishing boat was swooping across the seas towards us at a good 15 knots, its bright red-and-green prow high in the water.

'It's a Spanish tunny-man,' I said into her ear as the boat charged closer, its engine roaring. 'What's more, it could well have come out of Corunna. Corunna has been a tunny-fishing port for hundreds of years.'

The boat passed close across our stern, so close that we could see the white teeth gleaming in the dark faces of the crew as they waved and shouted at us cheerfully. And, in that moment everything changed. No longer in our minds were we somewhere off the coast of Cornwall. Now, suddenly, we were actually getting close to Spain. Eileen felt it too. She waved furiously back.

'Buenos dias,' she mimed extravagantly, mindful still of Iain. She turned back to me. 'Right, time to dig out me sombrero.' One hand flung upwards above her head, the other resting on her swaying hips, she flamencoed in tiny staccato steps towards the cabin, disappearing inside with a final snap of her fingers.

★   ★   ★

'Biscay, South Finisterre. North-easterly 4 or 5, but occasionally 6 off Cape Finisterre. Fair, good.' The cultured voice was crackly, indistinct.

'What was that forecast, Ron?' asked Iain sleepily from his bunk.

Damn, I thought, I've woken him. Still, I had to get the forecast, and it had needed most of the volume control to catch it, 500 miles from London. I read it back to him, then returned to the cockpit. Twenty minutes later he joined me.

'Feeling better?' I asked. He looked rested.

'Heaps better,' he replied with a smile. 'I've no idea what the problem was, but anyway. . . .' He was looking at the compass. 'Ah, I see you've changed course already.'

'Yes,' I replied. 'Just now, right after the forecast. As it's turned out, it looks as though we shall be spared a gale. But at least I was right about the north-easterly. And I still think it will make sense to cross the lanes now, before dark. Happy?'

'Absolutely fine,' said Iain quickly. 'You're the skipper.'

I have nearly always found the big ships to be remarkably good about small sailing boats crossing their path. Provided it is clear to them what you intend, they invariably behave impeccably, if necessary altering course well beforehand. Out here, of course, unconstrained either by their draft or by a constricted channel, they were obliged to give way to us under the rules. All the same, I was mindful of the succinct advice I had received in my army days from the hard-bitten captain of an American frigate, himself an experienced sailor. 'There's just one rule of the road you need to keep in mind, buddy: little ships give way to big ships.' Yet if he had meant it at all, he knew, as I did, that it applied only to a tiny minority.

Right through the afternoon, as the wind gradually picked up once more, a fair selection of the world's commercial shipping passed ahead or astern of us. The first group were all heading south, growing with surprising speed from small dots on the horizon to enormous, slab-sided leviathans as they thundered past. Super-tankers, tankers, container ships, flat-iron ships, ships with bridges astern or amidships, ships seemingly going backwards with bridges right in the bow; all of them seemed to be travelling at between 15 and 20 knots. I watched their bow-waves rising to bend like blue-green glass over the rounded bulbs blistered incongruously to the bottom of their bows. Then, after a pause of an hour or so, it all happened again, this time from the other direction.

On one of my brief visits to the chart table I looked over the top of the partition to where Eileen was yet again deeply engrossed in a paperback. This time it was a monster, and I could see that she had just started it. I waited until she looked up. 'Well, it shouldn't be long now, Eileen,' I called out. 'If the forecast is right, it's beginning to look like sometime tomorrow evening.' No exception to other seafarers where superstition is concerned, I made sure to grip the wooden partition hard as I spoke.

'Oh, that's lovely!' she replied brightly. 'Originally we were talking about Friday, weren't we?'

'That's right, we were. But we couldn't possibly have expected the weather we've had.' Now you're really tempting fate, I thought. 'Anyway, there are no guarantees, of course, but it does look promising.'

Her beaming smile followed me out into the cockpit. 'I know what she's doing right now,' I thought. 'She's flipping the pages, working out if she'll have time to discover who done it.'

★   ★   ★

'When do you reckon we'll see land, Ron?'

Iain was bending at the open door of the port-hand cabinet, the tiny crocodile clip in his left hand connected by a red wire to a voltmeter in the other. He had asked the question without looking at me. Wearing a larger version of Eileen's half-glasses right on the end of his nose, he was peering through them suspiciously at one of the fuses.

'Hard to tell with this sea haze – mist – whatever it is,' I replied, looking out beyond the port bow as I did so. 'Shouldn't be long now, though.'

By now our crossing of the shipping lanes and the delicious supper that followed it were but memories. The line of lights marking the ships in the north-bound lane had finally disappeared just after midnight, as our courses had continued to diverge, to be followed by a quiet night. Quiet, that is, until just before dawn when we started to approach the continental shelf once again. The relatively sudden change of depth over the next three or four hours had kicked up a choppy, petulant sea that had imparted a jerky, stilted quality to our motion. Little waves had slapped at the hulls from every conceivable direction, once in a while sending a playful bucket of water right into the cockpit. But that too had passed.

Now it was 1430 hours and we were bowling along once more, a brisk north-easterly on our port quarter. And once more we had the cruising chute up. Yes, I thought, the flaming cruising chute. Even as I remembered, I could feel my cheeks flushing once again with embarrassment. One way and another, I had made a real hash of getting the sail up. Altogether, it had taken me three goes to get it right. It was unforgivable really. A spinnaker would have been different, but a cruising chute! I tried to blot it from my memory.

I was feeling a bit flat. The truth was that I was getting tired, I realized. I was also a little disappointed that we had still not

38

sighted land. Yet if I had known then what I know now, I would have been half-expecting this sea mist. With or without a gale, the visibility is rarely good off the north-west tip of Spain; partly, I think, because of the spray dispersed into the air as the Atlantic swell meets its first obstruction for 3000 miles.

'Have a look at this, Ron.' Iain was standing in front of me, a heavy pair of binoculars in one hand, a bulky green box in the other. The two were connected by a thick black cable. 'It's a gyro-stabilized pair of binoculars. German-made, of course.'

'Good Lord,' I replied, 'I didn't know there was such a thing. How does it work?'

He showed me. First switching on the motor contained in the box, he waited a little to give the gyroscope time to run up to speed. Grinning, he handed them across to me. 'Try that for size,' he said.

It was quite astounding. What would normally have been a wildly moving kaleidoscope of sea and sky, was now a clear, distinct and remarkably steady image of a Spanish fishing dory. The image was big too, I realized; the magnification factor must have been enormous. 'Quite incredible,' I marvelled. 'It's a pity the visibility isn't better.' I looked out beyond the port bow again. 'If it was, we would see the. . . .' I stopped, looked again, then pointed. 'There we are, Iain. Take your first look at Spain.'

He swivelled suddenly round to follow my pointing finger. There was a pause. 'Ah . . . I'm not sure I. . . .' His voice trailed away.

'No, not down there,' I said, looking at him, 'higher up. Look much higher up.'

He did. 'Good God, there it is,' he said. Still only just discernible, the faintest of colour separations between grey-white and grey was resolving itself into the dim outline of a ragged mountain chain. 'I can't believe it's so high,' he said. 'You're sure it's not a cloud?'

'No, it's Spain all right. Remember, this is Spain, not Cornwall,' I replied. 'Those are the high Sierras you're looking at. They're above the worst of the sea mist, which is why we can see them. The coastal strip itself is much closer and lower. No, that's Spain all right.'

'Eileen!' called out Iain. 'Come and have a look at this!'
For once the paperback lost the battle.

★   ★   ★

Although we were all three in the cockpit, it was a time to
be silent. Before us lay the great sweep of Corunna Bay, while
to starboard the great Tower of Hercules was passing slowly
by on the end of its long promontory. Built originally by the
Romans as one of the first lighthouses in the world, it seemed
to be made of gold as its modern, clean-cut sandstone reflected
the yellow light of evening.

We had just lowered the sails, switching on the engine for
the last mile or so. With the decks cleared, it would be easier
to make out the two leading marks which, kept in line, would
give us the safe route into harbour.

'Ron, there's just one thing that Eileen and I would like to
say before we get in,' said Iain suddenly.

Here it comes, I thought. He evidently thought even less of
my cruising chute antics than I did. I waited.

'So far as we're concerned,' he continued, 'you have fulfilled
your task absolutely to the letter. We both feel we're very lucky
to have had you with us on this crossing. And we just wanted
to say so.'

Covered in confusion, I'm not sure what I said in reply. But
in the moments that followed, as I started to dig out the warps
and fenders that we would need when we reached the small
berthing pontoon, the warmth and significance of Iain's words
began to sink in. Even allowing for their natural generosity of
spirit, it was clear that I was looking at my first satisfied
customers. It was a great feeling.

★   ★   ★

I was digging up the garden when the postcard arrived.
On the front was a picture of Las Camarinas, a tiny fishing port 30 miles south-west of Corunna. On the back,
scrawled with a pen that I suspected I knew well, were
these words:

'Dear Mary and Ron. Greetings from Camarinas. Delightful

40

spot. We did miss you after you'd gone, Ron. La Corunna was a bit of all right. Adios. Iain and Eileen.'

Now, years later, I have three others to put beside it.

Even now, I still can't get over Eileen's total immunity to seasickness, especially after the way she so sorely provoked it. But at least now I think I know how she does it. She doesn't do it by taking pills. Nor, certainly, by abstinence. She does it with will-power.

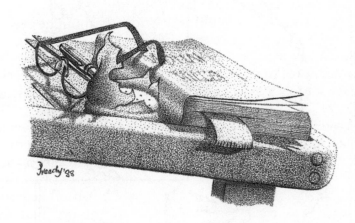

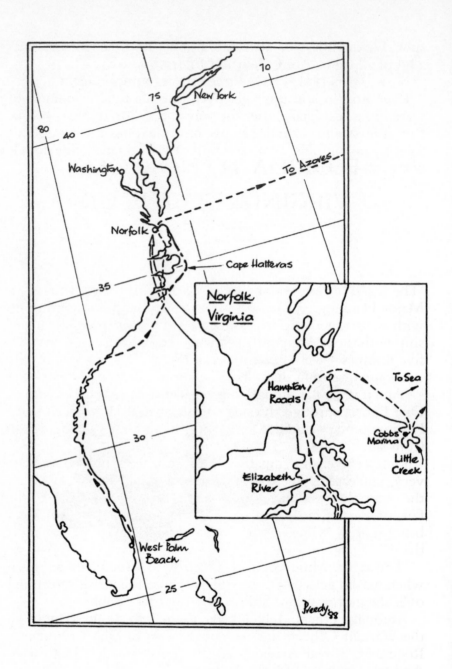

East Coast Of USA With Norfolk, Virginia
Inset

Chapter Three

FLORIDA TO NORFOLK, VIRGINIA, TO THE UK

'The worst bit was waiting to go ashore,' said Battery Sergeant Major Hanking. 'Once we were on dry land and getting on with it, it wasn't so bad. But just sitting out there on board ship with those Argentinian Super Étendards turning up every five minutes – well, it wasn't very funny, I can tell you.'

I waited, sensing that there was more to come.

'And it wasn't as though the ship had any real armour, either. One Exocet through the side and that would have been that.' His involuntary shudder set the beer in his glass swilling gently from side to side.

I felt a shiver of sympathy. 'No, I can see it must have been very unpleasant, to say the least,' I said. 'Funny, isn't it, the way that we have to re-learn the old lessons. To be fair, of course, more armour on a ship means less speed. But I bet I know which option you would have chosen right then.'

'Too right. Mind you,' he added with a rueful smile, 'even when we did get ashore, we still had those Étendards screaming over the gun position. Still, if you can't take a joke. . . .'

Amongst others, I had been invited to a guest night in the Warrant Officers and Sergeants Mess of 29th Commando Regiment, Royal Artillery at the Royal Citadel, Plymouth. And predictably, with the Falklands war still less than a year old, there was only one subject that we guests wanted to talk about. By some miracle, and despite being very much in the thick of things, not a single member of the Regiment had lost

43

his life. The most serious injury – a bad stomach wound caused by a mine – had been sustained by RQMS Armitage. But I had been talking to him only moments before and could see that, thankfully, he had made a complete recovery.

Although the conversation was continuing without a break around me, I found myself being diverted by, of all things, the matter of ship's armour. It wasn't that I was in any way technically inclined to the subject, quite the reverse. It was just that it had set me thinking of the very first armoured ships that had ever been constructed, both during the American Civil War: the *Merrimac* and the *Monitor*. It had been all of two years since those names had last chanced into my mind, yet the unusual context in which they had been set on that occasion was still sharp and clear. Despite the general hubbub around me, my thoughts were suddenly carrying me back across the Atlantic, to the very scene of their famous duel. . . .

*   *   *

It was just after three o'clock on a quiet Monday afternoon in late May, and I was climbing back aboard *Amélie*, a 36-foot Southerly 115, in Little Creek, Norfolk, Virginia. Five minutes before, I had rowed Chuck Johnson and his baggage to a little wooden landing stage 200 yards from the buoy to which *Amélie* was moored. Now, having returned to the empty boat, I was feeling suddenly lonely.

The twist of fate that had brought me here was, to say the least, a tortuous one. Originally, I had been asked by a delivery colleague in Southampton, England, if I would skipper the boat on the third stage of her voyage from Barbados to her new owner in Athens, the first two stages being Barbados to Norfolk and Norfolk to Gibraltar. Then, at the last minute, it had all been changed. Instead of the Mediterranean, I had joined the boat in West Palm Beach, Florida, to bring her up to Norfolk with Chuck Johnson. Now I was awaiting my two crew from England before setting off, via the Azores, for Gibraltar. There, in four weeks time or so, I would be handing over to someone else.

I won't be sorry either, I thought. Altogether, it will have meant nearly eight weeks away from home. All it needed now was for the plan to be changed yet again. I couldn't wait to ring the UK this evening in order to confirm the flight arrival time of the crew in Washington and to explain exactly where *Amélie* could be found. Provided everything went to plan, my two new shipmates would be on board by tomorrow night, and we would be leaving first thing the next day.

My decision to occupy a swinging mooring out in the creek rather than to go into one of the local marinas was, on the face of it, an unusual one. But quite apart from wanting a little peace and quiet after the noise and bustle of the American intra-coastal waterway, I particularly wanted to clean off *Amélie*'s underwater hull. Wearing masks and snorkel tubes, Chuck and I had done it once already, down in the Berry Islands. Yet it was time it was done again. An extra knot of speed across the Atlantic was not to be sneezed at.

Still, that will be something to occupy my time tomorrow morning, I decided. The first priority had to be my laundry. Despite all my attempts to stay abreast of the problem as we had come northwards, my clean clothes were now reduced to a light chequered shirt and a pair of blue shorts. And I was wearing both.

Ten minutes later I was embarked in the inflatable once more, rowing past the wooden jetty towards a small spur of land sticking out from the shoreline. A quick look at the *Compass Rose*, a boating services guide for Hampton Roads and the Lower Chesapeake, had indicated that Cobb's Marina lay just around the corner. 'W. W. Cobb at Little Creek Inlet since 1954,' it announced. 'Complete Haul-out and Repair; Ramp; Transient and Permanent Dockage; Fuel; Charter Boats.' Then, in case that wasn't enough of a 'grabber', it added: 'Fresh Seafood Market Features The Local Catch.' I was sold. True, it hadn't actually mentioned a washing machine, but the chances were that they had one, all the same.

Anyway, I thought, you're hardly in a position to pick and choose. Quite understandably, the bait which W. W. Cobb was dangling in the guide had been contrived to catch the kind of fish who would fill his finger berths with great big boats, not an itinerant scavenger looking for a fringe benefit. In my own defence, I had already half-decided to move into the marina tomorrow lunchtime anyway, once the bottom-scrubbing was finished, to refuel and then stay overnight. That would also make it easier for the crew to find the boat and load their luggage on board. Even so, I suspected that W. W. Cobb might have heard that cne before.

The fact that the marina was over 30 years old became more and more apparent as it slowly revealed itself round the headland. Certainly, it seemed to lack the superficial gloss that flattered many of the hundreds of marinas up and down the intra-coastal waterway. Yet, in my eyes, that was more a recommendation than otherwise, particularly as a closer in-spection indicated that all the things that mattered seemed to have been properly attended to. Thus, if the wooden pilings were unpainted and scuffed in appearance, they were also strong and substantial-looking. Nor were the berths themselves mean or cramped, while the well-sited life-saving equipment really looked as though it would work. The same informal, slightly haphazard appearance seemed to extend to the group of marina buildings scattered on the foreshore, I noticed as I beached the dinghy. Sited in no particular order, nor to any common design, they looked as if they had been added one by one as the marina had grown over the years. Indeed, the main shed, before which a large notice board repeated verbatim the words of the advertisement, appeared to be three buildings joined, end to end, into one. I pushed my way through the swing door into the first of them.

'Whaddya think, Elmer?' Immediately inside, a very large middle-aged lady wearing a white singlet, white shorts and sandals, was standing with her back to me. She was calling out shrilly to an elderly man standing some way down the long central aisle of what was evidently the chandlery department. As thin as a rake, the man I took to be her husband looked up from the large shackle he was inspecting to peer back at her over the top of his glasses. The lady accentuated her pose, tilting the peak of a dark blue yachting cap she was wearing one way, an intimidating hip the other.

Her partner side-stepped her question with an ease that suggested that he had done it before. 'You got somebody right behind you, Doris,' he growled, his voice weary rather than irritated.

'Oh gosh, excuse me!' exclaimed Doris in surprise, swinging round to fix me with a beaming smile. The long-tasselled price tag at the back of the cap oscillated wildly from side to side.

I smiled back. 'Please don't worry,' I said, holding my barrel bag in front of me to edge past her up the aisle. I made my way to the end, then stepped up two steps into the second room. There, a tall, thin lady with short, greying hair was standing behind a long counter, her pen flicking rapidly down a column of figures on the sheet of paper in front of her. I waited until she had scribbled the total at the bottom. The face that she raised to me looked careworn, a little ravaged by the passage of time, yet the kind, brown eyes and the quiet smile were encouraging me with their friendliness. I explained what it was I was looking for.

'A washing machine? Oh, sure,' she said nonchalantly. She pointed with her pen. 'If you go out of the door at the end there, you'll see a green trailer way over on the other side of the car park. The door's not locked, just go on in and you'll find the washing machine in the little alcove on the right-hand side.' She paused for a moment, studying me. 'I guess you're English, aren't you?'

'Yes, that's right,' I said.

'There y'are, Elmer, told you so,' came a furtive whisper from beyond.

'Well,' said the lady, appearing not to have heard the aside, 'I guess you won't know our machines over here, huh?'

'Not really, no,' I replied gratefully.

'OK, well, you'll want . . . hold on now, let me just have a look-see at what you've got in that bag.'

Feeling rather like a patient when the dentist says 'open wide', I drew back the zip of the barrel bag, pulling the sides about four inches apart to allow her a glimpse of the disgusting contents within. She leaned far over the counter to peer inside.

'Yeah, mostly cotton like I figured,' she said matter-of-factly. 'Alrighty, you want "Regular" and the "little pink shirt". Got it?'

'Regular and the little pink shirt,' I repeated, hurriedly closing the zip once more. 'Right, thanks very much.'

The green trailer was about 30 feet long, propped up on its legs on the other side of the unsurfaced car park. I opened the door and went in. Pleasantly surprised, I found myself in a spacious rest-room furnished with tables and chairs, including two armchairs. There was a pile of magazines on the table next to the door. Once again, it seemed, W. W. Cobb had concentrated on the things that really mattered, providing his customers with pleasant, relaxing surroundings while they waited for their clothes to be washed. Seen from the entrance, the entire left-hand end of the trailer was closed off by a partition, with a single door set into the middle of it. Clearly, another room lay beyond. On the right there was a similar arrangement, except that a narrow corridor led off further still to the right along the far side of the trailer. That, no doubt, led to the little alcove that the lady had mentioned.

The control panel on the enormous side-loading washing machine would have made Neil Armstrong suck his teeth. Thankful for my briefing, I emptied the clothes inside, shut the door, pressed the 'Regular' button and twisted the large dial clockwise to the little diagram of a pink shirt. Vaguely worried that there should also be an on/off button somewhere, I took a precautionary step backwards and waited. For 20 seconds or so nothing seemed to be happening. Then I heard a hissing noise and the sound of trickling water. Reassured, I made my way back to the rest-room.

From the moment I had seen the two armchairs I had been looking forward to trying them out. After all, it was not an item of furniture that I had seen much of recently, and I could already visualize the ease with which it would give, gloriously, under my weight. First, though, I headed for the periodicals on the table by the door. Noting wryly that a previous customer had left a pair of old socks beside them, I was just picking up the first magazine when I saw, half-hidden by a large table lamp, the picture on the wall behind.

I recognized the subject of the lithograph immediately from my history books. Yet in this case the artist's viewpoint was different from the famous one selected by Xanthier Smith. Seen from just above and behind the turreted platform of the *Monitor*, the severely truncated pyramid that was the *Merrimac* was depicted as lying barely 400 yards away across the scalloped water. Partially obscured by the smoke drifting from her guns and from her enormous chimney stack, *Merrimac*'s squat, angular profile contrasted crudely with the delicate tracery of a square-rigger anchored some distance beyond and to the right of her.

Fortunately for me, the American Civil War had been one of two campaigns that I had been obliged to study for the military history paper of my army staff college examination. Now, years later, and in a way that I could not possibly have envisaged then, the discipline of applied study paid off handsomely as I set about recalling the story of that momentous sea battle.

Originally one of the Federal Navy's steam frigates, *Merrimac*, had been promptly commandeered by the pro-Confederate community of Norfolk soon after war was declared. Raising her from the bottom of the Elizabeth River where the Unionists had scuttled her – and along which we had brought *Amélie* only yesterday afternoon – they soon turned the ship into a floating fortress, defiantly re-naming her the *Virginia*. That done, and with her decks awash under the enormous weight of her additional armour, *Merrimac* was then let loose, in early March 1862, on the enemy's wooden ships lying in nearby Hampton Roads. Before the end of that first day the Federal Navy's *Congress* and *Cumberland*, both powerless to resist the great iron juggernaut, had been destroyed, while the big steam frigate *Minnesota* had been driven aground.

The Union's reaction was swift. Aware of the potential threat for some months beforehand, the Federal Navy Department had literally just finished building the *Monitor*, described by some as 'a tin can on a shingle'. Consisting, again, of a platform barely a foot above the water, yet in this case with a central revolving turret mounting two 11-inch guns, a smoke pipe aft and a little navigating tower forward, the *Monitor* had been hurriedly towed down to Norfolk from New York. Arriving on the very evening of *Merrimac*'s victorious début, the two ships met next day face to face. The result of the duel was singularly indecisive. Both ships remained virtually intact despite the pounding of each by the other, the engagement was broken off towards the end of the day, never to be renewed.

In the end, it was only the Union army's occupation of Norfolk, right at the end of the war, that forced *Merrimac*'s captain to lower the Confederate flag and scuttle her once more. In naval terms she had remained undefeated. Yet that consolation would have been as nothing to the captain had he realized that the battle he had fought so doggedly against the *Monitor* had signalled nothing less than a wholesale revolution in naval warfare.

By the time I had flicked my way idly through the magazines, the intermittent rumbling of the washing machine was telling me that it was halfway through its washing cycle. Plenty of time yet, I thought, squirming a little deeper into the armchair. People really were kind over here, I acknowledged, thinking once again of how the lady had let me, a non-resident, use the marina's facilities without batting an eyelid. And I hadn't even had to mention my plans for tomorrow. Still, I shouldn't have been surprised. Time and again on our way up the intra-coastal waterway, people had gone out of their way to be friendly and to help us. The most obvious example had occurred only yesterday afternoon. In fact, it was that meeting that had led, indirectly, to my ending up at Little Creek.

We had been moored at the side of the waterway at Great Bridge, some twelve miles short of Norfolk, waiting for the lock gates to let us in to the mammoth, 660-foot lock. As on any Sunday afternoon the world over, the locals were out in force on the water. Amongst boats of every conceivable shape and size, one in particular had been engaging my attention. It was a small, two-seater racing boat, bright green in colour and sporting at the stern an enormous, chromium-plated, super-charged engine. Looking and sounding exactly like the marine equivalent of a dragster, its driver had been thrilling the attractive young brunette beside him for the last half hour with occasional rocket-like forays down the long, straight stretch of waterway behind us.

He had just returned, triumphant and breathless, from yet another run when I heard someone say something behind me. Knowing that Chuck was fast asleep in the cabin below, I turned round to see a dark, slight young man in shirt and slacks standing on the wooden quay beside the boat. Realizing that I hadn't heard him above the deep, throaty growl of the idling dragster, he said, 'I was saying, she's a little rascal, ain't she?'

'She certainly is,' I agreed, moving across to him. 'I've never seen anything like her before.'

'Hi, I'm Howdy Baily,' he said, holding out his hand with a smile. 'My sailboat's the third one behind you there.' He pointed towards a small sailing cruiser.

The name caught me a little off balance. Although I had heard it used in westerns, I had never actually met anyone called Howdy before. 'Ah . . . Ron Preedy,' I said, shaking his hand.

'I guess you're from England?' he said. I nodded. 'Not in that boat, though?' he asked.

'No.' I explained what Chuck and I were doing and went on to outline my plans for the trip across the Gibraltar.

'That must be quite a life,' said Howdy with a sigh. 'Still, I tell you, in another two or three years I'm planning on doing a little blue-water sailing myself.' He fished a business card out of his shirt pocket and handed it across to me. 'I make steel sailing boats for people, up in my boatyard at Little Creek. Anything up to 65 feet long. On my way back home now, as a matter of fact. Anyhow, I've finally decided that the next one is definitely going to be for me. Then I'm going to take off for a couple of years. Get across to Europe, down into the Mediterranean, that sort of thing. I've been waiting. . . .'

There was a sudden, loud squeaking noise that set my teeth on edge. The big swing bridge immediately in front of the lock gates, and after which the nearby town was named, was slowly pivoting upwards, warning that the lock gates were about to open.

'OK, well, I guess I'd better get back aboard,' said Howdy. 'But look, you find yourself anywhere near Little Creek when you get to Norfolk, be sure to look me up. Hell, I guess you're goin' to need to do some shopping and suchlike before you cut out for the Azores, and Norfolk's a big place, let me tell you. That means you'll be needing wheels. Come along and see me and, why, you can have the pick-up for as long as you need it. You all promise now?'

I had promised, delighted and touched by the generosity of his offer, by the trust which it implied on the strength of only five minutes' casual acquaintance. And tomorrow I was hoping to take him up on it. Quite apart from anything else, I needed two or three charts for the transatlantic trip, and of the two chart stockists mentioned in the *Compass Rose*, both were in downtown Norfolk.

The washing machine was just beginning a third, prolonged, drying spin. Almost finished, I thought, looking round to see where I had put the barrel bag. Even as I did so, I saw the door of the end room open slowly inwards.

Frozen to the armchair, I watched in blank amazement as an elderly, balding man gradually shuffled into the doorway from the room beyond. He was wearing a white, short-sleeved vest over which a pair of bright red braces curved generously downwards to a pair of grey flannel trousers. And he was bare-footed, I saw. Retaining hold of the door handle for support, he let a cavernous yawn escape him before padding, blinking, across the room towards the table by the door. Once there, he picked up the pair of socks, then turned to glance blearily in my direction. 'Hi,' he said, his voice still hoarse with sleep, before retracing his steps towards the room.

I awoke from my trance. 'Oh . . . ah, hello, good afternoon,' I stammered, appalled at the sudden dawning of light in my mind. Far from being the marina launderette, this trailer was actually somebody's home. No doubt the lady lived here herself, while, presumably, the man who had just disappeared into the end room was her husband. And I had calmly taken over their living room. Shocked into motion at last, I sprang out of the armchair and tore down the corridor to the washing machine. Thankfully, the circular glass door was already open. Seconds later, I was hurrying to the main door of the trailer, bits of laundry trailing from the open mouth of the barrel bag. Yet even as I did so, the elderly man reappeared in the doorway of the bedroom.

'Ah, I'm really terribly sorry,' I gabbled, my face hot with embarrassment. 'I honestly had no idea you were there. You see. . . .'

'No problem,' said the man, doing up his shirt. He had put his socks on by now. 'Git your washin' done?'

'Yes, fine thanks,' I replied. 'I really am very grateful. Well, I'll leave you in peace.' I made my escape.

Life is rarely what it seems, I grumbled, as I picked my way back across the car-park to the lady in the marina office. Still, one thing at least I can be pretty sure about. I've finally met W. W. Cobb.

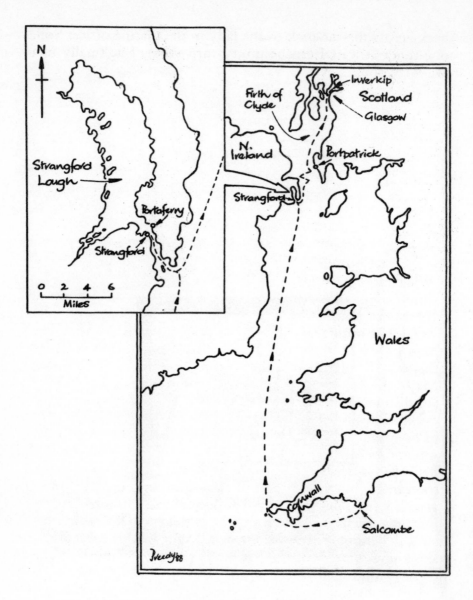

Within the inset map:

N

Strangford Lough

Portaferry

Strangford

0 2 4 6
Miles

Within the main map:

Firth of Clyde

Inverkip
Scotland
Glasgow

N. Ireland

Portpatrick

Strangford

Wales

Cornwall

Salcombe

Tweedy 88

Salcombe To The Clyde, With Strangford
Lough Inset

Chapter Four

NEWTON FERRERS TO
TROON, SCOTLAND

'What most persons consider virtue, after the age of forty is simply a loss of energy.'

I cannot claim to have read Voltaire. In this case his words were confronting me in bold black print from a page of my *Master Desk Diary*. Every double page carried a quotation, and this was the offering for the week beginning the fourteenth of May.

I dismissed the observation, anxious to record on paper the essential details of the telephone call while they were still fresh in my mind. It was Mary who had answered the phone a few minutes before. 'It's a Mrs Thurgood enquiring about a yacht delivery,' she had said noncommittally as I had hurried in from the garage. Now, putting my pen down once more, I glanced across at her. She was propped up with cushions on the settee, knitting. Feeling my gaze on her, she looked up quickly and smiled, her fingers still darting busily back and forth. As always, she knew that I would now fill in the gaps of the one-sided conversation she had just overheard.

'It's from Salcombe in Devon up to Inverkip marina on the Clyde,' I said. 'Leaving next Thursday.' I looked at my notes. 'Janet Thurgood. She and her husband are having to move up to Scotland at short notice because of his new job. He's already up there. Now they want to move the boat. It's a Sweden 36 – and very nice too, by the sound of it. Nearly new, all the usual gear plus automatic steering.' Mary always liked to hear that last bit; she knew how much physical effort it would save

55

me. She was waiting for me to continue. 'Anyway,' I said, 'she wants to come along as crew to save money. It looks as though she's done a bit of sailing.'

'So you won't be taking anyone else?' asked Mary.

'Well, not really,' I replied, aware that I was suddenly trying to justify the arrangement. 'As you probably heard, she feels she's quite capable of standing a watch on her own. Even if it's only three or four hours a day, that will be enough. After all, the whole thing should be over by Sunday evening. And apart from saving them a second return train fare, it will also save me the hassle of fixing up a crew.'

'Salcombe,' considered Mary thoughtfully. 'Gorgeous spot, but it's going to be a pain in the neck to get to, isn't it?'

'No, it's OK,' I said. 'She's going to pick me up from Plymouth by car. I'll have to ring her back with the train time. If possible, I want to be in Plymouth not much after nine o'clock on Thursday morning. That should get us to Salcombe by ten and then away, hopefully, by eleven.' I waited for her reaction.

Mary thought for a moment. 'You'll need your thick shirts,' she said.

Once again I found myself wondering about the woman I had been bright enough to marry 25 years ago. I could imagine what other wives might have said. Only a week ago, we had been enjoying lunchtime drinks at a neighbour's house when the subject of my yacht deliveries came up again. 'I really don't know how you can let him do it, Mary,' said one of the lady guests. 'I know I wouldn't.' I could see that she meant it. 'Sun, sea and sand – foreign parts – girls in bikinis – girls in half-bikinis, even. You don't know what he's getting up to.' Then she saw the look on my face. 'No,' she said, relenting, 'you mustn't mind my fun. I'm sure he's a model of good behaviour.'

'It's not that,' broke in Mary smoothly, the faint whiteness around her compressed lips betraying, to me at least, the irritation she felt. 'It's just that you obviously have no idea of what these deliveries are really like. You ought to see him when I pick him up at the station sometimes. He's absolutely on his knees.'

Mary must have read the quotation too, I thought flippantly,

56

my thoughts returning once more to the sitting-room. Yet she had spoken no more than the truth. At the risk of indulging in special pleading, I am convinced that most people, certainly those who do not sail themselves, do not, cannot, understand what yacht delivery is really like. Deliveries in the UK tend to be concentrated in the spring and autumn, as owners buy or sell boats or arrange for them to be brought back home after a holiday. It follows that for much of the time it is either blowing a gale, with seas to match, or it is foggy, or raining. Sometimes it is doing all three at once. Nor is this surprising. After all, it is often precisely in order to avoid a prolonged spell of bad weather himself that an owner engages a delivery skipper. In such circumstances, the rapid succession of one delivery after another soon takes on the character of a slogging-match, an unremitting test of endurance that deadens the senses, drains the energy. Nor – and this was the bit that people found hardest of all to swallow – are the foreign deliveries much better, notwithstanding the sunshine. Whether down to France, Spain, Portugal, Madeira, the Canaries, the Balearics or beyond, it is hard, at least for me, to summon up much enthusiasm for the aprés sail after a fortnight's regime of three hours sleep a night. Indeed, by then I have usually turned into a sort of nautical zombie, yearning for nothing more exciting than the first flight home.

Still, try convincing other people of that, I thought. Not that I could blame them. I had to admit that, on the face of it, it did appear to be a glamorous life-style.

'And your thermal underwear,' added Mary, absently.

★   ★   ★

'Why won't he pull over? God, these roads!'

Janet was driving, sitting well-forward on her seat, her small body hunched over the wheel. About 40 years old, blonde, blue-eyed, very attractive, she had tried twice to overtake the Tesco lorry on the outskirts of Salcombe. Now she was trying a third time. At the last moment a tractor appeared round the bend ahead of us. My right foot drove hard into the floor as I pushed backwards into my seat. Just in time, we managed to squeeze in behind the lorry again.

'Sorry,' she said, darting an apologetic look in my direction.

'Anyway, it doesn't matter now; we're nearly there.' Easing her foot off the pedal, she took a deep breath, then let it out again as she subsided backwards into her seat.

'So what's the programme now?' I asked, slowly releasing the handle on the passenger door.

'Paper shop first – that's on our way. Then back to the house for a couple of phone calls. Then, if you don't mind, I'll take you down to the jetty while I whizz off to sort out a few last-minute things. Now then, you should' – she emphasized the last word – 'find Henry Tattersall down there with his dinghy: elderly, tall, greying hair, probably wearing a donkey-jacket. He won't be long, anyway; I told him ten thirty. He's offered to take us out to *Harlot*, bless him, so we could pack up our own dinghy and stow it on board in advance. Anyway, I'll join you as soon as I can.'

It was the first time I had heard the name of the boat. Just as well that Mary hadn't, I thought.

The lady in the paper shop, her greying hair tied in a bun, was arranging packets of cornflakes when we burst in. 'Oh hello, Mrs Thurgood,' she said brightly, smiling through her glasses as she put the packets down. 'Today's the big day, then?'

'Yes,' replied Janet shortly. 'We're in a bit of a rush, I'm afraid. I'd like a packet of sugar and two boxes of matches please, Mrs Samens.'

'Right you are, m'dear.' She brought the items to the counter. 'And is this the gentleman that's going with you all the way to Scotland, then?' She leaned to one side to look past Janet, sending an arch smile beaming in my direction.

'That's right,' replied Janet, her face quite expressionless.

'Oh, very nice, I'm sure. And how's Mr Thurgood? Have you heard from him since he went up to Glasgow?'

'Yes, he's fine,' said Janet. 'Look, I'm sorry but I've just got to dash, Mrs Samens. What do I owe you?'

Henry Tattersall was not waiting at the jetty but turned up in his dinghy soon afterwards, complete with donkey-jacket. He was clearly sizing me up even as we shook hands over the pile of food and luggage I had unloaded from the car. He did not seem impressed. Evidently no man for beating about the bush, he got straight to the point in a way that suggested that he had already rehearsed what he wanted to say. 'Great friends of ours actually, the Thurgoods,' he asserted. 'Known young Janet for years. I would hate to see her come to any harm. I've done a bit of sailing myself, as a matter of fact, but I'm tied up at the moment. Otherwise I would have taken her up. Have you done many deliveries?'

Perfectly well aware of what was going on, I spent the next two or three minutes, as we loaded the dinghy, patiently answering one searching question after another. They ranged from navigation, through the rule of the road to the procedures for heaving-to in a storm. Whether I eventually passed the examination I do not know; I suspect not. Fortunately, however, Janet came hurrying round the corner just as we put the last box of food in the dinghy.

Half an hour later, *Harlot*'s engine was ticking over sweetly as Henry stepped carefully down into his dinghy once more, duty done. By now his manner toward me had softened somewhat, possibly because I had found him trying to bend on the mainsail upside down. 'Well, I'm sure she'll be in good hands,' he said to me as he pushed off with an oar, not making it clear whether he meant Janet or the boat. 'Look after yourself, Janet, and give my best to Stewart, won't you?'

'Yes I will, and thank you, Henry, for all your help. You've been a darling.' She blew him a kiss. For a moment Henry looked as though he was about to change his mind and come anyway.

'OK, Janet,' I said, 'if you can just keep the wheel steady, I'll slip the mooring. Then we'll let her just drift back off it a moment.'

Two minutes later we were on our way to Troon.

★   ★   ★

Harlot shuddered under the impact of yet another blow on her starboard bow. Even as I clung to the side of the chart table, I felt the boat fall away off the wind, heel over, then start to pick up speed once more as she clawed her way back on course.

No, I thought, this is no good. I looked again at the small cross I had just pencilled in on the chart. Some seven miles south-south-east of Strangford Lough, Northern Ireland, my date-time group entered beside the plot said '170500A May'.

59

Translated, that meant 0500 hours, British Summer Time, on 17 May. I'll wait for the 0555 hours forecast before making up my mind, I decided. But even now I was pretty sure what the man on Radio 4 was going to say.

It was the hour before dawn on Sunday morning, and so far we had been lucky. For three days we had made good progress, putting up mileages of well over a hundred miles a day as the wind had remained, cold but obliging, in the east. Then, just after midnight last night, it had backed anticlockwise to the north-east, so that now we had to stay hard on the wind in order to make good our course. There were three things wrong with that. First, if it backed even a tiny bit more, we would have to start tacking, and that would waste time. Second, even if it didn't back we would have the wind right on the nose anyway once we were through the North Channel and had turned north-east up the Firth of Clyde. And third, even as things were, we were starting to take a bit of a pounding. The wind-speed indicator was surging repeatedly from 24 to 28 knots, sometimes going higher still in gusts. Nor had it taken long for the sea to react.

For myself, this was nothing more than an uncomfortable nuisance, a little of the rough that goes with the smooth. Moreover, as things had worked out I had managed to get about three hours sleep per day, some at dawn, some before dusk. So I wasn't feeling specially tired. But Janet, now, that was different. Not that she had even come close to complaining, I recalled admiringly. Seventy-two hours on board, including an early bout of seasickness, had already confirmed my first impression of a tough-minded, resilient woman of considerable resolve and strength of character. All the same, I thought, this was not supposed to be the Sidney to Hobart race. What Stewart Thurgood undoubtedly wanted by the end of this trip was not only an undamaged boat, but a wife to match. All things considered, it began to look more and more as though we would have to run for shelter inside Strangford Lough.

Once again, I blessed my foresight in having brought along a number of large-scale charts of ports en route, of which Strangford Lough was one. I was certainly going to need it. Not only had I never made the passage inside before, but I was acutely aware that the entrance had an ugly reputation. Every six hours the tide squeezes through the bottle-neck entrance as it fills or empties the enormous inland lake behind it. Taken at spring tides and in winds above 25 knots – today's conditions precisely – the full force of the half-ebb tide would oppose the wind to kick up a roaring white-water chaos of a sea. The timing of one's approach was therefore crucial. Suddenly dry-mouthed, I looked again at the tide table. Allowing for the one-hour difference between GMT and BST, the ebbing tide in the entrance would go slack at 0628 hours precisely. That was the time to enter.

'Sole, Lundy, Fastnet, Irish Sea, Malin, Hebrides: north-easterly 6, occasionally 8 in Malin at first, decreasing 5 later. Fair, good.'

That settles it, I thought, as I put the pen back in the rack. In we go. Still, at least there's one thing; we shall be almost exactly on time arriving at the entrance. That really was a piece of luck. Usually, it worked the other way around, so that one had to lie off a bar or a harbour for three or four hours before being able to attempt entry. I climbed back out into the cockpit, a blast of cold air cutting into the back of my neck as I cleared the hatchway in the early light of dawn. Janet must have heard me. Suddenly, the hatch cover of the stern cabin slid back with a grating noise.

'Are we all right, Ron?' she called out anxiously, her face shadowed by the hood of her oilskin jacket.

'Yes fine, Janet,' I replied, trying to sound as casual as possible. 'I think we shall have to put in to Strangford Lough for a few hours, though. It's a bit of a nuisance, but I think it will be for the best. How do you feel about that?'

'Well, I would certainly much rather we were late arriving than take any chances,' she said. She saw me nod. 'Want any coffee or anything?'

'No, the thermos is still hot,' I replied. 'I should stay where you are for the time being if I were you.'

She raised her hand then disappeared below.

*   *   *

'Got it!' called out Janet from the bow.

Switching off the engine, I hurried forward to grab the mooring buoy from the end of her boat hook. Then I hauled in on the rope until I came to the heavy loop of chain. I made it fast around the samson post. 'Well,' I said, in the sudden silence, 'welcome to Strangford Lough.'

As so often at sea, the passage through the entrance that had so exercised my mind an hour before had turned out to be simplicity itself. We had caught slack water perfectly, the whirlpools on the surface the only augur of how things would be in three hours time. And now we were safe and sound inside, tied to a mooring not a hundred yards from the little village of Strangford itself. It was still only half-past seven, I saw, looking at my watch. It had taken no time at all to cover the three miles from the entrance on the first of the flood.

What a perfect spot this was. Further out in the middle of the channel, the wind was still shuddering across the surface of the water, as though some giant was scattering great handfuls of sand. But right here we seemed to be sheltered from all but the occasional eddy. I looked further afield. Half a mile away on the other side of the narrow channel, I could see Portaferry, basking in the morning sunshine. And now, turning to face the stern, I was able to enjoy my first real look at the quite stunning panorama of Strangford Lough. The further I looked, the more the verdant green shores fell back, as though deferring to the vastness of this natural inland lake, while of the far end of the lough there was no sign at all. For there, in the far distance, the sun had turned the water into a brilliant pool of yellow, drawing a veil of dazzling light over whatever lay beyond.

'Goodness, that is absolutely breathtaking,' said Janet. 'It was worth coming in just to see it.' Then, after a pause, she suddenly exclaimed, 'Oh my word, just look at this!'

Even before she spoke, I was already turning at the sudden sound of squabbling sea-birds. Directly in front of *Harlot*, and only 20 yards away, was a small rocky islet about ten yards in diameter, right in the centre of the harbour. And it was absolutely teeming with a breeding colony of arctic terns. I could only suppose that we had been too preoccupied to notice them before. But not now. Snowy-white, black-capped, fork-tailed, with red beaks and red webbed feet, the terns were suddenly protecting and proclaiming the limits of their territories. Not that they had far to go, I noted; each nest site was just about big enough for two birds and no more. Indeed, judging by another sudden squabble, over on the extreme left of the islet, one or two of them weren't even big enough for that.

The sight of a colony like this in a place as wild as Strangford Lough was hardly surprising in itself. But their precise choice of nesting site certainly was. I had no idea that they were so tolerant of people, let alone of the noise and bustle that would animate the village and harbour on any day other than Sunday. I tried hard to remember what I had read about them. Undisputed long-distance champions of the bird world, they had just spent our winter down in the Antarctic. There, enjoying the maximum period of daylight, they had first moulted, then grown a new coat of feathers, all the while building up their strength in the food-rich waters around them. That done, they had then flown a mere 8000 miles northwards to reach this precise spot in Strangford Lough, probably back in late March, before starting to breed about now. I smiled. There I'd been, moments before, thinking how well we had done in the three days since leaving Salcombe.

Janet dragged her eyes away at last. 'Well now, Skipper,' she said, 'I think one could say that you've earned a bit of breakfast.'

It was just after nine o'clock when I rowed us ashore in the dinghy. Even now, it seemed, Strangford was only just waking up to this Sunday morning. The first few people were walking across the village square, calling out to each other as they passed. 'Ah, there we are,' said Janet, climbing out of the dinghy, 'I can see a small grocer's shop from here. Lovely. Oh, and look, there's the phone box. Tell you what, why don't you ring Mary first while I get the bread and fruit? Then I'll go after you.'

Mary sounded relieved to hear my voice. 'I was watching the weather on the box,' she said. 'It didn't look too good for the top end.'

'Malin,' I supplied. 'No, they're talking about a possible gale, but at least it doesn't look like lasting very long. We'll just have to hope for the best. Meanwhile, I won't be sorry to catch up on a little sleep.'

'No, of course,' she said. 'Anyway, take care when you set off again, won't you?'

Janet was not so fortunate with her call. She pushed her way out of the telephone box, a frown on her face. 'No reply,' she said. 'My own fault, I suppose – I should have phoned earlier. He told me he would probably be working in the office today so as to have a little time for the boat once we get in.' She sighed heavily. 'Now, I do have the number of the next-door neighbour, he gave me that just in case. I'm just wondering if I should ring them.'

'That's your answer,' I replied. 'If you ask them to tell Stewart that you rang, he can call us up on the ship-to-shore telephone through Portpatrick once he comes home.'

'Of course,' she said, her face brightening. 'Then we won't have to come ashore again.'

★   ★   ★

It was four o'clock in the afternoon. Refreshed with sleep I emerged, blinking, from the main cabin into the brightness of a cockpit bathed in sunshine. Earlier, Janet too had been catching up on her sleep down in the stern cabin. But now, I saw, she was sitting up in the bow watching the terns. 'Good sleep?' she asked, smiling as she rose to make her way back towards me.

'Not bad at all,' I conceded, still only half-awake.

'You know,' she said, 'I could watch those birds for hours on end. They're such characters.' She stepped down into the cockpit, then started down the companionway steps into the main cabin.

'Oh, I hope I didn't keep you waiting,' I said. 'You shouldn't have bothered about me sleeping.'

'I didn't,' she replied. 'I came down twice before while you were asleep. I think it would have taken the local silver band to wake you up.' She laughed, then disappeared inside.

I listened to the welcome sound of the water pump whining away as Janet filled the kettle. Over to my left, the local car ferry was making its way, crabwise, across to Portaferry. Once again I found myself hardly believing how far to the left it had to shape its course in order to offset the tide. Now, as it met the full force of the ebb in mid-channel, I saw it drifting with surprising speed back to the right again. There was proof, if any were needed, of the strength of this half-tide current. Suddenly, I heard the sound of someone speaking on the radio down below.

'Ron, it's Portpatrick!' Janet called out urgently from the cabin. I hurried below.

'Yacht *Harlot*, this is Portpatrick radio, I say again I have a telephone call for you, over.'

'Hullo Portpatrick, this is yacht *Harlot*,' I replied, breathing hard. 'Please go ahead, over.' During the pause that followed I passed the handset over to Janet.

'Ah, this is Stewart Thurgood speaking,' said another voice. 'Please may I speak to Janet, over?'

'This is me speaking,' said his wife, smiling at the sound of his voice. 'How are you, darling, over?'

Deciding it was time to make myself scarce, I turned to climb out of the cabin once more. But Janet motioned me back again with a quick movement of her hand.

'Never mind me, how are you? What has happened, over?'

'I'll put Ron on to speak to you a moment,' she said. 'He'll explain.'

I kept the explanation short, concentrating on the strength and direction of the wind that had been forecast. I handed the telephone back to Janet.

'Odd, really,' said Stewart, 'there's hardly a breath of wind here in Glasgow, over.'

Janet paused for a split second. 'Well, there's plenty here,' she said, her voice suddenly sharp and brittle.

'So anyway, you're both OK, over?' returned Stewart smoothly.

'Yes, we're both fine but obviously waiting to get going again. Ron thinks we will be able to leave in the morning, over.'

There was a pause. Then, in a way that, even to me, sounded deliberately provocative, he said, 'So how are the two of you managing to pass the time together, over?'

I was halfway up the cabin steps when Janet replied. 'Sleeping,' she said acidly, her indignation given even greater force by her refusal to add another word.

My head was still spinning as I sat down on the foredeck. It really was a bit much, I thought. First of all she has Mrs Thingummy with her heavy innuendo in the shop back in Salcombe. Then she is knocked around for three days at sea and is sick into the bargain. And now for good measure her husband has just added insult to injury, wounding her with words as only a partner can. Uncomfortably aware that I had more than once reacted in much the same way towards Mary, I guessed that his comments, however distorted by feelings of impotence, even jealousy, at our enforced isolation, were nevertheless evidence of the depth of his feeling for her. Right now, though, she would find it hard to see it that way. Nor could I try to show her without taking far too much for granted. Admittedly, over the past three days we had built up an easy, companionable relationship in a way that would have been quite impossible in more normal surroundings. But these were much deeper waters.

Ten minutes later she came up into the bow, the redness around her eyes ample evidence that she had been crying. Just at that moment I wanted very badly to meet Mr Stewart Thurgood. At a loss to know how to comfort her, and mindful of the embarrassment she must be feeling, I transferred my attention once more to the terns. She sat down quietly beside me.

At the very top of the little islet there was a tiny platform of rock just large enough for one nest. At this moment only one of the pair was in residence, sitting well-down on the eggs beneath. Then, even as I watched, its partner turned up. Slightly smaller, she landed right beside him, immediately making the little movements that signified her readiness to take over incubation duty. I had witnessed the same performance a hundred times already on a hundred different nesting sites. This time, though, there was a twist at the end. Suddenly, another larger bird approached from behind the crest, bobbing and weaving at her in the full ritual of courtship. The reaction was swift and violent. The male on the nest suddenly flew at the intruder, pecking with all the instinctive venom inside him. Then, as his victim quickly retreated, he turned round again to deliver another vicious peck, this time at his mate.

'Hoy, that's not fair,' protested Janet loudly. 'She didn't do anything!'

'No, she didn't,' I agreed. Then I managed to say something right for once. 'It's funny, isn't it, they could almost be human sometimes.'

For a long moment Janet said nothing. Then I heard her quiet laugh beside me. 'Yes, you're absolutely right,' she said with feeling, looking at me at last. I saw her shoulders suddenly relax. 'Well now, Skipper,' she said with a smile, 'what time are we off in the morning?'

★   ★   ★

Mary was waiting for me in the small reception hall of Newquay airport. I had managed to fly down from Glasgow to London and then catch a Brymon Airways flight on to Cornwall. I hurried across to her, took her in my arms and kissed her. Then, as she always did, she pushed back slightly to look into my eyes and measure my tiredness. This time, though, I fancied that she paused a little longer. 'How was it?' she asked.

'Not too bad,' I replied. 'I hadn't expected the Strangford Lough episode, of course. But it worked out OK. It was just a question of sticking to the rules.'

She kissed me again, a little longer this time. 'Right, sailor,' she said, 'let's find your bag and then get you home.'

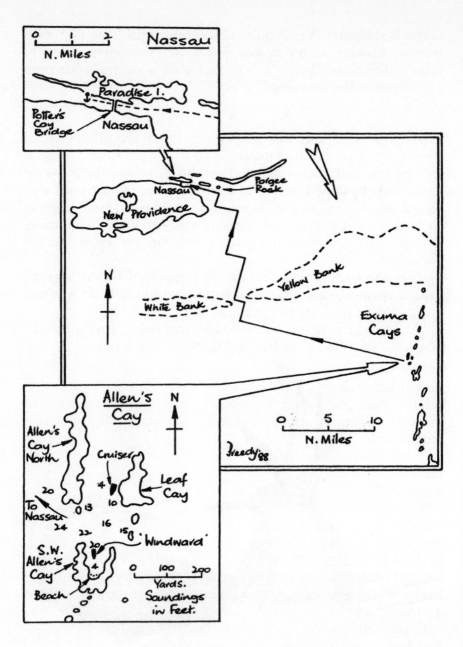

Allen's Cay To Nassau, Bahamas

Chapter Five

BARBADOS TO FLORIDA

'Watch out furry daggons, buddy.'

I was halfway down the boarding ladder, one leg bent, the other already knee-deep in the water. Pulling myself up again, I peered through my face mask over the top of the high stern.

'What was that again, Fozz?' I asked. From here the only bit of him I could see was his bandaged hand resting on top of the port-hand cockpit coaming. The rest was hidden by the stern cabin. I had left him a moment before, enjoying a beer in the sort of sunny, late afternoon for which the Bahamas are renowned.

'I said "watch out for the dragons," ' he said more loudly, carefully articulating his words in his east coast American accent.

'Oh, right . . . will do,' I replied lamely, unable to think of a better one or to put off any longer the pleasure that awaited me. I lowered myself slowly back into the water, luxuriating in the delicious coolness as it rose up my body. Then, clamping the end of the breathing tube between my teeth, I let go of the ladder to paddle gently, head down, along the side of the 45-foot ketch.

Even from the deck, the dappled white sand 20 feet below had been quite startling in its clarity. Now, listening to the magnified sound of my own breathing, I just seemed to be suspended in space. Nearing the bow, I floated lazily on to where the heavy anchor cable curved steeply downwards to the sand, every link sharp and clear. That was the nice thing about the Bahamas, I decided: it was so easy to check the anchor. In this case the twin flukes of the big Danforth were well and truly embedded in the sand, the result of a quick burst astern with the engine when we had dropped anchor in this deserted bay half an hour earlier.

And to think I'm being paid for this, I marvelled. I didn't even have to lift my head to see where I was going. *Windward* was looking straight at the little beach not a hundred yards away. All I had to do was to follow where the anchor cable had pointed. Now, the white sand plain below me was gradually rising up as the water shallowed, giving way to the first foothills of slowly waving sea grass. Here and there among the dark green blades I picked out the beige cornucopia of a conch shell, a branch of pale yellow finger coral, the delicious lilac tinting of a venus sea fan. Further away to my left, three or four red-finned fish patrolled the top of the forest, their mouths slowly opening and closing. Beyond them again there was a brief flash of silver.

Suddenly my sublime serenity was shattered with all the force of a physical blow. Dead ahead, exposed on a patch of sand in all its ugliness, was a discarded Coca-Cola can. The indignation almost choking me, I forced my legs downwards to stand up in water chest-high. It's quite incredible, I thought as I stripped off the face mask, how some people's minds work. They come to an idyllic spot like this, then promptly desecrate it by. . . .

There was a sudden scuffling in the dry scrub at the back of the beach. Now there was another, a little further to the right. And another. Heart suddenly beating faster, I waded through the shallows towards the shore, hardly daring to hope. Then, all of a sudden, there they were, breaking through the screen of scrub, bouncing from side to side as they ran, helter-skelter, down the sand towards me.

Wild creatures are seldom so appealing as when they come close for food. Whether a robin in the garden or ponies on Dartmoor, we respond immediately to the trust implicit in their action, while postcards the world over testify to the enduring charm of the scene they present. The same could hardly be said of the great marine iguana. The nearest one had stopped about eight feet away. No, I thought, still heady with delight, 'charming' was hardly the word to apply to this five-foot specimen as he presented himself, quite motionless, for my inspection. From his heavy-lidded eyes, his splayed, claw-toed forelegs, right down the whole narrowing wedge of his leathery hide to the end of his long tail, he looked for all the world as though he had stepped straight out of pre-history. Now there were at least half a dozen on the beach, ranging in size from about two feet long to the big chap right in front of me. The others had stayed a little further away; not from fear of me, I sensed. They just knew their place.

Sadly for them, though, their quest was a fruitless one. It hadn't been the physical difficulty of bringing food with me; it was more that, like the ponies on Dartmoor, feeding the iguanas on Allen's Cay – the second word is pronounced 'key' – is strongly discouraged. Yet the stampede of a few moments before had clearly demonstrated that it still happened. Part of the problem, I suspected, was that most people couldn't see how the iguanas could possibly survive on an island totally devoid of food of any kind. So they fed them. Yet if my memory served me correctly, these creatures lived on weed lying well below the low-water mark. Hence the name 'marine iguana'. The big one seemed to have been reading my mind. Suddenly he turned away again to head, disgusted, back into the scrubby hinterland. In less than a minute the beach was deserted once more, the distinctive feet and tail marks the only evidence of what I had seen.

At the far end of the beach the ribbed skeleton of a wooden dinghy lay stranded just beyond the high-water mark. Unlike the Coca-Cola can, this piece of refuse offended me not at all as I walked slowly towards it. On the contrary, in a place that Captain Henry Morgan might have known well, it seemed entirely in character with its surroundings. But the filthy pile of rubbish in the scrub just behind it was a different matter. Thrown onto a patch of earth scorched black by fire were all the sordid remains of someone's barbecue: wine bottles, spirit bottles, tin cans, cardboard cartons, even a discarded pair of flip-flops. The sight depressed me beyond measure. For the second time in less than ten minutes the afternoon had been blighted by the unacceptable face of modern civilization.

I had more or less recovered my spirits by the time I returned to the boat. Fozz was down below in the cabin. 'That was really something,' I called down to him, throwing the mask and tube onto the cockpit seat. 'About seven of them altogether.'

'Yep, saw 'em from here,' said Fozz. He delivered the words slowly, with his usual economy of effort. 'Any fish?' Unlike me, he was a fully qualified sub-aqua diver, and I knew that he habitually caught more meals than he paid for. Not right now, though, given his injured hand.

'Three or four mutton fish,' I replied. 'And what may have been a bonefish. Nothing else.' I rubbed myself down with the towel he had thrown out to me. 'There's something else ashore, though,' I added bitterly. 'Some bright sparks have had a party and left a pile of rubbish behind. Can you believe it?'

I watched his shoulders rise, then fall again in a heavy sigh. 'Yeah, I can believe it all right,' he said wearily. 'Pity, though; last time I came through here it was as clean as a whistle.' He put down the can opener he was holding to come towards the hatchway, gripping the sill with his long brown hands. A little younger than me, he was tall and lean with lank black hair, his skin the colour of stained teak. He looked up at me, concern in his grey eyes. 'How bad is it?' he asked.

'Bad enough,' I replied. 'Certainly too bad to leave. Which is why I'm going straight back in the dinghy to bury it before it gets dark. I'll just put a pair of shorts on first. I don't suppose you've got a shovel aboard, have you?'

'Somewhere,' he replied, looking away and frowning. 'Now then, where . . .?'

The loose sand made the digging easy, allowing my mind to range free. I had turned down Fozz's offer of help, not so much because he couldn't use his hand; he could at a pinch. But it was essential that he should keep it as clean as possible. After all, I reflected somewhat callously, I owed it a lot. It was the hand that had brought me out of the wind and rain of a Cornish January in the first place.

Cast your bread upon the waters, I thought. Back in Cornwall six months before, I had been in a position to respond immediately to a delivery request from Falmouth Marina. That same evening I was on board *Windward* bound for Guernsey, along with her owner, Mr Stanley Haber of Long Island, New York, and her permanent professional skipper, Martin, or

'Fozz' Fosdick, originally of Atlantic City, New Jersey. The journey over, I had returned to St Agnes by air and thought no more about it. Then, just two weeks ago, had come the call from Antigua. It was Fozz. Very quickly he had explained that he had put his hand on a spiny sea urchin while skin diving. Despite applying the standard remedy – removing all the spines that could be easily extracted and covering what was left with hot candle wax to neutralize the toxin and cushion the area – the hand had quickly become swollen and inflamed. In the end it had meant hospital. But the real problem was that he had to leave in seven days' time to meet Stanley Haber in Fort Lauderdale, Florida. Hence his request – one confirmed by the owner – that I fly out to join him.

Over the phone there hadn't been time, nor was I inclined, to ask why a delivery skipper had not been sought from Nicholsons, the big Antigua-based yacht agency. It couldn't be my natural charm, I thought. In the end I had had to wait five days for my answer. Sitting in the cockpit of *Windward* as we left Falmouth harbour, Antigua, bound directly for the Turk and Caicos islands, Fozz had considered the question for a moment.

'Well, I guess you're the devil I know, Ron,' he said with his quiet smile. 'And Stanley went for it straight away.'

'But what about the air fares?' I persisted. 'On top of my fee it's not peanuts, is it?'

'It is to him,' he said with a laugh. 'That's what he deals in, partly: peanuts – real ones. No, I guess our idea of a lot of money is a whole lot different to his. He'll probably make it up in a day. Meantime he's much more concerned about his boat. Anyway, to borrow one of your English sayings, it's no skin off your nose, is it?'

No, I thought with a rueful smile, as I trod the last can into a hole that I hoped was deep enough to deter the iguanas, no skin off my nose, not then. But plenty now. We had been going hard for the last week and my winter complexion had taken quite a beating. Today, in fact, had been the first day that I had dared to strip off; and only then in the late afternoon.

It was almost dark by the time I brought the rubber dinghy alongside *Windward*'s port quarter. Fozz took the painter. 'See that guy over there?' he asked quietly.

I turned to follow his pointing finger. Three hundred yards

away, on the far side of the channel separating us from two other small cays, I could just make out the dim outline of a substantial motor cruiser. It was unlit and at anchor. 'Well, well, when did she turn up?' I asked.

'Just as you were landing in the dinghy. But I'm not surprised you didn't see her. They came in slow and quiet, dropped the hook and that was it. I haven't seen a sign of them since. She's a scruffy-looking tub, too. I guess you can't tell now, but they sure don't spend a whole lot of time cleaning her. Anyhow, come on – chow.'

We ate in silence for most of the meal, each aware of what the other was thinking. On the afternoon of the previous day the standard chat show, broadcast by a Florida radio station, had concentrated on what was undoubtedly the single most important issue in this part of the world: drug running. It was old news as far as Fozz was concerned, but it had certainly opened my eyes. Progressing from the early days of small motor boats, the drug barons were now smuggling large quantities of narcotics into Florida on board cargo ships. More to the point though, they were continuing to supplement this with small boat landings. Yet now they were no longer using their own craft; these were too easily traced and monitored. Instead, they had taken to piracy, commandeering small pleasure boats, including sailing boats, belonging to innocent tourists. There had been three or four cases of this in the last six months alone, most of them well-documented. Nor had many of the victims escaped with their lives.

Not surprisingly, with the programme still fresh in our minds, there was an obvious temptation to read more into our situation than there actually was. It was at least a thousand to one, I reminded myself, that this was just one more of the swarm of cruising boats that invaded the Bahamas at this time of the year. Still, he had turned up very late. Rule number one in the Bahamas, one I had learnt quickly during my first passage in 1985, is not to attempt to sail at night. In water so shallow, the only safe way to proceed is by day, preferably with the sun behind you. That way it is relatively easy to read the colour of the water ahead. Distracted for a moment by the thought of tomorrow, I rehearsed the general principles in my mind. A green patch means a white sandy bottom at least eight feet deep; the darker the colour, the greater the depth. A darkish blue-green patch means a grassy bottom, probably of at least the same depth. But ivory-white water shading to a pale turquoise warns of a sand shallow only one or two feet beneath the surface, while brown water, more ominous by far, signifies coral heads. Hard enough to pierce a boat's hull, the darkest of them would be less than a foot below the surface.

Really, it took a lifetime to learn all the secrets of these waters. Even now I was only moderately experienced, despite my earlier voyage. Thankfully, though, Fozz was an expert. But even he wouldn't have cut his arrival time as fine as the motor cruiser had, I reasoned, returning to my theme. I was about to make the point to him as he unlocked a strong wooden cabinet on the starboard bulkhead amidships. The next moment he had opened the door, reached inside and extracted a hefty-looking revolver.

We were ready for bed. Normally, Fozz slept in the other cabin but not tonight. About to switch off the cabin light and climb into my quarter bunk, I had a final look at him on the opposite settee berth to see if he was comfortable. Even now, he still had to rest his arm on cushions. But he seemed happy enough. 'How's that hand doing, Fozz?' I asked, nodding at the cushions.

'Not too bad, buddy,' he replied. 'I guess I'll survive.' The phrase seemed to hang in the air between us, charged with unwanted meaning. 'OK,' he said, 'you can hit the lights when you're ready.'

Even as I flipped off the switch, a strange, wavering bird-like call broke the silence of the late evening. It was immediately answered by another. 'I didn't realize there were any birds on the island,' I said; 'I certainly didn't see any.'

Fozz chuckled softly. 'Everybody's fooled the first time they hear it. I was too. That, my friend, is your regulation marine iguana about to ensure the survival of the species.'

'It can't be,' I said in disbelief, trying to relate the fragility of the call to the armoured amphibian I had seen earlier.

'It surely is, believe me. And I have a nasty feeling you're going to hear a lot more of it before the morning. Night.'

★　　　★　　　★

75

'Green for a long way now.'

Fozz walked carefully back from the bow along the windward side deck as the ketch cut her way, close-hauled, through the transparent green water. It was 1100 hours on another beautiful morning, and we were steering a course of 295° magnetic under all plain sail. After a quiet start, the breeze had picked up gradually to settle at about 12 knots from the north-west, just enough to let *Windward* show off again. She was a beautiful boat, beautifully maintained. By now I had long since learned to look beyond the superficial gloss that most boats can affect to the things that really mattered. Every moving part was well-maintained and well-lubricated. Every part that might move, but shouldn't – such as a bottle-screw or a shackle pin – was properly secured and bowsed down. All areas of potential chafing, whether on sails or running rigging, had been properly protected. And so on. She was certainly worth the trouble. From her clean-cut bow all the way down her teak-lined deck to the Stars and Stripes flying bravely at the stern, she was every inch a thoroughbred with a performance to match her looks.

No place for automatic steering systems, given the underwater hazards all around us, I had taken over the wheel from Fozz half an hour earlier. Earlier still, I had winched up the anchor just after sunrise, leaving him to manoeuvre the boat carefully out of the cay entrance before heading her north-westwards towards Nassau, capital of the Bahamas. Nassau was to be our next overnight stop, and almost certainly our only one before we set out across the deeper waters of the Great Bahama Bank, through the tumble of the Gulf Stream, to our destination: Fort Lauderdale, USA.

Fozz had stopped here and there to check the rigging. Now he stopped again, shading his eyes to look astern before stepping down into the centre cockpit. 'Well, I'll be damned,' he said. 'Don't look now but I think that's her behind us.'

For a moment I thought he was indulging his somewhat distressing tendency to get me going. The motor cruiser, dirty and unkempt in the morning light, had still been lying to anchor when we left. Nor had she moved for some time after that, as both of us knew from our frequent looks astern. But she was there now all right, about three miles behind us and closing. Even as the tension mounted inside me, \I was telling myself

76

not to be stupid. Nearly 15 miles out from Allen's Cay, we were only 20 miles now from Nassau, home of the Bahamian Defence Force. The radio was tuned to Channel 16 on listening watch and we had already heard C6N3, the Nassau marine operator, talking to a patrol boat in our area. All the same. . . .

'Would you mind taking the wheel again for a bit, Fozz?' I said. 'The log's almost up to 1463 – that's our safe distance limit for Yellow Bank. I'd better just go and have a look at the chart.' We had taken turns with the navigation all the way from Antigua. Today it was my turn. The satellite navigator confirmed that we were about two miles short of the junction between Yellow and White Banks. This was the recommended crossing point over a treacherous belt of shallows stretching right across our path. In places, coral heads rose to within two feet of the surface. It wouldn't do to get this wrong. Yet as things stood, I could see that the northerly breeze had pushed us about three miles or so to the south-west of our desired course. Clearly, we would have to put in a tack to starboard before attempting the gap. 'Time we went on to the other tack,' I called out to Fozz as I climbed back into the cockpit.

Fozz had evidently been expecting it. 'Ready about,' he called out immediately. The manoeuvre completed, we settled down on to the new tack. Now then, I thought as I fiddled with the tension on the starboard sheet, let's wait and see if the cruiser does the same thing.

'Let's see if the cruiser does the same thing,' said Fozz, looking behind him. Even as he spoke, the big white hull behind us heeled slowly over to starboard, sending its port-side bow wave high into the air.

'Well, it still might not mean anything,' I said. 'After all, he wants to find the gap just as much as we do.'

'Sure, but why follow us?' said Fozz. 'We had no option but to finish up to the left of the gap; hell, we're sailing hard on the wind. But he's not. He could have gone straight for the gap from the moment he left Allen's Cay.'

The cruiser had suddenly slowed down about two miles astern of us. 'True,' I agreed. I considered for a moment. 'The only other possible explanation, I suppose, is that he doesn't have good enough chart coverage for this area. So he's relying on us to show him the way.' Even as I said it, I realized with a

77

feeling of some relief that this theory really did fit all the facts. Time and again I had met owners who, reluctant to spend on their charts a tiny fraction of what they lavished on their boats, made a habit of following others. They obviously hadn't heard the one about the boat that followed a dredger on its way to unload its cargo on a nearby sand-bank. Then again, I could remember another bright sunny morning like this one; two years ago, off the north-west tip of Spain. On that occasion I had been doggedly pursued for well over an hour by a large white Bermudan sloop under full sail plus engine. Bound for the nearby fishing village of Las Camarinas, I had eventually stopped just short of the Cape Villano lighthouse to see what he wanted. 'Which way to Corunna?' had yelled the man in the bow as soon as he was close enough. Having told him to turn left and follow the coast for 20 miles – I had thought it better to keep it simple – he waved happily at me before the boat sheered off to the north-east. So it did happen.

But that was then; this was now. The cruiser was keeping station about two miles astern of us. Half an hour later he did exactly the same thing as before. As we tacked to head straight for the gap, so he turned to follow us. The passage through the gap was quite exciting. Standing at the wheel, my eyes moving constantly between the echo-sounder, the compass and Fozz's hand signals up in the bow, we were through in less than ten minutes. Then it was time to tack again, this time in order to make good our new mean course of 355° magnetic, almost directly into wind. From this point onwards we would have to make short tacks all the way to Nassau. But at least there would be no more worries about shallow water.

It was nearly 1600 hours by the time we downed sail just one mile short of the Porgee Rock light tower, at the eastern end of New Providence island. All that remained now was to turn to port under engine and head up the channel between New Providence and little Paradise island, to our chosen anchorage off the great city of Nassau.

By this time the motor cruiser had been relegated in our minds to little more than an object of mild curosity. It had continued to shadow us right through the afternoon, always hanging back two miles or so behind us. Indeed, we were passing under the huge centre span of Potter's Cay bridge, less than a mile from where we would drop anchor, before I suddenly realized that they – whoever they were – no longer required our services. Almost before we were aware of it, the motor cruiser was roaring past, about a hundred yards away on the port side. The man on the wheel was just visible through the tinted glass of the side window. He was looking straight ahead.

Ten minutes later we were lying at anchor, 200 yards off Paradise island. Even with the engine off I soon realized that, if it was a paradise at all, it was a noisy one. From somewhere close ashore an amplifier was broadcasting a selection of the latest pop songs, seemingly without a break. No, I thought, I'll take the peace and quiet of the Exuma Cays any time. Suddenly I felt glad that we would be leaving first thing in the morning.

For now, though, we decided to seek refuge below. Yet even as I turned to follow Fozz down the steps, I noticed something out of the corner of my eye. About 200 yards astern of us, the cruiser, unmistakable in its shabbiness, had suddenly reappeared to drop anchor. The man on the bow still refused to look in our direction. Having secured the anchor cable, he turned in a single movement, his eyes glued to the deck, before hurrying back aft.

'Guess who's just turned up astern?' I called out.

Fozz came up into the cockpit once more. 'He sure seems to enjoy our company, doesn't he?' he said. 'Still, let's forget it. What about a beer?'

We were halfway through the first can when something bumped us hard on the starboard side. Immediately there was the sound of feet landing on the side deck. Fozz and I reached the companionway at the same moment. Even as we did so, two black men in naval working blues, berets on their heads, jumped down into the cockpit. They turned to face us, automatic weapons pointing downwards. The next moment another, larger, black man joined them. There were two bars on his shoulder epaulettes; otherwise he was dressed the same.

'What in God's name is going on?' demanded Fozz angrily, about to climb up out of the cabin.

'Just stay where you are, sir, if you don't mind,' said the officer, raising both hands, palms towards us, in a calming motion. His English was impeccable, I noticed. 'I am an officer of the Bahamian Defence Force,' he continued, seemingly quite unruffled. 'I now wish to come below to search your vessel.' As we fell back before him he made his way carefully down the companionway steps. 'Now, gentlemen,' he said, 'may I ask which one of you is the owner of this boat?'

'Neither of us,' said Fozz, 'but I'm the skipper. This boat belongs to Mr Stanley J. Haber of Long Island, New York. I work for him. My name is Martin Fosdick.' The use of his proper Christian name caught me out for a moment. 'Fozz' suited him much better, I thought.

'I see. And you, sir?' He turned to me, catching me unprepared. I explained who I was. He seemed satisfied. 'Well now,' he continued calmly, 'you will save time if you just allow my men to go about their work unimpeded. Meanwhile, I suggest you take a seat.' Still the same perfect English, I noted. Whether in terms of diction or usage, I was pretty sure which one of us the BBC would have chosen.

At a signal from him one of the ratings slid back the hatch of the after-cabin, then disappeared inside. The other joined us in the main cabin before making his way discreetly forward into the forepeak. Now the officer turned his attention to his immediate surroundings. Opening up lockers here, lifting bunk seats there, he carried out a systematic search. Finally, he came to the locked wooden cupboard on the bulkhead amidships. I had the feeling that it was the first thing he had noticed, but he had been in no hurry to get to it. 'Have you the key to this, sir?' he asked, turning to Fozz. Fozz lifted the top of the chart table to fish out the key from a little hook. He also removed at the same time an official-looking document which he promptly thrust towards the officer.

'These are the official ship's papers,' he said. 'Don't you want to check them out?' He's playing for time, I thought in horror. He's got no licence for the revolver.

'All in good time, sir,' said the officer, his eyes never wavering for a moment. 'I'll just have the key if I may?' Fozz handed it over. 'You have a licence for this weapon, I take it?' said the officer a moment later, holding the revolver flat in the palm of his hand.

'Yes sir, I do,' said Fozz quickly, anticipating the question. 'It's right there in the cupboard.' I could see he meant it. Good old Fozz, I thought with a sigh of relief.

The officer looked inside, found the piece of paper and

examined it carefully. 'And the weapon is also listed on the transire?' he continued. 'One moment,' he added before Fozz could speak, 'I see you also have it here in the cupboard.'

'Officer, would you mind explaining what all this is about?' asked Fozz, the impatience evident in his voice.

'Yes, sir, of course,' said the officer as calmly as ever, replacing the documents in the cupboard. 'We have reason to believe that you may be carrying prohibited substances on board your vessel.'

'Prohibited substances?' echoed Fozz. 'Drugs, you mean?'

'Drugs sir, yes. Perhaps I could ask you where you have just come from? Today, that is.'

'We left Allen's Cay this morning, about eight o'clock,' replied Fozz.

'Yes, that ties in with our information. We also understand that you were seen digging on the smaller southern cay, South-West Allen's Cay, at last light yesterday evening. Would that be correct?'

Fozz and I looked at each other, the penny dropping at last. No wonder the cruiser had shadowed us. He thought we were smuggling. He had found us on an otherwise deserted island, digging in the darkness, and he thought we were smuggling.

'No, no, that was me, officer,' I broke in with a rush. 'You see, I found a pile of litter on the beach when we arrived there yesterday afternoon. I was just burying it, that was all.' Even to me it sounded hopelessly implausible.

He studied me for a moment. 'Burying litter, sir?' he asked. I nodded. 'Don't you know that all litter should be disposed of in deep water?'

'No, he didn't know that,' interrupted Fozz, getting angry. 'Nor did I. Anyway, it wasn't ours – we just found it there. Look, we were just trying to tidy up your island, for Chrissakes!'

'Quite, sir.' He seemed completely unaffected by the outburst. 'Well, I should soon be able to verify your story – we have a patrol boat checking the cay right now. They know where to look.' The rating in the forepeak appeared once more, looking hot and dishevelled. He looked at the officer, shook his head briefly.

Suddenly, I saw that Fozz was laughing quietly. Leaning

against the back-rest, he was looking up at the cabin roof, slowly shaking his head from side to side. When he looked at the officer once more there was a gleam in his eye that I thought I recognized. Steady, Fozz, I pleaded silently.

'Well now, officer,' he said, his voice suddenly heavy with affected charm, 'why don't you make yourself comfortable while you're waiting? What can we get you? A double whisky? Or something stronger, perhaps? What about a needle?'

'Fozz, for God's sake,' I cried. . . .

'It's all right, sir,' said the officer, the faintest suggestion of a smile at the corner of his lips. He put his official face on again. 'I am quite sure, sir,' he said, looking Fozz straight in the eye, 'that you understand why we have acted as we have, particularly in view of the report that we received.' As he finished speaking there was the sound of someone else landing on the side deck.

'Oh sure, I understand all right,' said Fozz contritely, his mood over. 'I'm sorry, it's just that it's not every day that. . . .' His voice trailed away as a face appeared round the corner of the hatchway.

'You're wanted on the radio, sir,' said the rating.

With the officer gone, we were glad to step up into the cockpit for some fresh air. We were just in time to see two heads disappearing below the top of the cruiser's white superstructure. 'Interested onlookers,' I observed. 'Mind you, I suppose when you come to think about it, we've really got nothing to complain about. Let's face it, of the two of us, they had much more reason to be suspicious of us than we of them.'

'Yeah, I guess so,' said Fozz. 'Still, it just goes to show. I always thought you were too fastidious for your own good, Ron!' He slapped me on the shoulder, laughing.

'You'll just have to blame my army upbringing,' I protested. 'First rule of sanitation in the field: always bury your rubbish.'

We turned our attention to the patrol launch alongside us. She was enormous: fully 100 feet long from stem to stern, I estimated. Painted on her battleship-grey topsides on the port quarter was the single word *Marlin*. 'If he's going to stick around much longer I'm going to ask him to stand off and drop his own anchor,' said Fozz. 'Right now he must be bending ours double.' He jumped up on the cockpit seat to look towards her bow. 'Nope – cancel that; he already has.'

Suddenly, the officer appeared once more around the stern superstructure, a millboard in his hand. Remaining on board the patrol vessel, he walked across to the lifeline immediately opposite us. 'Right, gentlemen,' he said, 'everything seems to be in order. And you may be glad to hear that the rubbish is about to be dumped in deep water. Could I ask you to sign this, sir?' he said, handing the millboard across to Fozz. 'It asks you to confirm that the boarding procedure was carried out correctly. Finally,' he continued, 'perhaps you would allow me to thank you for showing such concern for the beauty of our island cays. As for the search, you will realize that such procedures have sadly become more and more necessary these days. I can't promise you it won't happen again if you visit us in the future – as I hope you will.' He took back the millboard. 'I wish you pleasant sailing, gentlemen,' he ended, saluting with a smile.

We were still in the cockpit when *Marlin* slowed down opposite the white cruiser. We saw the officer lean out of the bridge window to shout something. Then the patrol boat sheered away again to go roaring up the channel.

There was a faint rumbling noise from astern. The white cruiser was weighing anchor. 'Quick, where are the binoculars?' said Fozz, reaching inside the hatchway. He held them up to his eyes. Already the cruiser was turning away from us, the anchor still not clear of the water. Suddenly, Fozz was laughing again. 'You'll never guess what she's called,' he said.

'No, go on, tell me.'

'*Vigilant.*'

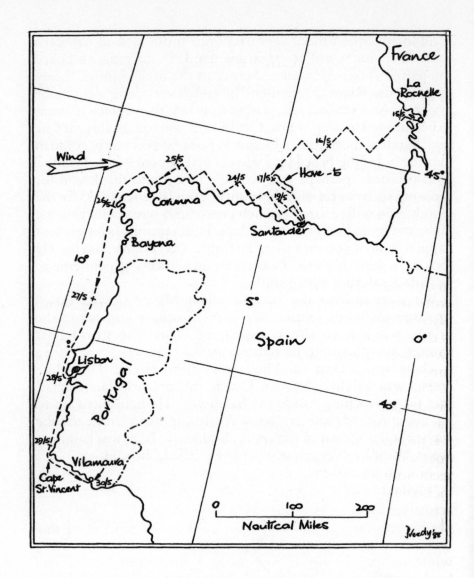

France
La Rochelle
15/5
16/5
45°
25/5
24/5 17/5 Hove-to
Wind
25/5 Corunna 19/5
Bayona Santander
10°
27/5
5°
Spain 0°
Lisbon
28/5
Portugal 40°
29/5
Vilamoura
Cape 30/5
St.Vincent

0   100   200
Nautical Miles

JVerdy'88

La Rochelle To Vilamoura

Chapter Six

LES SABLES D'OLONNE
TO VILAMOURA

In any discussion of the factors contributing to a boat's sea-worthiness, the dividing line between fact and assertion seems often to be no more than paper-thin, so complex and emotive is the subject. But after years of sailing a whole range of boats, two observations at least seem to me to have stood the test of time.

The first is that, while bigger boats pay a corresponding dividend in terms of comfort, confidence and speed, size alone has surprisingly little to do with seaworthiness. For, provided it is properly designed and strongly constructed, even a 20-foot boat will survive a storm in a way that, to the uninitiated, may seem nothing short of miraculous. More than that, I have been increasingly persuaded by experience that such a craft may actually stand less, not more, chance of sustaining damage than her bigger and heavier counterpart. Thus, the same wave that will move a small boat bodily sideways five yards or more, while leaving it virtually unscathed, will think nothing of buckling the guardrails of a nearby coaster or gouging a great chunk out of a sea wall. Clearly, the key to this seeming enigma is the matter of inertia, in this case the ability of the small boat to yield to a sudden, powerful impact.

The second observation is that, whatever the size of boat, the quality of design and construction matter much more than the type of materials used. Of course, such a generalization cannot be sustained in cases where the material has subsequently been neglected. Otherwise, though, given modern professional standards, the evidence seems to be overwhelming. Thus, I have seen – though thankfully never at first hand – too many fibreglass hulls that have been pounded on rocks to doubt any longer their enormous strength, just as I have seen the remains of too many wooden ones to take theirs for granted. Nor am I prepared to condemn, as some do out of hand, the growing number of ferro-cement boats, for the New Zealanders in particular have demonstrated that such craft can be very strong and seaworthy. Here again, it seems to me, the problem arises more with the standard of construction in less professional, less conscientious hands.

I recall, for instance, a night during my two-year tour of military loan service in Brunei when an Australian father and son attempted to enter the local port of Muara from Singapore in their ferro-cement ketch. Following the lights of a local fishing boat into the outer fairway channel, they committed the classic error of cutting the corner, thus striking a rock under the water. Seconds later the boat had sunk, leaving father and son clinging to a buoy for the rest of the night. Subsequent recovery of the boat revealed that, at least at the point where the hull had shattered, the cement was barely more than half an inch thick. Without question, that boat had been an accident waiting to happen.

Now, seven years later, on 19 July 1985, it was this memory that had returned to add to my worries as my crew – Bombardier Steve Richardson – and I headed away from Santander in northern Spain bound for Vilamoura in southern Portugal. For *Azure Lady* was a 45-foot, heavy-displacement, ferro-cement ketch. And she had already tried me sorely.

Setting out originally from La Rochelle five days earlier into a stiff west-south-westerly wind, the first calamity occurred around teatime the next day when the big furling headsail had jammed solid, halfway out. Unable, despite all our efforts, either to strip off the sail or to reach the site of the trouble some eight feet from the top of the forestay, I had resorted in the end to motoring the ketch around in a circle in order to furl the sail as tightly as possible. That done, and reassured by a 1750 hours forecast that promised no increase in the Force 5 to 6 wind, we had pressed on towards Corunna under staysail and reefed main, helped occasionally by the engine. Once inside the harbour, I promised myself, we would be able to sort things out.

But all that was before the arrival of the intense secondary depression. Regrettably indifferent to what the man on Radio 4 had prescribed, the mean wind speed had increased from 24 knots at 2000 hours to 34, gusting to 42 knots, by 2300 hours. Nor had the barometer given more than an hour's warning of what was coming. There was worse still to follow. Just after midnight, and long before the seas had fully responded to the sudden increase in wind, we were knocked absolutely flat by a rogue wave. Whether it had been any more severe than the one which had struck *Allez Cat II* in the same area the previous year I rather doubted. But *Azure Lady* was much heavier in displacement, and because of this, I believe, she absorbed far more of the impact. Quite apart from the severity of the knockdown itself, there was plenty of other evidence to support this hypothesis. Both canvas dodgers had been badly torn towards the stern, while the teak rail around the stern deck, measuring 4½ by 1½ inches, was split apart along 18 inches of scarfed joint on the port quarter. Even more sobering was the damage sustained by the outboard engine, mounted on the rail close by. Its metal tiller bar had been torn clean off and was lying on deck beneath the engine, the shorn bolt alongside it. These and other more minor items of damage demonstrated that *Azure Lady* had met the wave without flinching – and had paid for it.

Even then, though, the fates had not finished with us. Gradually over the previous two or three hours the wind had been seeking out and exploiting every tiny imperfection it could find in the furling of the genoa. Unable, safely, to unfurl it again in winds that were now gusting well into Force 9, it wasn't long before a small tear appeared in the luff of the sail some fifteen feet above the deck. In the end I decided to turn and run for Santander, hoping to save the sail before it became too badly damaged. However, by the time we had gained the shelter of the north-easterly facing entrance, a substantial part of it was already in tatters. It had been a depressing sight.

Very often, depression is as much a symptom of tiredness as of anything else. But not this time. Next morning the black cloud was still sitting there on my shoulders as I contemplated the ruined sail spread out on the deck. Wear and tear was one thing, but serious damage of this kind quite another, particularly when it was someone else's boat. Appalled at the knowledge that this was, far and away, the worst damage that any boat in my care had ever sustained, it didn't really help that the sail itself was far from new. Unbidden, my brain began yet another post-mortem.

Blessed with hindsight, I had little doubt that I should have turned back to La Rochelle as soon as I had established that the furling gear was irretrievably jammed. But at the time the deliberate sacrifice of 150 nautical miles, bought so dearly over the past 36 hours, had seemed an inordinate price to pay, particularly in view of what both forecaster and barometer were telling me. As for the other damage, it was impossible to see how I could have avoided it. For until the big wave hit us, *Azure Lady* had been serenely content in her hove-to state, fore-reaching hardly at all.

Deciding to put it all down to experience, I thereafter firmly dismissed any further retrospection in favour of sorting out the boat and preparing for our re-start.

Now, as midday approached, 24 hours later, the black cloud was starting to lift at last. It wasn't simply that we were on our way once again. It was more that, for the first time in days, the wind had moved marginally out of its dead-ahead position, backing towards the south-west sometime during last night. Still not enough to allow us to make our new course to Corunna without tacking, at least it meant that now we would only have to put in the occasional short leg back towards the coast. The rest would be distance made good. I was also heartened by the way *Azure Lady* was performing to windward under her modified rig. Having bent a small No. 1. jib on to the inner stay, I had been doubtful of how well I could get her to respond, unbalanced as she now was. But the loss in speed had been less than I had feared, about 1½ knots, I judged. All in all, I decided as I looked around me, things could be a lot worse.

'Not a very pleasant bit of coastline, is it?' called out Steve from his position at the wheel. Swaying as the boat heeled even further over to a sudden gust of wind, he nodded briefly out to the port side.

I turned to peer above the raised gunwhale towards the

ragged range of black cliffs stretching away into the distance. By now we were some miles away from them as our offshore tack gradually took us further and further from the axis of the coast. But the ominous line of white at their feet was still plainly visible. 'No, it's not,' I agreed. 'No wonder the locals still call it the *Costa del Morte* – the coast of death.'

'Really?'

'Yes. You see, it's not just the cliffs themselves. It's also the lack of safe harbours between here and Corunna. That, and the fact that a bad northerly will quickly turn this into a very nasty lee shore.'

'Mm. Exciting,' said Steve, with a grin. Clearly unconcerned, he concentrated once more on his steering. Despite the pronounced degree of heel, he still preferred the interest and activity of steering to the automatic pilot.

I might have expected that reaction, I thought with a smile. With another crew I would have been far more circumspect with my colourful remarks, but not with 'The Prof'. For once again 29th Commando Regiment, Royal Artillery had done me proud. Not only was Steve a commando and parachute-trained member of 148 Forward Observation Battery, each of whose men was hand-picked, but the last five days had provided ample proof of his steadiness, endurance and quiet good humour under difficult conditions. That he was known in the battery as 'The Prof' I had discovered from Major Guy Gillett, his battery commander, over the telephone some days before. And it wasn't hard to see why. Somewhat introverted and reserved by nature, his habitually studious expression seemed somehow to belong more to the laboratory than to the end of an abseiling rope. Even so, having omitted to ask Guy whether Steve himself liked the nickname, I had so far hesitated to use it myself. Unwarranted assumptions of that kind could be surprisingly irritating on a small boat at sea.

Over the next hour or so the wind started to gust more and more, gradually raising the mean wind speed past the threshold of Force 6. By now I had given up wondering when the weather would let up and give us a chance. It had been blowing like this – or worse – ever since we had left La Rochelle, so that now it was becoming difficult to remember what an even keel was like, even for me.

Steve had been reading my thoughts, apparently. 'Do you ever get used to this?' he called out, regaining his footing after a particularly savage gust of wind. Looking across at his dark, heavily built figure I just smiled.

'No,' he said, answering his own question, 'I thought not. Never mind, I'd still rather be here than back in Poole. We've got a big technical inspection coming up in a week's time. At least I'll miss that – won't I?'

'Yes, I think you will now,' I acknowledged, recalling with a stab of guilt the estimate I had given the battery commander of our return date. 'Originally, I had hoped we might make Vilamoura inside a week. But now it looks more and more like ten days, I'm afraid.' I looked at my watch. 'Almost time for the 1355 forecast. I'll just take it down; then I'll come up again to take over the wheel.'

'Biscay, South Finisterre. South-westerly, veering westerly, 5 or 6, fair, good.' So much for that, I thought. No wonder this coast had a reputation for being one of the hardest to escape from.

At that moment there was a sudden bang from somewhere up in the bow, followed almost immediately by a cry of alarm from Steve. My heart in my mouth, I rushed up the companionway steps, aware as I did so that the boat was righting herself and that there was the noise of flogging sailcloth from up front. Noting the wheel spinning unattended in the empty cockpit, I turned to look forward.

The inner stay carrying the No. 1 jib had parted from the deck, and right at this moment Steve was hanging on to it like grim death, trying to gather in armfuls of sail as he did so. Yet, serious though the damage was, it was not that which was bothering me. Far more alarming was the fact that Steve was swinging around like the weight on the end of a pendulum as the boat bounced in the waves. And his safety harness wasn't clipped on. Even as I watched, he was swung hard into the starboard lifelines as the boat lurched sharply over once more.

'Let it go, Steve,' I roared at the top of my voice, realizing even as I did so that he simply couldn't hear me above the din. Resisting the almost overwhelming temptation to rush forward myself, I decided I must first try to stabilize the boat, stop it from sheering repeatedly either side of the wind. Thankfully, the engine started almost immediately. Pushing it into gear, I headed the boat directly into the wind, then eased back slightly on the throttle and engaged the automatic pilot. That done, I leapt out of the cockpit and started to scramble forward as fast as I could. I was not a moment too soon. Just as I came level with the mast, Steve was thrown against the starboard lifelines once again, this time harder. Suddenly he was hanging right out over the side, with only his feet still hooked into the upper lifeline.

The next moment I had reached him. Pulling hard on his legs, I managed to get him inboard again, then clipped my safety harness onto the base of the guardrail stanchion.

Altogether, it took about ten minutes to sort out the mess. Thankful for the small hank of nylon cord that I always carry in the pocket of my oilskin jacket, I managed to anchor the bottom of the stay to a nearby ringbolt as Steve tried to damp down the snatch loading with his arms. Next we lowered the sail and unhanked it. After that it was easy. Sending Steve down to open the forehatch and bring back a stouter piece of line, I was soon stuffing the sail down through the opening in the deck. All that remained then was to bowse down the inner stay more securely onto the ringbolt with the second piece of line.

Pausing to draw breath at last I took my first real look at the stay and its associated terminal gear. What I saw confirmed what I had remembered from my routine inspection yesterday. It was immensely strong, all of it. Thus, the stainless steel stay itself was a good eight millimetres thick, sufficient to lift a ten-ton lorry all on its own, while the bottle-screw at the end of it was absolutely massive. Again, the other end of the bottle-screw was double swivel-mounted directly onto a T-section, stainless steel deck plate, at least three-eighths of an inch thick all round, the base of the plate having a hole of the same size at either end to take the through-deck bolts.

Certainly no problems there, I concluded. All that remained now was to examine the two bolts themselves, assuming, of course, that they hadn't gone over the side. I was lucky. One, complete but badly bent, was lodged between the toe-rail and the bottom of the starboard topmast shroud. The other I found sliding up and down the same toe-rail further aft, its shaft ending with ragged abruptness one inch below the head. Returning to the bow, I tried the longer bolt in one of the holes, already certain of what I would find. Sure enough, there was so much play between the shaft and the edge of the hole that I almost felt I could squeeze another one in beside it.

There remained just one other matter to check. Edging forward on hands and knees onto the short plank bowsprit, I bent down to examine one of the bolts in the forestay deck plate. It didn't matter that I couldn't see the shaft, the size of the head alone told me all I needed to know. Once again I was looking at a quarter-inch bolt.

Moments later I had turned *Azure Lady* downwind. 'No good trying to go on, Steve,' I said by way of explanation. 'Next thing we know, we'll lose the forestay too – and that'll mean a dismasting. No, it's back to Santander, I'm afraid,' I said apologetically, appalled at the prospect even as I spoke.

Running downwind, it had suddenly become a different world. No longer did we have to grit our teeth against the constant, jarring crashes, shield our faces from the wind, close our ears to the mind-numbing cacophony of sound. Now we were swooping gloriously before the seas, luxuriating in the blissful quiet all around us. I had known it would be so, of course; indeed, I had nearly turned the boat downwind when the crisis first occurred, realizing the difference it would make up in the bow. But in my mind had been the dreadful image of Steve swinging far out over the sea on the end of the stay as we came round. Right or wrong, I had decided to keep the boat headed up into the wind.

That my repeated inspections of the last few days had over-looked the chronic inadequacy of the bolts was less easy to justify. Granted, only the heads had been visible. Granted, too, my pre-sailing inspection in La Rochelle had been more than a little distracted by the general air of *joie de vivre* generated by Bastille Day. But that was no excuse; I should have picked it up. Yet if that knowledge had in some way contributed to the anger still smouldering inside me, it was as nothing compared with my feelings towards the unknown person who had rigged the boat. Somewhere, sometime, a man who should have known better had behaved with criminal stupidity. Confronted with the designer's clear intentions in the shape of two, three-eighths holes in the deck plate, he had promptly ignored them. Instead, he had substituted two bolts that were patently too weak to bear the load he knew would be imposed on them.

Here again, I concluded grimly, had been an accident waiting to happen. And the consequences had nearly been disastrous. But for the grace of God I could have been, even now, criss-crossing the seas in a desperate search for my crewman. That reminded me. 'Steve, why were you hanging on to the stay like that?' I asked. 'You nearly went over the side.'

He shrugged, his face breaking into a quiet, slightly embarrassed, smile. 'Well, it was banging against the mast and rigging quite badly,' he explained. 'And I was worried that the gear at the bottom – you know, the bottle-screw and so on – was going to come off and go over the side. Still, it was a bit exciting, I must admit.'

Understatement of the year, I thought. Yet at least there was one consolation. At long last I could confront squarely something that had been niggling at me for days now, even before the trip started, in fact. As early as my first telephone conversation with the owner I had somehow picked up a vague feeling of unease about the boat. Perhaps it was the knowledge that the owner had brought her in easy stages down to La Rochelle. Or, again, maybe it was the mass of unnecessary, even frivolous, bits and pieces, particularly in terms of electrical gadgets, that my pre-sailing inspection had uncovered; the boat had more the appearance of a floating home than of a sea-going vessel. Whatever the case, I had gradually formed an impression of 'softness', a suggestion that she had rarely, if ever, been asked to face the stern test of serious offshore sailing.

It was nearly dark by the time we rounded Cabo Major, the great headland guarding the approaches to Santander. Of all the ports that I would have chosen to witness our ignominious return, I think this would have been one of the last, for Santander boasts an illustrious pedigree in the eyes of British yachtsmen. It was here, for instance, that Adlard Coles finished the Royal Ocean Racing Club race from Brixham in 1948 after surviving a storm in the western approaches to the English Channel. Two years later Patrick Ellam and Colin Mudie had completed the same voyage in their 20-foot sloop *Sopranino*, using the race as a proving trial for their Atlantic crossing a year later. I wondered what they would have thought of this performance. Not a lot, I suspected. Then I remembered that at one point in the 1948 race Adlard Coles and one of his crew had actually been washed overboard. So it happened to the best of them, once in a while.

I prefer to touch only briefly on the worry and frustration of the next three days. Fortunately for us, an extremely helpful local chandler, himself a member of the Royal Cruising Club, overlooked the fact that it was a weekend, opening all sorts of doors that would otherwise have been closed to us. It was just as well. It took nothing less than an industrial drill to enlarge the two holes in the deck; and nothing larger than a diminutive Spanish rigger to screw the nuts onto the bolts in the tunnel-like interior of the bowsprit. In the end, though, it was done.

Perched like a statue on top of a nearby post, a cormorant offered his black silhouette to the first of the light as we set off for the third time on the morning of 23 May. It was a little strange to see him, in fact; cormorants were not supposed to be this far south in the summer months. But perhaps he didn't know that. Had we been Romans, I reflected fancifully, we would be calling it an omen.

Determined to obstruct us to the last, the wind fluctuated obstinately between south-west and west all the way to Corunna. Finally, however – battered, bruised yet grimly triumphant – we watched the western arm of Corunna bay snuff out the shore lights one by one as we turned the corner.

'You know what will happen now,' said Steve, indulging his weakness for black humour. 'Now that we've got this far, the wind's going to. . . .'

'Don't even think it!'

My warning must have appeased the gods. By dawn next morning – 26 May – we were broad-reaching at 7 knots past the Cape Villano lighthouse, sunlit and imposing on the end of its serrated backbone of land. After that, the landmarks just seemed to flash by. Eventually, in the lull before dawn two days later, we were slipping carefully under engine between Cape Carveiro and the Berlingas islands.

Because the gap between the Berlingas and the mainland

always seems to act like a funnel for shipping, I extended my watch until we were well clear of the traffic on the other side. At last, though, the extra chill that always seems to come with first light persuaded me that it was time to hand over to Steve and go below. Even before I climbed into my sleeping bag I knew that I was going to fall asleep within seconds. For quite apart from my accumulated tiredness, now I was feeling relaxed for the first time since leaving La Rochelle a fortnight ago. At last, it seemed, our luck had changed.

It was not a noise that woke me but a sudden silence. The engine had stopped. The next moment Steve was calling from the cockpit, the urgency in his voice jolting me wide awake in an instant. I was still wriggling out of my sleeping bag when I smelled something burning, saw the cloud of blue smoke invading the cabin from above. Recognizing immediately the peculiarly distinctive odour that signifies an electrical fire, I was not altogether surprised to find Steve bending over the control console as I reached the top of the companionway. Prepared for the worst, I was profoundly relieved to see that the smoke was already dying away. I dismissed for the moment any thoughts of fire extinguishers, looked instead at the engine stop button. He had pulled it out, I saw. And he had turned off the ignition switch. I turned towards him.

'What happened, Steve?'

'Well, just like you see, really. One moment we were going along quite happily on automatic pilot, the next there was blue smoke coming out all round the sides of the panel. There was no sign of anything wrong before that, I can promise you.'

I thought for a long moment. 'OK, first things first. If you'd like to turn the fuel off, I'll get the sails up again. There's still not much breeze yet, but it's better than nothing, I suppose. Then we'd better get that panel off and see what the damage is.'

Ten minutes later I had managed to coax *Azure Lady* up to 3 knots in the light north-westerly wind. By this time too, Steve had removed the control panel to reveal a tangled spaghetti of wiring beneath, some of it burnt and blackened, some of it still intact. Now comes the tricky bit, I thought. The only way to tackle this lot will be by following the wiring diagram, step by step. It would be a slow process, but I had done it before and I could do it again. Even if we only succeeded in restoring the ignition system and navigation lights, that would be enough for our purposes.

Preoccupied with steering, it was a moment or two before I realized that Steve was no longer just standing there at the control console, studying its contents. All at once he had started to disconnect leads all over the place, working at a pace that made my head spin.

'Hang on, Steve,' I called out, horrified. 'Are you sure you know what you're doing? It might be best to work from the wiring diagram, you know.'

'Don't think it'll be much good to us,' he said, his fingers moving with confident ease from one part of the panel to another. Suddenly he pulled a blackened ball of wire clear of the console altogether, dropping it disdainfully behind him onto the floor of the cockpit. 'Quite honestly,' he continued, 'there's so much extra wiring here, I don't think the diagram would help us anyway at this stage. Look at this.' He paused for a moment, pointing at something that looked like an engineer's plan of Clapham Junction. 'There's a whole sheaf of wires going into this single junction box. No wonder it overheated.' Now he was off again, this time to the accompaniment of a thin, tuneless whistle.

I was beginning to see the light at the end of the tunnel. 'You've done this sort of thing before, then?'

'Not on boats,' he replied carelessly. 'But I play around with car electrics a fair bit. There's not much difference really.'

An hour later the engine was going once again, driving *Azure Lady* through the water at a good 6 knots towards Cascais, on the outskirts of Lisbon. Contemplating my ragged nerves, I resisted the temptation to appeal out loud against the severity of this latest manifestation of Murphy's Law. After all, we still had another 200 miles to go, and I had no wish to forfeit any remission of sentence.

There were three reasons for calling in at Cascais. First, although we still had plenty of fuel left, there was just too little to see us all the way to Vilamoura. And the way our luck had been going, I was certainly not going to risk the onset of a total calm over the next two days. Second, now that we were close enough to our destination to calculate our time of arrival with reasonable confidence, I wanted the owner to try and book our two return flights in advance. Steve, after all, was already overdue, while I had another delivery coming up in five days' time. And third, since I would be speaking to the owner anyway, I had to tell him about the electrical fire.

The north-westerly had veered slightly and freshened by the time we weighed anchor at 1500 hours. Soon we were running sweetly before it, heading due south for Cape St Vincent. No longer prepared to be tempted into optimism at any price, we were nevertheless hard put to contain it when the wind, far from dying as it often did with the onset of dusk, actually increased slightly. What followed was one of the best runs from Lisbon down to Cape St Vincent that I have ever known. As a result, it was just before noon the following day when we first sighted the Cape St Vincent lighthouse, perched like a five-storey hotel at the top of its vertical, 500-feet-high cliff. Struck as always by the fitness of its grandeur, marking as it does the south-west corner of Europe, it wasn't long before the table-top of Sagrés came into view around the corner. An hour after that we had broken out into the wide bay beyond, rejoicing at the lushness of the Portuguese southern Algarve stretching away to port into the blue distance.

Now, with just 30 miles to go, it was all over bar the shouting; time, perhaps, calmly to reflect on the voyage before we became embroiled in the fuss and formality of arrival. Two false starts, two emergencies at sea, an interminable head wind almost wilful in its obstinacy, one week overdue: by any standards it had been an impressive combination of bad weather and bad luck. Perhaps the Romans knew a thing or two about omens after all, I thought wryly.

Yet for all that, it might have been worse. The fire might easily have been far more serious than it was. We might have lost the mast. And immeasurably worse than either possibility, I acknowledged with a gulp, I might actually have lost my crewman. Then again, without the trials and tribulations of the last fortnight, I knew I would not be sensing the same satisfaction that was warming me even at this moment. Acknowledging to myself that I had actually contemplated giving up the delivery altogether during the black hours following our return to Santander, I could only be thankful that, sustained as I was by the admirable phlegm of 'The Prof', I had decided to press on.

Once again, the cormorant came to mind. No, I decided; he wasn't an omen, good or bad. He was just a cormorant.

Chapter Seven

PLYMOUTH TO POOLE
(WITH MEMORIES)

'You stubborn sod!'

Normally, Lance-Bombardier Andrew Wightman, Royal Artillery, was not given to strong language. A likeable, self-possessed young man in his early twenties, he was already too mature to regard swearing as an obligatory accessory to the green beret he wore so proudly. But this time his patience had been tried once too often.

Mine too. Even as his anger exploded, I was still recovering on the starboard bunk of the Dufour 28, the salt sweat stinging my eyes. I glanced across at Andrew's blurred image on the opposite bunk. Slumped against the cushioned back-rest, he was staring unseeing at the white roof of the cabin, his chest pumping in and out, the starting cord still in his hand.

I forced myself to look again at the object of our wrath. The blue-painted diesel engine seemed to be resting, gathering its strength for the next round. Really, I should have known. Over the telephone from Dover the new owner had hinted that the batteries might be 'a bit low'. Yet the boat had looked so attractive as she waited patiently for us on the end of the pontoon that I had once again allowed optimism to triumph over experience. It didn't last long. It had taken just five minutes to discover that the batteries were completely flat. There was worse to come. A brief glance at the handbook had disclosed that the engine boasted a compression ratio of 13 to 1, calling for the services of a double-jointed gorilla to start it by hand. Certainly, it had been quite beyond us to turn the engine

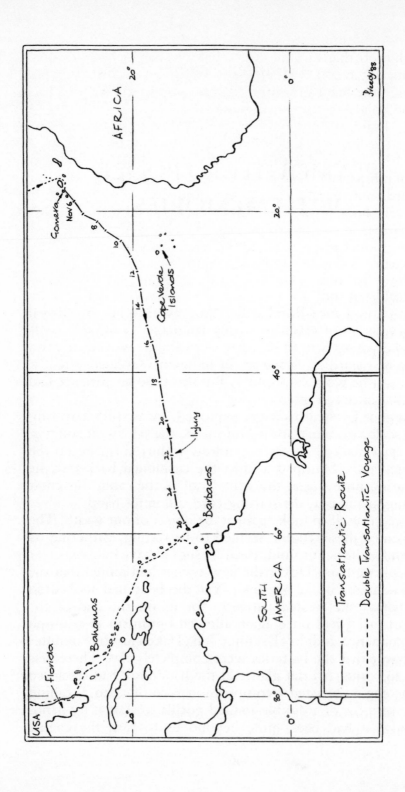

Track Of Miss Fidget From The Canaries To The West Indies, November 1984

through more than one revolution before it had kicked viciously back, its single cough an eloquent comment on our attempts to change the habit of a lifetime. No wonder the vendor had gone on holiday to the Portuguese Algarve.

'OK,' I said, turning once more to Andrew, 'we're going to need . . . a little outside assistance. I'll go up to the marina office. It's just possible they've got a charged battery . . . and a pair of jump leads. That ought to do it.' Yet even as I squeezed the words out, I realized that my optimism was at it again. It was seven thirty in the evening. Obliging as they were in this new marina, it was ten to one that the workshop was closed by now. Nor, I suspected, had the attractive young lady in the office swung too many engines in her time.

Andrew had obviously been thinking along the same lines. 'Tell you what, Skipper,' he said, 'why don't I nip back to the Citadel a minute?' He paused, still breathing hard himself. 'I've got the bike outside, it won't take me long. I'm pretty sure I can sort something out.'

I was heartened by his offer. The Royal Citadel, home of 29th Commando Regiment, Royal Artillery, was looking down on us at this very moment from the commanding heights of Plymouth Hoe. 'Well, fine by me, Andrew,' I said, 'but you do realize we can't use army gear, don't you?'

'Oh, I know that,' he replied, 'I wasn't planning to. But there are usually one or two of the REME lads around in the evenings. Perhaps they can come up with something.' The regiment was fortunate in numbering among its permanent strength a detachment of the Royal Electrical and Mechanical Engineers.

Moments later, the sound of Andrew's running footsteps had faded away down the pontoon. What it is to be young, I thought as I filled the kettle for a cup of coffee. At that moment I could no more have broken into a run than fly in the air. That reminded me. Standing up straight in the cabin for a moment, I gingerly twisted my upper body around my hips, first one way, then the other. Battered over many years by rugby, parachuting and abseiling, my lower back had always been a somewhat reluctant partner in my sailing. Now I knew that I provoked it at my peril. Thankfully, all seemed well. It would be sore tomorrow, of course, but soreness alone didn't matter.

It was the prospect of a slipped disc that really worried me.

Not without reason either, I conceded, trying to summon the memories of three years ago from a reluctant corner of my mind. For it was then that my back had nearly cost me my life. Without really being aware of it, I subsided onto the bunk once more as the memories came flooding out. One way and another, I had been lucky to come out of it in one piece. . . .

It was 1984. Taking an extended break from professional yacht delivery, I had finally decided to realize the sailing ambition of a lifetime: to attempt single-handed a double crossing of the Atlantic Ocean in my own 26-foot Super Seal Bermudan sloop *Miss Fidget*. While careful to stress my primary motive, I was simultaneously hoping to raise money for the St Agnes branch of the RNLI. The 'Blue Peter' inshore lifeboat provided by the BBC children's programme was crewed by young men whose commitment to their dangerous calling was largely unconditional and wholly unpaid. More than that, I was deeply conscious that the little boat embodied an organization to which all yachtsmen owe a standing debt of gratitude. Here, it seemed to me, was a chance to repay a small part of that debt.

So it was that, at 1300 hours on Monday, 5 November 1984, after a two-month journey from St Agnes down to the Canary Islands, *Miss Fidget* and I set off from the little island of Gomera, bound for the West Indies.

Despite the date, there were no fireworks to signal my departure. But I didn't need any; my stomach was telling me all I needed to know. Gradually, however, over the next two or three days, the knowledge that I was about to realize a long-standing dream managed to settle me down. During that first week at sea my basic tactics were to go as far to the south-west as necessary – even as far as the Cape Verde islands – to ensure that I was well into the trade-wind belt. In those latitudes the trade winds have been blowing from east to west, day in, day out, for thousands of years. Yet too often I had read accounts by those who had turned almost due west at their first encounter with them. As a result, they had soon sailed out again to the north, to spend many days becalmed. Anne Davison came to mind. In 1948 she had been the first woman to cross the Atlantic single-handed – an outstanding physical and mental achievement by any standards. Yet it had taken her nearly ten weeks to do it, mainly as a result of staying too far north. I was hoping to do it in four weeks, in a small but fast lifting-keel sloop designed by Ron Holland and built by John and Pat Baker at Starcross in Devon.

By the first Sunday morning *Miss Fidget* and I had covered just over 700 miles in six days. The Cape Verde islands were already abaft the beam, some 180 miles to the south-east. Just after nine o'clock I prepared to take the first morning sextant sight which, together with a noonday transit, would give me my daily fix of position. Using my legs to steady me, I sat astride the top of the main hatchway and began a square search for the sun. Suddenly the boat did one of its occasional sharp lurches to port and, as I jack-knifed my body to retain balance, I felt something odd happen in my lower back.

The pain in my right leg started about two minutes later. Gradually over the next 45 minutes – and notwithstanding two painkillers – it grew from a dull ache to something close to agony. Then, just as I was really starting to panic, the pain receded again, to be replaced by pins and needles. Half an hour later, only the dull but persistent ache remained. I spent the rest of the day worrying, debating whether or not to cut and run for the Cape Verdes. In the end I decided against it. For one thing, I was already sufficiently far downwind to face a really hard, perhaps impossible, beat back to windward. For another, I was doubtful about my chances of obtaining expert treatment. So I pressed on, taking two pain killers a day to help things along. Before long I discovered that the pain could be almost eliminated if I kept my right leg above the level of the rest of my body.

Later that day the trade wind arrived with its puffy white clouds, its lively blue sea, and by teatime I had set the poled-out genoa headsail goose-winged with the double-reefed mainsail. For the next eight days I touched neither sail nor tiller in what for me, notwithstanding my aching leg, was the most marvellous sailing experience of my life. Now and then I adjusted the Navik self-steering gear a touch, and twice I had to renew the rubber shock-cords damping down tiller movement in seas that were often close to gale force. But apart from that, my daily celestial navigation and my twice daily check of sails and rigging, I had little to do.

Happily, though, along with the trade winds had come

the flying fish, clearly intent on providing a diversion. Right through the day I would watch them skimming 50 yards or more across the dancing blue and white sea, their wings held out stiffly at right angles to their tiny silver bodies, before disappearing again with a tiny splash. And just in case even that sparkling exhibition was beginning to pall, now and then they would stage their show-stopper. Completing the first 30 yards or so through the air, they would dip one wing fractionally into a wave, pivot, then shoot off in a completely different direction for almost the same distance again. For them, of course, the tactic was a desperate one, designed to throw the pursuing dorado off their trail. For me, selfishly, it was sheer delight. Indeed, the only sadness I felt derived from the fact that the dorado's appetite seemed in no way to diminish with the setting sun; so that it was rare indeed not to find flying fish lying on the deck in the morning, struck down by *Miss Fidget* as she ploughed, uncaring, through the darkness.

As for other signs of life, so precious in my isolation, these were very few. Of dolphins I saw nothing. Nor was there any great variety of bird life. Altogether I identified three different types of bird in the entire crossing. The first and most common was a rather nondescript gull with a dirty brown back. Then, whenever the wind piped up near to gale force, out of nowhere would appear those most enigmatic of birds: the little stormy petrels. As I watched them pattering down the waves with their tiny feet, black wings beating fast, two questions perplexed me. The first was where they went when the weather wasn't stormy, for I never saw them. And the second was how, if, as some suggest, they spend their entire life on the wing, there were still any stormy petrels around anyway.

But it was the third type of bird that stole the show. With admirable timing, a pair of them made their debut on the very day that *Miss Fidget* and I were celebrating our passing of the halfway point. Sitting in the cockpit recording a tape for Radio Cornwall, I suddenly heard a high-pitched squeaking above. I looked up even as I was speaking. Then the words just failed me. Two snowy-white tropic birds were hovering just over the top of the mast, their red beaks pointing downwards as they looked at me, their four-foot long tails streaming out in the wind like fine lace behind them. The presence of these delicate-looking creatures in a place so far from land, so forbidding in its loneliness, seemed somehow unreal. Recovering at last, I gabbled into the microphone, trying – and failing miserably – to capture the sheer wonder of the moment. Then, in no time at all, they were gone, shooting away downwind until they were lost in the distance.

My Stowe log, recording the distance run, packed up when we were 16 days out of Gomera. Pulling in the rotator, I discovered tooth marks around the end of the cable. But my spare cable made no difference; clearly, the trouble lay elsewhere. The reading showed that we had covered 1974 miles, leaving about 800 miles to go to Barbados, my chosen destination. From now on, I realized, I would have to estimate my daily run, confirming it with my sun sights. In fact, this proved to be much easier than it sounds, and I was rarely more than five miles out in my guess.

By now the weather had become rather unsettled again. Rain squalls began to occur and the wind, though still strong, began to vary more in direction. Still, we were continuing to make excellent progress and I came to realize that we might well complete the crossing in 21 or 22 days, some five days less than I had originally estimated.

The world fell apart the next day – on Thursday, 22 November. Just after 0800 hours I suddenly noticed an ominous-looking line squall overhauling us fast on the starboard quarter. I had just got the mainsail down and secured to the boom when it hit us. Immediately we began to yaw wildly as the poled-out genoa up front took the full force of the squall. Letting go the sheet to take the strain off the sail, I went quickly forward. I had just pushed the genoa down through the forehatch and was hanking on the little No. 1 jib when the pain in my leg came back. And this time it really meant it. Within seconds I was lying on my back in agony, my right leg propped up on the starboard lifeline.

I could not possibly put any time-scale to what happened next. Suffice it to say that eventually I managed to hoist the sail and get below. There followed the experience which, even now, my subconscious prefers to keep hidden. Whatever I did, whatever position I adopted, nothing seemed able to diminish the quite agonizing pain in my leg; not even, I realized with a flicker of real panic, holding the leg high above me as before. Altogether I took eight painkillers in what I now judge to have been about two hours. Far too many, of course, but by now I was way past caring. Bathed in sweat, I rolled around the bunk trying to control the pain – and what lay waiting just behind it. Finally, in sheer desperation I reached for the SARBE: the automatic homing distress beacon.

The prospect of alerting the entire international search and rescue organization appalled me – yet I could see no alternative. I ripped off the black plastic strip which prevents accidental activation and for a moment more just held it, inert, in my hand. Then, in that brief instant, either inspiration struck on its own or I had a little help from elsewhere. I found a strong strop that I had brought along on the voyage 'just in case' – six feet of webbing in a continuous loop – and hung it from one of the levers securing the centre hatch in the cabin roof. I then lay on the port bunk, raised my right leg into the loop and let the strop take the weight.

Almost immediately the pain eased slightly and after 15 minutes it was under control for the first time. Gradually I realized why. For as long as I was using my muscles to keep the leg upraised and balanced above me as the boat see-sawed from side to side, the pain had continued to be aggravated. Now, at last, the leg was completely relaxed.

By the end of 24 hours I had worked out the ground rules. They were very precise. I could spend just under two minutes out of the strop and not a second more. Twice I tried to be greedy by extending this period but each time regretted it bitterly for the next 15 minutes or so. I soon came to learn what this meant in practical terms. Changing headsails up in the bow took three separate sessions out of the strop – four if there was any snag. Sight taking also took three sessions: one to remove the sextant from its box and prepare it; one to get the sun somewhere near the horizon; and one to take three or four sights. I could then work the sights out in the strop. Making coffee: two sessions. Going to the toilet: one or two sessions. And so on.

I didn't sleep at all that first night, nor through the long day that followed. By dusk on Friday evening, therefore, I was looking forward to making up for this. It just seemed to be a question of when sheer exhaustion would outweigh the residual dull pain and I felt fairly certain that the balance would shift sometime during the coming night. Sure enough, by 0200 hours, I was feeling very drowsy indeed. My eyes started to close. . . .

I am in a large, completely bare room, dragging myself across the floor towards a single door set into the far wall. Once through the door and the pain will stop. I reach it, open it and pass through. Another room, another door. Somewhere a faint voice is saying 'Get your leg back into the strop!'

I set off across the second room, the pain worse, more insistent. No matter, this will be the one. Just get to this next door. Finally I do so, open it and pull myself through. Another room, another door. No time for disappointment; too much pain for that. Just concentrate on getting through the next door. This will be the one.

So it continues. More rooms, more doors, more pain, more desperation. Can't be helped. Must keep going.

'Get your leg back in the strop!'

The voice is louder, clearer now. But it doesn't seem to be making any sense. My one overriding aim is to get through the next door. That's the only way to stop the pain.

'No! Get your leg back in the strop! That will stop the pain.'

I keep moving. 'What strop, for God's sake?'

'The strop. You remember the strop. Get your leg back in the strop!'

'But I can't, not while I'm trying to reach the door.'

'Forget the door. Concentrate on the strop. Wake yourself up, get your leg back into the strop and the pain will go!'

Little by little, I come to realize where I am. I am in the cabin, writhing around on a port settee soaked in sweat. It is completely dark. It is night and the oil lamp has gone out. I try to collect my thoughts through the mist of pain. The strop, that's it, my leg is no longer suspended above me. It must have fallen out while I was asleep. I turn on my back, raise my right leg and feel for the strop in the darkness. After two or three misses my heel finally catches in the loop. The pain continues unabated, but I am fully awake now and know that, if I can just stay as I am, it will soon start to ease off. Meanwhile, I swallow two painkillers dry and try to relax my leg muscles.

By the time the pain has subsided enough for me to push it from the front of my mind, to think about the time and look at my watch, it is 0330 hours. I can hardly believe it. It seems incredible that the eternity of my nightmare had actually spanned little more than an hour.

At the time this experience, however illusory, was so vivid in its impact, so unpleasant in its recollection, as to influence my subsequent actions quite significantly. For as I lay there counting off the long minutes until dawn, I realized that, if I once fell asleep again, exactly the same thing would happen. There was simply no way of ensuring that my foot remained secure in the strop. At some stage, therefore, as the boat bounced it would fall out again, again without actually waking me up. And then my nightmare would return to torment me. Yet I had to admit that I felt considerably more rested, demonstrating that a little sleep was worth having. But not at that price. From now on I would stay awake, no matter what.

Thankfully, the dawn that Saturday morning was clear and relatively quiet with a lively trade wind freshening to Force 6 soon after 0800 hours. Later that morning I tried to pick up the BBC World Service on short wave, but it had been getting fainter every day, and now I couldn't hear it at all. Then, just after midday, I thought about trying to find Radio Barbados on medium wave. Seconds later, incredulous and delighted, I was listening to someone interviewing shoppers in a furnishing store in Bridgetown, ending each interview by playing a record of their choice. This memory, like all the others, was razor sharp:

'OK, petal,' coaxed the male West Indian voice, 'jus' stan' a little closer to the microphone, it's not goin' to bite you. So tell all the listeners now, what you come for?'

By way of reply there was a sudden high-pitched giggle, its rich resonance indicating a more substantial frame than the term 'petal' had suggested. Another lady was laughing in the background.

'Come on, sweetheart, you must have come here for some-thin',' persisted the interviewer, an edge of impatience just apparent beneath the heavy charm.

'Well . . . ,' her voice was absurdly high in pitch, 'see, I jus' come to change this here . . . this cushion,' she managed eventually, to another whoop from her friend.

'Of course you have, petal,' replied the interviewer quickly, evidently relieved that he could now move on. 'OK now, honey, I wanna know all about you in just a moment. But let's do the record first. What you like to hear?'

This time she was ready. 'Strangers in the Night,' she said coyly. Her friend found that even funnier.

'You got it, sweetheart. OK, Buzz,' he was talking back to the studio now, 'you heard the lady, "Strangers in the Night".' He turned on the charm again. 'Well now, jus' tell all the people at home your name and. . . .'

This programme was followed by the Barbadian – or, more correctly, Bajan – equivalent of 'Grandstand': an afternoon of horse racing alternating with live cricket commentary with occasional summaries by that greatest of all cricketers, Sir Garfield Sobers. Punctuating everything, a commercial break every ten minutes demonstrated that Christmas in Barbados is even more commercialized than in the UK.

It is an indication of how slowly my brain was working that it was late afternoon before I even considered searching for the Barbados aircraft homing beacon on my radio direction finder (RDF). Granted that its rated range was only 200 miles, but I was aware that most stations can be picked up, if inaccurately, well beyond the official maximum. And so it proved. The moment I finished keying in 345 kilocycles, the continuous signal came clearly through the headphones.

These contacts with Barbados, with their sounds of normal people doing normal things, raised my morale enormously, creating the comforting illusion that we were much closer to our goal than we actually were. Yet my sextant sight at 1410 hours local time had disclosed that we were still some 270 nautical miles away – about 300 land miles. So we were not there yet by any means.

I noted the approach of dusk with something close to dread. Another twelve hours of darkness were about to begin and now there was not even the prospect of sleep to break it up. In the event, however, that Saturday night proved to be much less of a trial than I had feared. Not only did Radio Barbados continue to provide a welcome diversion until nearly 0200 hours but, surprisingly, I had little or no trouble staying awake thereafter. I can only conclude that my subconscious was as worried about falling asleep as the rest of me. Yet to offset this, I had to admit that I was now very tired indeed. The slightest physical effort tended to exhaust me, while I was finding it increasingly difficult to sustain my concentration. Never mind, I thought, with any luck, tomorrow night – my twenty-first – would be my last at sea.

Sunday brought another fine, sunny day of steady trade wind. By now, though, it had veered quite markedly and as the day wore on I realized from the RDF that we were being pushed more and more to the north of our track. This could be remedied, of course, by coming off our dead run and going on to a broad port reach. But I resisted the idea. The wind might yet back again in the next few hours and needless struggling with the booming-out pole was something I could do without. So I decided to leave things as they were until evening. Then, if the wind direction still had not changed, I could alter on to a broad reach and head directly for Barbados on what would be *Miss Fidget*'s fastest point of sailing.

I had known for some time that my painkillers were not going to last out. At my already reduced rate of consumption I would swallow the last one just after midnight. That would help get me through the night. Thereafter I would have to rely on aspirin instead of Paramol. Partly to take my mind off this problem, I decided to tackle another. Basic common sense dictated that, once night fell, I would have to maintain a proper watch in the cockpit. So far my path across this deserted part of the Atlantic had been devoid of shipping of any kind; this despite crossing over two or three shipping routes where I had kept a continuous watch. But now the noon sight at 1442 hours local time this Sunday afternoon had shown that there were just 138 nautical miles to go to Ragged Point on the eastern coast of Barbados. So although we were not going to close the land or even raise the light until well after dawn, the nearer we got, the greater the chance of meeting up with other ships. Somehow or other, I had to find a way of remaining in the cockpit.

Repeated experiments during that hot afternoon eventually produced a solution. I found that by lying at a certain angle along the top of the starboard cockpit locker with my right leg raised, bent and resting between two halyard winches on the cabin roof, I could sustain a tolerable watch position for up to an hour at a time. Better still – and somewhat to my surprise – I found that I only needed about ten minutes in the strop down below to recover.

As one source of worry faded, another appeared to replace it. As much as I had been trying to ignore the fact, the wind had been gradually dropping during the early evening. The prospect of a 24-hour calm was just too appalling to contemplate in my present state. But even light winds would be serious. In some way that I could not explain, I knew that I really couldn't go on much longer without starting to lose contact with my surroundings. And with land ahead, that could be disastrous.

At dusk I trimmed the sails to put *Miss Fidget* onto a broad port reach. Then, just after dark, I had to start the outboard engine. By then the mainsail had started to slat to and fro, while the genoa was spilling its wind with every swell that passed. Amazingly, the engine started on the third pull – and this from a lying position on the starboard cockpit seat. For the next hour we motored on at 5 knots. At last, as I watched a substantial bank of cloud overtake us in the starlight, the breeze picked up once more.

It was just after this as I was enjoying the quiet after the engine's noisy clatter that I saw, for the first time in 19 days, the lights of a ship. It was about three miles away on the port beam and for a fleeting moment I considered whether to try and stop her with a red flare. But I quickly rejected the idea. The boisterous trade-wind sea was still high despite the recent lull, and I had a horrible vision of scraping *Miss Fidget*'s hull and spreaders down the side of the ship. And anyway, I thought, what am I expecting her to do? Granted, I could probably get some painkillers, but it wasn't worth the trouble. We were nearly there now.

Fortunately, after two or three more sessions under the engine, the wind picked up convincingly soon after midnight and thereafter blew steadily for the rest of that seemingly endless Sunday night. By now the desire to sleep was almost overpowering, particularly when down in the cabin in the strop. It was just as well that I was spending most of the time in the cooler, breezier cockpit. At last, however, the first glimmerings of dawn appeared. I had never been more thankful to see it. Soon after 0700 hours I was taking a final set of sights as the sun cleared the horizon. Crossed with my radio bearing, they showed that there were just over 40 miles to go – about seven hours' sailing. Assuming that I sighted land about 15 miles away, that ought to mean a landfall around noon.

Just after 1000 hours I passed out. It can't have been for long, but it scared me. I can remember feeling a bit dizzy when filling the kettle for a cup of coffee. Then I got back into the strop while the kettle boiled. When the whistle went I got out again and was reaching for the coffee jar when the dizziness returned. The next thing I knew, I was lying crumpled up on the floor, my leg burning like a red hot poker. The coffee jar, thankfully still with its lid on, was rolling to and fro beside me, while the whistling noise in my ears was actually coming from the kettle, still boiling away on the stove. As I pulled myself back into the bunk, I realized that it was now very important indeed to get into Bridgetown as quickly as possible. Either that or stop the first ship I saw.

I spent that dull, cloudy morning alternating between cockpit and cabin, looking ahead every 20 minutes or so for any sign of land. Noon came – 1300 hours – 1400 hours; still nothing. By now I was really worried. Clearly, I concluded, there was something wrong with my sights – or even with the sextant itself. Otherwise I must have sighted land by now. Had I been more alert, more aware of my surroundings, I would undoubtedly have realized how poor the visibility had become. As it was, I could only conclude that we were still a long way from Barbados, a thought that brought me very close to despair.

Soon after 1400 hours I must have fallen into a kind of stupor while lying in the cockpit. The next thing I knew something wet was splashing my face. It was raining. I pulled myself up into an upright position to peer, blinking, at what lay ahead. For a few seconds I could see nothing. Then, as a black rain squall up ahead moved gradually away to the right, I saw it. Through the murk appeared the dark, blissfully solid bulk of land. Barbados at last!

There are no safe anchorages or harbours on the windward side of the island, so that it was close to dusk when the lights of Bridgetown finally appeared around the last headland. It would be pitch dark by the time I arrived. But I wasn't worried. Once I reached the anchorage in Carlisle Bay I would be able to attract someone's attention – and my troubles would be over. Somebody else could worry about anchoring, getting me ashore, into hospital and so on. It was just not my problem.

The bay was full of ships, the shoreline studded with thousands of lights. But there were no people. Altogether it took me an hour to start the engine, drop the sails and find the yacht anchorage; and another thirty minutes to assemble my collapsible dinghy and secure the boat. There was still no one around. Yet by now, perversely, I was almost glad. At least, I thought, I'll have the satisfaction of getting into port and ashore unaided. Even now, though, one more hurdle lay ahead. Presumably because of the physical exertion involved in rowing, I found that my working time was reduced to less than a minute, at the end of which the pain would force me to lie down in the bottom of the dinghy, my leg propped up on the side. Altogether, it took about a dozen sessions. Then, at last, I was right alongside the pier of the Holiday Inn, the shore only yards away. I made one final effort before the wave surge picked up the boat and swept me ashore onto the steeply shelving beach.

I called out to a group of people I could see enjoying a Monday evening drink on the patio of the Holiday Inn. Moments later, a large, bearded man had run across to me. He turned out to be an American doctor on holiday. That was fortunate because he was able quickly to assess my condition and send for an ambulance.

'Don't mind me asking,' he said hesitantly as we waited, 'but I guess you do have another boat besides that dinghy, don't you?' He actually suspected that I might have crossed the Atlantic in a 7-foot collapsible dinghy. Amusing as it was, his question sparked off a thrill of pleasure inside me as I realized that, despite all my trials and tribulations, I had actually crossed the Atlantic Ocean. Although I didn't know it then, I had sailed 2773 miles in 21 days and six hours, averaging 5.4 knots and daily runs of just over 130 miles.

The kettle was boiling. My mind still firmly back in Barbados, I went through the motions of making the coffee.

There are some moments in life when it is much better not to know what lies ahead. Certainly, lying there on the beach enjoying the warm evening breeze, my leg resting on the stranded dinghy, I would devoutly not have welcomed the faintest inkling of what lay in wait for me at the Queen Elizabeth hospital.

Even before I was pushed on my trolley through the double doors leading from the ambulance bay, the sheer volume of noise from within warned me that all might not be well. The next moment I was immersed in pandemonium. Suddenly, there were coloured people all around me, hundreds of them. Filling the reception hall, they spilled over into the long corridor behind, some trying to waylay the sisters and nurses as they came hurrying by, others just standing in small groups, most of them shouting at the top of their voices. The young Bajan orderly looking after me stopped the trolley in the middle of the crowd, then fought his way through it in the direction of the reception desk. He returned two minutes later with a chubby, bespectacled black sister carrying a white card. She was looking tired and harassed.

'Can you please explain what has happened to you?' she shouted, bending over to catch my reply. I told her as briefly as I could. There followed more questions as she completed the card. 'We'll try and get a doctor to see you as soon as we can,' she said, placing a hand on my arm. She spoke briefly to the orderly, then disappeared once more into the crowd. Now we were off again up the long corridor. Eventually, we came to a long line of about 20 trolleys parked one behind the other down the left-hand wall, all of them occupied. I was parked on the end of the queue. Even this far down the corridor there were people standing all around us, some staring curiously at me.

'OK,' said the orderly, 'I'll have to leave you now. Just stay here on the trolley. The doctors will see you when they can.' I thanked him as he hurried away.

By now my mind had picked up all the turmoil of my surroundings. Quite apart from my growing suspicion that this was yet another nightmare, three other thoughts were chasing each other round my brain. First and least, I could still, despite my condition, find a wry amusement at the bizarre change in my circumstances compared to just one hour ago. Then, I hadn't seen or heard another human being for over 21 days; now, I had been inundated by hundreds of them all at once. Second, I was only too guiltily aware that this hospital, chronically over-extended as it was, could emphatically have done without an injured transatlantic yachtsman to add to the fun. But last, and most of all, I just wanted to know when someone was going to stop this pain.

Since boarding the trolley I had lain on my back, using the inverted 'V' of my doubled left leg as a prop for the other. But the steady increase in pain was telling me that this was far from an ideal solution. Willing to try anything, I turned slightly on the trolley and tried to raise my leg to a resting position against the wall. This worked just so long as I didn't rest it too heavily; otherwise the trolley would just glide away on its wheels towards the centre of the corridor. Trying to take my mind off my troubles, I glanced at my watch; it was nearly eight o'clock. Ah well, I thought, just hang on a bit longer. It can't be long now.

By nine o'clock I had moved up four places; by ten o'clock, a further three. I was now very low indeed. I managed to waylay a small, slim nurse as she hurried by. 'Excuse me,' I said, 'but can you tell me when someone might be able to see me?'

'Sorry, jus' can't say,' she said. 'I know you been waitin' a long time but, see, we've had a lot of trauma cases in tonight. Traffic accidents, that sort of thing.'

'Well, in that case,' I replied, 'do you think the sister might be able to give me something for the pain in my leg?' I had swallowed the last aspirin at lunchtime.

'No, she can't do that,' she said, not without sympathy. 'See, the doctor may want to operate or somethin'. We give you somethin' now, it could hold up his treatment.' Even as she said it, I knew that she was right. But it didn't help.

All right, I thought, as she almost ran off down the corridor in her haste, if nothing else, at least I'm going to make myself as comfortable as possible. I eased off the trolley, lay flat on the floor facing the wall and raised my right leg to rest against it.

That was much better. The next moment there was a sudden scuffling noise behind me.

'Quick, Lonnie, jump up, quick!' said a woman's voice urgently.

I looked around. My trolley was right out in the middle of the corridor, surrounded by a group of people. Reluctantly, they moved away, revealing a young teenage boy lying flat and tense on the white sheet, his hands gripping the sides of the trolley tightly. Evidently, he had won the musical chair. Now his mother was pushing the trolley back into place on the end of the queue, studiously avoiding my gaze as she did so. That's it, I thought. Any minute now a white rabbit will come hurrying down the corridor consulting his watch.

But it wasn't a white rabbit; it was a black sister. I recognized her as the same one who had completed my card earlier in the evening. Her obvious preoccupation almost carried her right past me. But not quite. Suddenly, she registered the sight of me lying on the floor. Stopping in her tracks, she fixed me with a horrified stare, then placed both hands on her hips. 'What you doin' down there?' she demanded indignantly.

'Ah . . . well, you see, Sister. . . .' I began.

'Didn' the orderly tell you to stay on the trolley?'

'Well, yes, I think he did, as a matter of fact. But. . . .'

'Well, you lost it now. Don' know when the doctor will see you now. No one gets to see the doctor unless they're on a trolley. Don' you understan' that?'

'Well, I didn't realize. . . .'

'My God,' she said, shaking her head as she appealed to the ceiling. 'Well, nothin' I can do about it now,' she finished with a shrug of her shoulders. She stumped off up the corridor.

Right, I thought, that settles it. There's only one person who can help you now, and that's you. I had one card to play. As a member of the Royal Naval Sailing Association (RNSA), I had written before leaving the UK, and again from the Canaries, to the honorary RNSA liaison officer in Barbados, Commander Ted Sworder, Royal Navy. A distinguished and much decorated leader of minesweeping flotillas in World War II, he had retired to Barbados with his Philadelphian-born wife and had kindly offered to do what he could to welcome visiting members. Originally, I had planned simply to get in touch with him

116

once I arrived in Bridgetown in order that we might enjoy a casual drink together. Nor had I seen any reason to alter that plan when I had finished up on the beach earlier in the evening. The first priority had to be the hospital. Now, however, things were very different. It was ten thirty at night and, right now, I needed help as I had never needed it before.

Remembering from my arrival that I had seen yet another sister besieged at a desk in a small alcove halfway down the corridor, I limped my way towards it. She was still there, beleaguered by about 30 people, all of them apparently talking at the same time. Pushing my way through, I saw what I was looking for: a white telephone at the edge of the desk with a directory beside it. I waited until the sister looked fleetingly in my direction. 'Can I use the telephone?' I yelled, pointing at it.

'The telephone? What do you want . . .?' she started to say, before someone on the other side tugged hard on her sleeve, demanding her attention.

I seized my chance. Picking up the telephone and the directory, I retreated as far as the cable would allow, then subsided onto the floor. My leg was already insisting that I lie down again. Propping it on my doubled left leg once more, I started to leaf through the directory. Eventually, and notwithstanding my difficulty in reading the small print – I had left my reading glasses on the boat – I made out the name of Sworder. I dialled the number.

'Good evening, this is the American Embassy,' said a voice whose accent left no room for doubt. Apologizing, I put the phone down to consult the directory once more. I realized that I had misread a '5' for a '6'. I tried again. Just hold on a bit longer, I told myself.

'This is Peggy Sworder speaking,' said a pleasant, confident voice, again American.

From that moment things started to look up. Ten minutes later an anxious Ted Sworder drove up to the hospital to find me still lying in the corridor. It took him just two minutes to size up the situation, speak to a sister and arrange for my discharge. After a short car journey, in which I lay in the back with my foot propped up on the front passenger seat, I staggered up the stairs into the Sworders' pleasant seaside apartment.

From there, Peggy quickly rang a doctor friend who prescribed four of the powerful painkillers she had in the house and asked to see me first thing in the morning.

After the pills and a marvellous cup of coffee, I was ready for bed in the empty holiday flat on the ground floor. I tried to thank Peggy before going downstairs with Ted, but she cut me short. 'You know,' she said in her beautifully dry way, 'I guess this is the first time I have ever held a conversation in my own house with a strange man who was lying on the floor – sober!'

I could not possibly list the hundreds of things that they did for me over the next nine days, but at least I can mention a few. Peggy cooked most of my meals, which Ted brought down to me on a tray (I had rented the downstairs flat from them). Peggy washed my clothes. They took me in the car for my visits to the doctor. They did my shopping. And so on. Most of all, they kept my morale up with their irrepressible good humour.

Doctor Gale is a very able general practitioner with, fortunately for me, a particular interest in neurology. After concluding from his first general examination that complete physical collapse had been very close, he quickly diagnosed a slipped disc and explained that my right leg was reacting to a referred pain caused by the disc pinching the sciatic nerve in my lower back. He went on to stress the potential danger to my spinal cord, and the dire consequences that would attend any further displacement. After two prolonged epidural sessions, involving the injection of cortisone into the nerve endings in my lower back, he noted without surprise that it did little to relieve the pain. He then advised me strongly to return to the UK for an operation.

Once again the Sworders swung into action. Ted set about arranging for me to return to the UK by air on a British West Indian Airways DC9. There followed hours more work for him in sorting out my bank draft from the UK to pay for the three seats required for the stretcher, cashing travellers' cheques and so on. Thankfully, I had taken out medical insurance before leaving the UK. Three days later I was back in England, in the Devonport Naval Hospital, Plymouth. . . .

With the thought of Plymouth I was suddenly back in the Dufour 28, the coffee mug empty in my hands. I stood up to wash it out, part of me still clinging to the recollections of three years ago. By great good fortune, a month of traction had rendered any operation unnecessary. Better still, I learnt that my disc, a nagging acquaintance of some years' standing, had now taken up a permanently displaced but stable position. So it was that I was able to return to Barbados in early February to continue my voyage. In the months that followed, I sailed up past the Windward and Leeward islands, through the Bahamas, across to the USA and from there, via the Azores, back to St Agnes by early August, 1985.

I nearly overbalanced as the starboard side of the boat suddenly dipped sharply. It felt as though three people had stepped aboard all at once. Peering up over the top of the hatchway, I saw a giant making his way towards me, followed closely by Andrew.

'Skipper, this is Staff Sergeant Roger Carpenter,' called out Andrew. My outstretched hand was suddenly enveloped by a huge paw.

'Nice to meet you, Colonel,' said Roger, grinning. He was about six foot four and built in proportion, with honey-coloured crinkly hair, blue eyes and a slightly tanned complexion. 'I hear you've got a bit of engine trouble.'

'Yes, the batteries are flat, I'm afraid,' I replied wonderingly, still awed at the sheer size of the man. I was about to ask Andrew where the charged battery and jumper leads were. Then I thought better of it.

'Staff Carpenter's in the REME, Skipper. Supervises the vehicle mechanics in the Regiment,' supplied Andrew, completely invisible behind the great hulking figure filling the cockpit.

'Oh, that's marvellous,' I replied. 'It is good of you to take the trouble, I must say.'

Two minutes later Roger had examined the engine, adjusting here, tapping there. Now he was ready, the starting cord in his hand. Fancying that the engine had already retreated a good inch inside its compartment, I watched him plant his great feet solidly on the cabin sole either side of it. He wound on the cord, then crouched slightly, coiling himself like a spring.

'Aaaarrrrgggghhhh!'

Slowly at first, then faster, the spring uncoiled as Roger let the roar escape him, pulling upwards with both arms in one enormous effort.

'Put . . . , put . . . , put . . . , put, put, put, put, put, put, ...'

Yes, I thought. Not much wrong with his back.

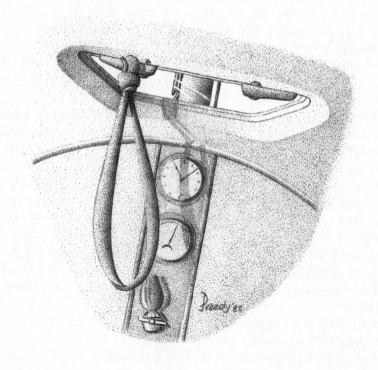

Chapter Eight

CLYDE TO PLYMOUTH

Naturally enough, most of my yacht deliveries are memorable because of what happened whilst actually at sea. Yet one or two will always be associated in my mind with comparatively minor incidents ashore.

It was early May 1987, and I was bringing *Armelia*, a Sadler 26, from the Clyde to Plymouth. It had been hard going from the start, as one shallow depression chased another across the Irish Sea. But Sadlers perform well to windward, and I had managed to keep going. Then my luck ran out. Half-way between St David's Head and Land's End I met up with a severe gale from the south-south-west – right on the nose. To be honest, I had only myself to blame. The man on Radio 4 had already foretold a possible gale for sea areas Lundy and Fastnet. But too often I had found such warnings to be exaggerated, and I had been tempted to push on. After all, I knew that if I could just get round Land's End my problems would be over. Then it could blow as hard as it liked – well, almost – while I ran before it up the English Channel. It was not to be. The severe gale had duly arrived while I was still well short of Land's End, and despite heaving-to for twelve hours the gloomy shipping forecast at 0555 hours that morning was a carbon copy of the last, offering no let-up whatsoever. That decided me. By early evening I had run 40 miles back to Milford Haven and with the last of the light reached the Camper and Nicholson yacht marina up-river.

By eleven o'clock I had squared things away, showered and

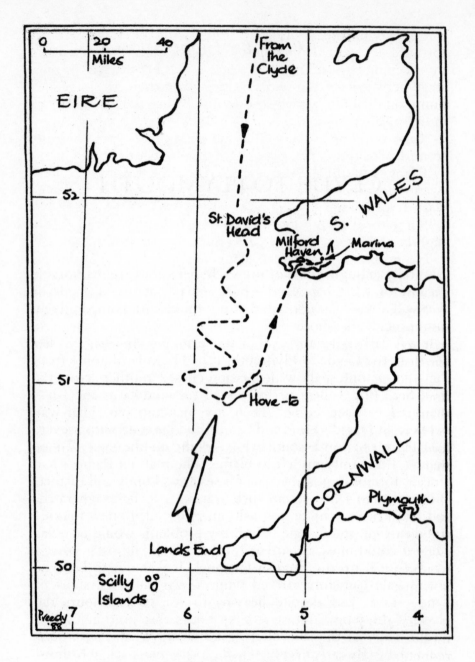

Running Back To Milford Haven For Shelter

eaten. Having finally come to terms with this reverse in my fortunes, I was tired and ready for a quiet night. I climbed into my sleeping bag and had just reached that luxuriously drowsy stage between waking and sleeping when there was a sudden bump on the hull. In two seconds flat I was on deck, shivering in my pyjamas. Mistake Number One.

'Take our line, will you!' shouted someone peremptorily from the cockpit of the large yacht now outside me.

'Right,' I mumbled, moving like a zombie towards the bow. A crew member – there seemed to be two of them – threw a warp across to me.

'Sorry to disturb you,' he said quietly with a sympathetic, slightly embarrassed smile. 'You must have been fast asleep.'

'No problem,' I replied, feeling better, 'I'd better make fast ashore.' Yet even as I stepped down onto the wooden pontoon the voice called again from the cockpit.

'No, no, not there, just make fast to your bow, that's all you need to do.' The skipper, for such he had to be, sounded faintly irritated. Before I could say anything the crew member on the foredeck spoke up.

'Hold on, Skipper, he's right, you know. Our bow and stern lines ought to be taken on to the pontoon. We're a lot bigger than he is.'

He was right. The other boat was at least ten feet longer. It looked a bit like a Sweden 36, but only daylight would confirm that. Right now I didn't care.

'Oh, have it your own way,' came the petulant rejoinder.

Duty done, I retreated below. Yet not, alas, to sleep. For the next hour or so the same strident voice could be heard breaking the silence of the night with one instruction or another. Of the two crew members I could hear nothing. They, at least, seemed to understand that others might be trying to sleep. Then, at last, my fatigue won the battle, and I knew no more.

My inner alarm clock woke me for the 0555 hours forecast. It was better – but not much. Granted the wind would be moderating to a 6 or 7 – it already had, I realized, noting the reduction of noise in the rigging – but it was still going to come from the south or south-south-west. Even if I reefed right down and just bashed away towards Land's End, the sea would still be very lumpy and confused. Every third wave would stop us dead and it would be impossible to make any real progress. Much better to accept the inevitable and stay put. I turned over and went back to sleep.

I woke just before eight o'clock. He's at it again, I thought, as I slowly realized what had disturbed me.

'I don't want to have to ask you again, John. I'd like this deck washed down before breakfast.'

A skipper myself, my natural inclination was to side with him. Yet once again I found myself sympathizing with the crew. Not that there was anything wrong with rousting them out first thing in the morning. I had done it myself countless times. But to wash down the deck? That suggested that the boat was not about to put to sea again; at least, not straight away. In which case why the rush? They had looked pretty tired the night before and would doubtless have welcomed the chance to catch up on their sleep. Still, perhaps they were going to leave the boat there and catch a train or something. It was really none of my business.

I kept my head down as long as I could that morning. Eventually, however, nature called and, since boats in harbour follow the same rule as trains standing in the station, I dressed and set off under lowering skies towards the marina amenities complex. As I did so, I noticed two things. First, the boat alongside me was indeed a Sweden 36, and very nice too. Second, and more to the point, there was now an empty space in front of me alongside the pontoon itself. Clearly, its occupant had left earlier that morning, no doubt heading north with the wind behind him. My spirits rose. With a bit of luck my close neighbour would have moved his boat by the time I got back. Especially if I took my time.

No such luck. The Sweden 36 was still rafted alongside when I emerged from the showers. As I clambered aboard *Armelia* the crew were busy stowing away their mops and buckets, while the man I took to be the skipper was standing on his foredeck, coiling a warp. He was in his forties, I judged, short and dark with prematurely balding hair and a suspicion of a paunch.

'Good morning,' I called across. 'Not much of a day, is it?'

He didn't look up. 'Bloody,' he said shortly.

'Ah . . . I see the chap in front has decided to move on,' I persevered. 'Must be heading north, lucky devil. Still, at least it makes a bit more room.'

'Yes,' he said, finally looking up and staring straight through me. I felt suddenly confused. 'Well, I'd better get on with my chores, I suppose,' I muttered lamely. I escaped below.

He did move the boat in the end. But not until it was almost lunchtime. Until then our close proximity cast me once more in the role of involuntary eavesdropper. It was not one I welcomed. Apart from anything else, it's very easy for one skipper, particularly when single-handed as I was on this occasion, to pick mental holes in another. So I spent as much time as possible below. Even there, however, it was far too easy to hear that penetrating voice. For the most part I was able to ignore it. But now and then the hairs would prickle on the back of my neck. One of the crew was very young, about eighteen or so, I guessed, and I soon realized that the skipper rather enjoyed humiliating him, preferably in front of others. Thus, in the same weary voice that I recognized only too readily:

'Not like that, John. God, you're awkward! Did you have trouble learning to ride a bike or something?'

These and similar comments from time to time managed to blight the morning for me. Correcting a member of the crew is one thing, but it can be done far more effectively without sarcasm and in a helpful, private manner. Thankfully, there was one brief respite mid-morning when I invited the three of them aboard *Armelia* for a coffee, an invitation which the skipper refused. The younger of the crew, fresh-faced, fair-haired, was John Waring, and the other, a short, powerfully built man in his thirties, Tim Sender. To this day their names are in the address book that I always carry with me on delivery trips. Our conversation was friendly, relaxed and, by mutual and tacit consent, very general in nature. It ended abruptly in response to a summons from alongside. Thereafter it was the mixture as before. At last, however, the skipper apparently decided that he could delay moving the boat no longer; I was left in peace.

I was washing up when the 1355 hours forecast came through. Happily, it was much more encouraging, and I realized that I could be on my way next morning. Even the barometer was showing signs of turning upwards. I went up on deck to see if there was yet any sign of the promised improvement. The grey clouds were still around, but now there were patches of blue between them. Suddenly, a broad shaft of sunlight broke through, eliciting an immediate, glittering response from the water.

It's amazing what a little warm sunshine will do. Within moments people were climbing out of cabins all over the place to stretch their arms and look about them. One of the marina berthing attendants was walking casually down the pontoon, stopping here and there for a chat. Nearby, at the edge of the marina, a small van pulled up in the car park. 'Martin's Express Bakery' it said on the side. The driver switched off the engine but did not get out. Instead, I could see him open his shirt, lean back in his seat and close his eyes. The customers were going to have to wait.

'Right, time we sorted out that aerial. You go up the mast, John. Tim and I will do the winching.' Just in front of me the skipper was standing in his cockpit. John was on the foredeck.

'No good doing it yet, Skipper,' said John. 'Tim's still away getting the shopping, remember.'

There was a pause. Then:

'OK, in that case we'll just have to do without him.' Clearly, the skipper was not a man to be diverted.

'Don't see how,' rejoined the youngster, starting to look worried. 'We need two on deck, don't we? One winching and one taking up the tension on the halyard.'

The berthing attendant had reached their boat and was standing patiently on the pontoon, hoping to attract the skipper's attention.

'Good Lord, no,' said the skipper. 'All we need is a little ingenuity. Now, where are those jerrycans?' He dived below.

I was becoming interested. In fact it is perfectly possible for one man to hoist another up the mast; yet this was going to be something new, I realized. At this point, however, the berthing attendant gave up and moved on towards me.

'Afternoon, sir. Leaving today?'

Having settled up with him, we spent a few minutes chatting and enjoying the sunshine. Then, no doubt realizing from the frenetic activity up front that he would just have to come back later, he retraced his steps up the pontoon. Meanwhile, on the Sweden 36, the bosun's chair had been hoisted empty on the spinnaker halyard to a point about three feet from the top of the mast. That was also new. The bosun's chair was evidently homemade and consisted of a flat, rectangular board – the seat – from which four ropes, one from each corner, rose to a central D-ring suspended about two feet above it. It was the D-ring that was connected to the spinnaker halyard itself. Another light line was attached by some means to the bottom of the seat and hung down to the deck. Obviously, that would perform the function of a down-haul. Finally, at the base of the mast, four large plastic jerrycans full of water had been positioned. The skipper was in the act of threading the other end of the spinnaker halyard through the handles of the jerrycans and making them fast. Daylight began to dawn. He was planning to use the jerrycans as a counter-weight. Ingenious – in theory, at least. I found myself wondering if he'd done it before.

John had patently not done it before, judging by the expression on his face. Nor did he much want to start now.

'Look, Skipper . . . ,' he began.

'Right, all set.' The skipper stood up, his face red. 'Now the next step is to haul the jerrycans up.' He was almost whistling. 'Come on, give me a hand.'

John had clearly learnt from experience the futility of argument once the skipper had the bit between his teeth. With a long sigh he joined him on the down-haul. Together they started to heave. Slowly the jerrycans rose from the deck, swaying slightly as they jerked upwards towards the lower spreaders. The two of them had to rest twice during the operation but eventually, as the bosun's chair descended almost to the deck, the jerrycans were clustered like an enormous bunch of grapes immediately below the block at the top of the mast. Suspended from them, the long tail of the spinnaker halyard hung down to the deck.

For a brief moment I tore my gaze away and looked around me. The hoisting operation had attracted quite a lot of attention. On a dozen boats around the marina, people had left what they were doing to gaze expectantly towards us, while in the car-park the van's engine, started a few moments earlier, suddenly stopped again.

I turned back to see John pointing down the pontoon.

'Look, here comes Tim,' he shouted, the relief obvious in his voice. Just in time, I thought. Tim was walking along the pontoon towards the boat, laden with shopping bags. Oblivious to the danger of a ducking, he was staring fixedly upwards as he walked, obviously not too sure of what he was seeing.

'What the hell's all that?' he exclaimed, as he reached the boat.

'It's the Skipper's idea,' said John, his voice suddenly flat and weary. 'It's for going up the mast.'

'You're not serious?' gasped Tim, dropping the shopping down on the pontoon to gaze once more skywards.

'Nothing the matter with it,' rejoined the skipper defensively, still recovering from the hoisting operation.

'Nothing the matter with it?' echoed Tim incredulously. 'Who was going up anyway?'

'Me,' said John.

Tim turned back to the skipper. 'Why him? You're both about the same weight. Anyway, it's madness. Look, just give me a hand with this shopping and then we can do it the proper way. I don't mind going up.'

Perhaps it was the word 'madness' that stung the skipper. Or perhaps he resented the implication that he had been about to invite a member of his crew to do something he wasn't prepared to do himself. Or again, maybe he just couldn't bring himself to back down in front of his ever-growing audience. Whatever the case. . . .

'Alright then, I'll go up myself. Can't imagine what all the fuss is about. Come on, don't just stand there. John, you take hold of the spinnaker halyard and just haul the jerrycans down when I tell you. Gently, mind. Tim, I want you to hold on to this line on the bosun's chair. You're the brake man.'

So saying, he put his head through the inverted V of the bosun's chair and pulled the wooden seat under his bottom from behind. On his face was a look of grim determination.

'Look, Skipper,' said Tim, 'are you really sure about this? Why don't we just. . . .'

'Take the strain!' rapped out the other. 'Right, haul away gently.'

His crew obeyed. For the first few feet or so things went beautifully. John applied the first gentle downward pressure on the spinnaker halyard. Beside him Tim kept a light tension on the brake line. As the jerrycans gently descended, the skipper just seemed to float upwards.

'Hold it there!' he called, once he had cleared the cluster of cleats and winches at the base of the mast. John stopped pulling. Tim checked firmly on his brake line. The skipper stopped rising, suspended in perfect equilibrium some six feet above the deck. He shifted into a more comfortable position on the board, looked up to see that all was well and took a fresh grip on the D-ring in front of his face. 'Piece of cake,' he declared triumphantly. 'Right then, haul away.'

Once again he started to rise. Then it happened. As Tim applied more tension to the brake line, suddenly it went slack, the end dropping away from the bosun's chair. Somehow or other the knot had come undone. Tim just stood there horrified, the other end of the line useless in his hand, as he watched his skipper, gradually but inexorably, start to pick up speed.

'Don't pull so hard, John!' yelled the skipper, his voice tinged with panic. But John had already let go. 'Brake, Tim!'

In March 1985 I was fortunate enough to stand on the cabin roof of my own 26-foot Super Seal at Cape Canaveral to watch Challenger lift its astronauts, monkeys and rats into space. What had impressed me most on that occasion was the sensation of sheer power as the space shuttle accelerated remorselessly into the clear blue sky. Suddenly, here in this marina in South Wales, I could see it all over again.

By the time the skipper reached the level of the lower spreaders he was already moving fast. That was a pity because his only real hope would have been somehow to grab one of them as he went by. Granted, the jerk would have almost pulled his arm out of its socket, but even so. . . . As it was, he could only hang on tight as he shot, terrified, upwards. Now he was really shifting. The jerrycans came hurtling down towards the deck, missing him by the barest whisker. A thin, terror-stricken scream escaped his lips. My heart rose into my mouth.

It was his crew who saved him from serious injury – or worse. In the nick of time John and Tim managed to impede, though certainly not stop completely, the fall of the jerrycans, and at no little risk to themselves. It was just enough to damp things down. The skipper was no more than six feet from the top of the mast when the spinnaker halyard above him went suddenly slack, sending the bosun's chair careering outwards from the mast and then back again with a clatter. As for its occupant, he just continued upwards like the second stage of the Apollo moon rocket. Thankfully, however, he was no longer being propelled through the seat of his pants. By the time he came level with the mast-head his momentum had virtually spent itself. He grabbed frantically for the mast truck and the surrounding group of shroud terminals – and stuck.

For a moment there was silence. Then, as it became increasingly clear from the skipper's language that he was unhurt, there came the inevitable reaction.

When at last I was able to see through my tears, I looked around me. Although soaked through with water from one of the jerrycans that had split on impact, Tim and John were leaning against each other for support, quite unable to control themselves. Nor were they alone. The reaction was exactly the same elsewhere, the helpless laughter echoing all around the marina. As for the man in the bread van, he had disappeared completely. Only the slight quivering of the vehicle on its springs betrayed his presence, evidently prostrate on the front seat. No doubt he felt it had been worth the wait.

Eventually the laughter died away, and things started to return to normal. The skipper clambered gingerly back into the bosun's chair before his crew lowered him gently to the deck. Judging by the look on his face, he at least had not thought it funny.

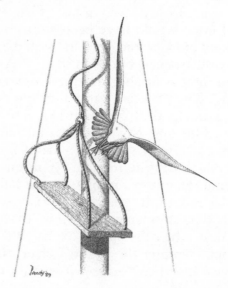

'What the bloody hell were you playing at, Tim?' he demanded acidly as he extricated himself from the bosun's chair. 'You were supposed to be the brake man, for God's sake.'

'Sorry, Skipper, but the rope came off,' explained Tim, showing him the rope's end. 'Not my fault, really.'

'Nothing we could do, Skipper, honestly,' chipped in John, his voice a little uneven. 'And you did tie that rope on yourself, remember.'

I slept well that night. It was beautifully quiet.

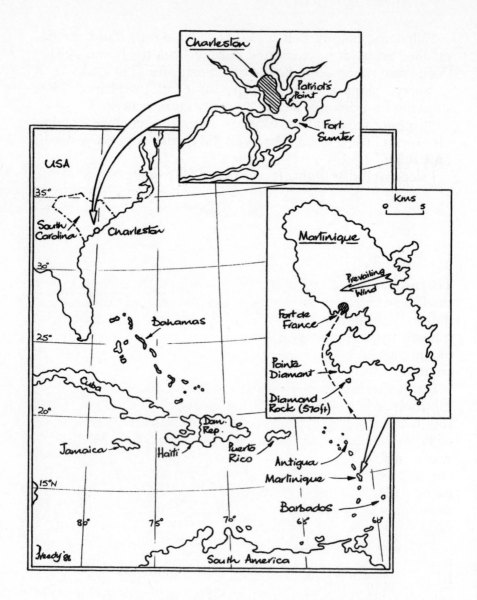

Western Atlantic Coast With Martinique And
Charleston Inset

Chapter Nine

MARTINIQUE TO CHARLESTON, SOUTH CAROLINA

Toothache is a painful nuisance at the best of times. But in a small boat at sea it quickly becomes something worse, and if the sea is rough, worse still. Every jolt and jar seems to be transmitted directly through the hull of the boat to the source of the pain in a way that makes it very difficult to think of anything else.

It was therefore with heartfelt relief that, on a hot and humid morning early in February 1985, I managed at last to escape the rough and tumble of the trade-wind sea as I came into the lee of Pointe Diamant, on the south-eastern tip of Martinique. It was a pity, really. In other circumstances I would have been entranced by all the sights, sounds and smells of a new island, particularly a French one. But not today. Right now my only ambition was to get into Fort de France as quickly as possible, drop the anchor and find a dentist.

Fort de France itself, the capital of Martinique, lies on the northern shore of the large natural harbour of the same name. Its low-lying, flat-roofed buildings started to multiply fast as I came round Cap Solomon, while a thick cluster of yachts made the landing place easy to identify. Picking my way amongst them, I eventually found a space just large enough for *Miss Fidget*, my 26-foot Super Seal sloop, to swing in. Minutes later I was stepping down into my collapsible dinghy.

The big yacht alongside me to starboard was called *Seacup*. It was flying a large Stars and Stripes proudly from the stern. As always, the American flag looked as if it was brand new, a silent reproach to other nationalities, particularly the British and the French, who often appear to have used theirs for wiping the floor of the cockpit. Even as I admired it, a wiry, middle-aged man in shirt and shorts clambered down the stern ladder into a large inflatable. Having settled himself on the seat, he looked across at me, smiled a welcome.

'Hi there,' he called out. 'Whereya from?'

'Bar-hay-hos,' I managed, the need to keep my jaw from moving making the word impossible to articulate.

'Barbados?' he echoed. I nodded. 'Single-handed?' I nodded again. Then he realized that something was wrong. 'Say, are you OK?'

'Tooh-ahe,' I replied, dropping an oar for a moment to point at my mouth.

'Gee, that's too bad,' he said. He thought for a moment. 'Can't say I know any dentists here myself, but I guess they'll be able to give you the good word in the harbour office. Anyhow, I'll let 'em know you're comin'. So long.' As he pulled away with short, jabbing strokes of his paddles I saw, painted on the stern of the dinghy, the name *B-Cup*. I was halfway ashore before I got the point – but right then I wasn't in the mood for humour anyway.

Forty minutes later, hot, perspiring, breathless, I was climbing a flight of rickety stairs under an archway of bougain-villaea up the side of a wooden house somewhere in the centre of the town. Pushing the gauze-covered swing door open at the top, I entered what was obviously a combined reception and waiting room. Ventilated by a large fan rotating slowly on the ceiling, it was empty, shaded and deliciously cool after the sticky heat and dust of the streets. I pressed the buzzer on the desk. Moments later a door at the back of the room opened, and a slim, strikingly attractive, black girl wearing a crisp white uniform walked through it. Against her smooth, coffee-coloured skin the fine chiselling of her features was intriguing.

'M'sieu?' she enquired, her teeth flashing in an exemplary smile.

I pointed at my mouth. 'Je suis anglais, mademoiselle. J'ai douleur ici,' I managed with my rehearsed speech, dismally aware that facial paralysis had combined with my execrable

French to render me totally incomprehensible. She took it in her stride.

'C'est bien, m'sieu, assayez-vous, s'il vous plâit. Un moment.' She disappeared again.

Grateful for the way in which she had confined herself to my schoolboy level of French, I subsided heavily into an armchair. Nor did I move for some time. Normally in a dentist's waiting room I would have sought distraction by thumbing, however perfunctorily, through the magazines on the table. Yet in this case they would all have been in French. Anyway, as things were, I was glad just to be able to sit down in peace and quiet for a bit, thankful for the chance to prepare myself mentally for what lay ahead. Reasonably composed at last, and trying to ignore the throbbing from the back of my lower jaw, my gaze wandered across the room to a large framed picture on the opposite wall. It was a print showing a number of eighteenth century ships of war clustered around a massive, faintly familiar, tower of rock. Trying to read the title strip mounted on the frame on the bottom, I could just make out two words: 'gagnée' – captured; and 'Rocher du Diamante' – Rock of Diamonds. Then I had it. Of course. This was the famous Diamond Rock that Commander Ted Sworder had told me about back in Barbados. You idiot, I thought suddenly; two hours ago you actually sailed right past it without even registering what it was.

The image of the real rock that I now managed to recall to mind was a lot sharper than I might reasonably have expected. For at the time it had been far more important in my eyes for the shelter which it had afforded me than for any other reason. All the same, it had been impossible to ignore its dramatic appearance even then. Towering, incredibly, to something close to 600 feet, the sheer-sided pinnacle of rock had risen from the sea like a stone sentinel, less than a mile from the mainland. Indeed, unless my recollection deceived me, it had actually been marginally higher than the coastline behind it. Resolving firmly to have another look at it when I left Fort de France in a few days' time, I tried to remember what Ted had told me about its unique role in Napoleonic naval history.

'It was all to do with the vital need for timely naval intelligence,' said Ted over an evening drink on the veranda of his beach house in Bridgetown. 'At all costs you had to know where the enemy was and what he was doing. The thing was, you see, the British ships on the West Indian station were either based up in English Harbour, Antigua, about 250 miles to the north-west, or over here in Barbados. So in order to know what the French were up to, Admiral Hood had been obliged to keep a frigate constantly on station within sight of Fort de France, where the French fleet was based. Anyway, a point eventually came in 1803 when the Lords of the Admiralty were stretched to the limit with naval commitments all over the world. And that was when the Admiral hit on the idea of saving on the frigate by using Diamond Rock as a permanent reporting station instead. Somehow or other they managed to put about 120 men with cannon, balls, powder, lots of food and water up on top of the rock, commissioned it as 'Her Majesty's Sloop-of-War Diamond' and just left the detachment there to observe and report on enemy movements in and out of the port.'

'But surely the French tried to remove them?' I asked.

'Oh, they tried, certainly, but you only have to see the rock to realize how difficult it must have been to recapture it. The French tried to bombard it from the mainland, but Hood pushed their guns into the sea before they could get started. As for storming it from the bottom, well, it must have been a bit like the Greeks at the Pass of Thermopylae, only worse. A handful of men at the top could have held off an army if they wanted to. Anyway, that's exactly what they did, for well over a year.'

'What a story!' I exclaimed, picturing the scene as it must have been. 'And every so often one of our ships would turn up to resupply them and get the latest news on enemy naval movements?'

'Exactly; either that or Commander Maurice, the officer in command, would send his small sloop over to St Lucia. It was quite an achievement, I can tell you. When you actually get close to it, just have a look at how high it is – and then think about what it must have meant in terms of effort and ingenuity to get four two-ton cannons to the top in those days. Compared to that, even the gun race at Earls Court seems pretty tame.'

Now, back in the waiting room, I looked again at the print, marvelled at the sheer audacity of the venture. Yet it didn't really need the French tricoleur at the stern of one of the ships to tell me that this picture was not glorifying the British achievement; far from it. It was actually commemorating the subsequent recapture of the rock by the French. Nor, given my present surroundings, was this surprising. I was just about to walk across to the picture to discover when the recapture had actually taken place when the door opened once more.

'S'il vous plâit, m'sieu,' said the girl, somehow managing to make her smile inviting and sympathetic at the same time as she held the door open for me.

Later, in the pleasantly relaxed aftermath of my encounter with the dentist, I wandered slowly round the town, my jaw still frozen with anaesthetic, soaking in the atmosphere of this ancient Caribbean seaport and doing some desultory shopping at the same time. It was three o'clock in the afternoon when I returned to *Miss Fidget*. I was just making the dinghy fast to the stern rail before stepping aboard when the American on *Seacup* invited me over for a drink. Moments later I was seated comfortably in the palatial cockpit of the 40-foot ketch talking to Arnie Sealam and his wife Tina, both from New England.

'I guess the visit to the dentist worked out OK?' enquired Arnie, taking in my relaxed slouch with a smile.

'Yes, he was marvellous,' I replied, sipping something that tasted a bit like Pimms behind its icy coldness. Then I laughed. 'You know, as a matter of fact I wasn't too sure how he would receive me after what I saw in the waiting room.' I explained about the picture. 'You never know,' I added, 'after 200 years or so he might have seen his chance to get even with the Brits for the Diamond Rock episode!'

Arnie looked quickly at Tina without speaking. Then they both laughed. 'Ron, I don't think you know the half of it,' said Tina, still giggling. 'But I guess that may have been as well in the circumstances.'

I looked at her, puzzled.

'Tina's talking about what happened here just a few years back,' put in Arnie, smiling. 'That was when one of the anniversaries of the French recapture of the rock came up. Anyhow, seems they decided to commemorate the occasion in true Napoleonic style with an official sail past the rock. It was quite a flotilla, by all accounts: lots of official ships and launches joined by just about every French yacht in the neighbourhood. All the pomp and ceremony they could come up with.' He paused for effect. 'There was just one problem.'

'What was that?' I asked.

'Well, a couple of Brits on a yacht here in Fort de France got to hear about it ahead of time. Anyhow, comes the morning of the sail past, out goes the fleet in stately procession – and then they see it. Right up on top of the rock, fluttering bravely in the breeze, is a Union Jack!'

★ ★ ★

It was just 18 months later that, once again, I found myself in need of a dentist, this time in the middle of a delivery trip. Chuck Johnson, an engaging young Californian, and I were taking a Southerly 115 called *Amélie* from West Palm Beach, Florida, to Norfolk, Virginia. There Chuck was due to leave the boat, while I would be joined by two crew from England to sail the boat, via the Azores, to Gibraltar.

Unlike most deliveries, this one was not under pressure of time, not at this stage, at any rate. Thus, Chuck himself had been in no great hurry to reach Norfolk, while the comfortably-timed flight date for my crew meant that he and I could afford to take our time heading northwards. As things turned out it was just as well. Threading our way up the beautiful intra-coastal waterway, we had just reached the pretty town of Beaufort, South Carolina, when the very same tooth that had been filled in Martinique started to nag once more.

Suspecting quite unjustly for a moment that the French dentist might have had his revenge after all, I tried to ignore the warning signs right through that day and for most of the next. But the dull pain was still there when we reached the city marina at Charleston, South Carolina, at teatime; by then commonsense had asserted itself. Whatever else, I knew I had to get the tooth attended to before starting across the Atlantic. With Chuck's ready agreement, therefore, I set off into the town during the early evening to try and arrange a dentist appointment for the following morning.

It was nearly seven thirty by the time one of the city buses dropped me off again outside the marina. And it was immediately apparent that something was happening inside. Joining the steady stream of people talking and laughing their way through the entrance, I soon began to pick up the distant strains of a Dixieland jazz band. Moments later I had discovered its source. Berthed alongside the pier immediately opposite *Amélie* was a large, Mississippi-type paddle boat, its lights already bright and welcoming in the gathering dusk.

Reaching her at last, I stopped for a moment to listen to the music as the customers jostled their way happily past me and up the wooden gangway. Then I saw the billboard propped up against the side. 'See Fort Sumter where the Civil War began!' it prescribed. 'Tours daily from Charleston City Marina and Patriot's Point.' This was evidently the more relaxed, evening version of the daytime tour. And the uninhibited whoops and laughter from the passengers already embarked suggested strongly that music was not the only item on the menu.

'Get fixed up?'

Preoccupied with the paddle boat, I hadn't even noticed that Chuck was standing up in the cockpit of *Amélie* behind me, the better to enjoy the music. 'Oh, hello Chuck,' I replied, trying to make myself heard over the final repetend of 'Sweet Annabelle Lee'. 'Yes, nine thirty tomorrow morning. OK by you?'

'You bet,' he replied. He nodded towards the paddle boat. 'They're pretty good, aren't they?'

It was another half-hour before the great paddle wheels started to turn at last. By then the total volume of noise had become almost deafening. Yet the band had certainly known how to play, and it was with some disappointment that, over our supper in the cabin below, we noted the gradual fading of the music into the night.

'You know, over on the west coast I guess we don't know as much about Fort Sumter as we should,' admitted Chuck, a trifle sheepishly. 'Oh sure, it triggered off the Civil War in 1861 and all that stuff, but I'm not too clear about the details. So I can't really fill you in on it like I should, Ron.'

'Don't worry, Chuck,' I replied. 'Believe it or not, I had to study the American Civil War in my army days, so I could easily bore you stiff about it if you're not careful! Not that there's a lot to tell, really. It was all over in 36 hours.'

'Hey, go ahead and bore!' said Chuck, suddenly all attention. 'What happened?'

'Well, during the run-up to the war the fort was still garrisoned by the Federal Army, about 70 soldiers under the command of a Major Robert Anderson – I think that was the name. Then came the declaration of war itself. From Anderson's point of view it must have been quite a shock. One moment he had been enjoying one of the most peaceful, least demanding jobs that the army could offer; the next, he found himself suddenly surrounded by thousands of rebel troops in the very heart of the Confederacy. Mind, the writing had been on the wall for some time. Abraham Lincoln had steadfastly refused to hand over the fort when he was asked to do so by Jefferson Davis. Then he added insult to injury by sending word that he was going to resupply the fort, demonstrating that he meant to keep it. And that did it.'

'What then?'

'Well, by that time the Southern troops under General Beauregard were dug in with batteries of guns all around the harbour here. So they just opened up. Anyway, 36 hours later Anderson surrendered, and in no time he and his men were on their way back to New York by steamer.'

'Many casualties?'

'Only one, apparently, and even that was accidental. Anderson was firing a last salute to the Union flag, before lowering it, when a charge of powder exploded, killing one of the gunners.'

'It's a hell of a thing when you think of all the carnage and misery that followed,' said Chuck soberly. 'Still, I guess Fort Sumter was only the spark. The whole thing was going to explode anyway by that stage.'

It was just after eleven o'clock when, dozing in my bunk, I picked up the first faint sounds of the band once more. Evidently, the Fort Sumter tour party was on its way home. It was just 20 minutes or so before we felt the paddle boat bump heavily against the pier, another 40 before the last inebriated group of revellers stumbled noisily down the gangway. Still, at least the band had kept on playing right to the end. Nor had they quite finished even now. As they launched themselves into what I suspected would be their finale, I recognized with delight something I had been waiting to hear all evening: 'The Charleston'.

★　　　★　　　★

'Looks like it'll have to come out, I'm afraid. I'll just give you a shot of local.'

The tall, bespectacled dentist picked up the hypodermic syringe from the tray which his young female assistant was holding in front of her. He advanced towards me. Moments later my jaw started to go numb.

'I really don't think it would have been worth saving – and I guess it's better out anyway if you're headed out across the Atlantic,' continued the dentist. The assistant having left the room, he strolled across to a chair and sat down. 'So, have you had a chance to take in the sights here in Charleston?' he asked conversationally, waiting for the anaesthetic to take effect.

'Not really, I'm afraid,' I replied, faintly aware of a sensation of *déja vu*. 'We only arrived yesterday afternoon, and we'll have to push on again pretty soon if we're going to reach Norfolk in good time.'

'That's a pity,' he said. 'Charleston has a lot of history going for it. Not like in Britain, of course,' he added hastily, 'but colonial beginnings, American Civil War, that sort of thing. That was quite a war, you know. Maybe you wouldn't believe it, but it's still felt pretty keenly in this neck of the woods.'

Things were getting a bit tricky. Once again I tried to decide whether he looked like a Unionist or a Confederate, a carpetbagger or a Johnny Reb'. Ten to one it was the latter, but even those odds were far from reassuring in my present circumstances. Then, at last, I saw the clue I had been looking for. On a low table near the window was a little plastic cylinder containing pens and pencils. And there on the side of it was a transfer print of the Confederate flag. It wasn't much – but it was enough.

'Yes,' I said, suddenly expansive, 'I can believe it. I do know a little about it, as a matter of fact. And I must say that, as an ex-army man myself, I have always considered Robert E. Lee to have been one of the finest generals that the world has ever seen.'

Chapter Ten

LYMINGTON TO GIBRALTAR

'When I win the pools, I'm goin' to get 'old of the biggest wooden sailing boat I can lay me 'ands on – and give it to me worst enemy.'

In my mind's eye I could see again the huge frame of Garry Harris standing beside me on Loe Beach, at the northern end of Falmouth harbour. An ex-Cornwall rugby player, he spent much of his time moving boats or concrete moorings in and out of the water, though not, as some suspected, with his bare hands. And he had been summing up in his own, uniquely pungent way, the tyranny which any wooden boat imposes on her owner.

On that day, I recalled, I had shivered under layers of clothing as a typically raw March wind had threatened to cut my head off. Now, months later, my bare feet could hardly stand the heat of the wooden fuelling pontoon at the 'Bon Successo' marina, Belem, on the outskirts of Lisbon. The contrast could hardly be more marked. On decks all around me people were stretched out on their backs in the sun, their eyes closed, their arms by their sides, serene in the knowledge that they were doing the only sensible thing. Yet, impatient as I was to join them, first I had to see to the refuelling and berthing of the sleeping wooden giant beside me.

I wondered what Garry would say if he could see this one. Fully 55 feet long from her raked bow to her half-counter stern, *Thunderer* was a true thoroughbred from the Nicholson stable and a past winner of the Fastnet race to boot. Yet really, I thought, she ought to be called *Phoenix*, given the way that her

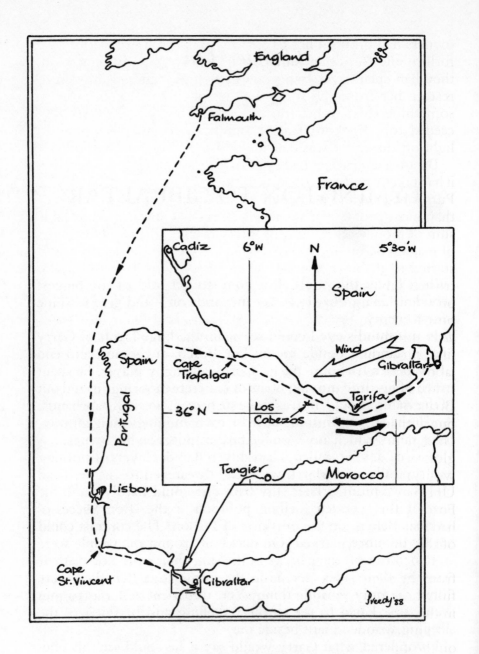

Falmouth To Gibraltar With Approaches To
Straits Inset

owners had brought her back from the dead. Discovering her, forlorn and forgotten, in a corner of a South Coast boatyard, they had spent over two years in a single-minded mission to restore her from the sorry wooden shell she had become to something close to her former glory. They had certainly succeeded too, I acknowledged, admiring the way the dappled light off the water was dancing on her gently curving hull.

By any standards it had been an impressive achievement; and it had taken a pretty impressive couple to do it. Richard and Janine Purser had already packed more into their 30 years or so apiece than most people manage in a lifetime. Having made a sizeable sum of money on the UK property market, they had lost most of it again before moving to Canada, where they had promptly started to make another. Leaving their affairs in the hands of trusted subordinates, they had then returned to England, intent on acquiring a second-hand wooden boat of character and shipping it straight back to Canada. But that had been before *Thunderer*. From what they had told me since, it had taken the boat little more than half a day to sentence them to two years' hard labour, not to mention life imprisonment thereafter.

I had been looking forward to the trip to Gibraltar for weeks. Boats of this size did not come my way very often, still less one with her pedigree. For days on end before leaving St Agnes, I had pictured her hammering down the Bay of Biscay, reaching gloriously across a brisk westerly wind. Yet from the moment we had left Falmouth fate had set her face cruelly against us. Unbelievably, the wind had steadfastly refused to pipe up above Force 4 for more than about 20 of the 722 nautical miles we had so far covered. Small wonder that we had spent nearly half of the time under engine.

'OK, ready when you are.' Richard was calling out to me from the companionway of the main cabin. Short, dark, powerfully built, he was wiping his hands with a rag. 'Got it undone in the end,' he said. 'What about the filler cap?'

'No problem,' I replied. 'Right, if you'd like to keep an eye on the dipstick down below, I'll start filling up. I've swilled the deck down, so if I do spill any diesel it shouldn't stain. I'll scrub it down afterwards anyway – or rather, 'Roo will. Where is he, by the way?'

'Last time I saw him he was showing a lively interest in that motor cruiser over there,' said Richard with a smile. Looking where he pointed, I caught a glimpse of 'Roo's blond head behind the windscreen of the cruiser, and another, with hair much longer, beside it. Making up for lost time, I thought.

The fuelling pontoon actually doubled as a filling station for the busy road flanking the other side of the short stone parapet. Having just sent another car on its way, the unshaven Portuguese attendant twiddled a match between his stained teeth as he picked up the diesel fuel line and handed it across to me. Faintly alarmed at the sight, I carried the hose across to *Thunderer*, pushed the nozzle well down into the fuel pipe and squeezed the pistol grip. Even as I did so, the musical sound of a girl laughing drew my attention back to the cruiser. 'Roo was clearly making progress.

I had been lucky where he was concerned, I acknowledged. Normally, I made a point of picking my own crew; or rather, 29th Commando Regiment picked them for me. But this time the decision had already been made. A young Australian bachelor in his twenties, free-wheeling across Europe, 'Roo had met up with the Pursers towards the end of their restoration work. They had quickly taken to each other, and before long the couple had invited 'Roo to accompany them on their Mediterranean cruise. As for me, any preconceived ideas I may have had about him soon proved to be quite wrong. No less a prey to stereotyped images than most people, I suppose I had expected a younger version of Crocodile Dundee. Instead, over the last week I had gradually come to know and like a pleasant, alert and fun-loving young man evincing all the quiet self-confidence that travel cultivates in the young. His nickname, I learned, was a relatively new acquisition; in fact it was Janine, a devotee of Pooh Bear and friends since childhood, who had first applied it. Nor, I soon discovered, did he seem to mind its use by others.

'Oy, Pedro, what time do you close?' I turned at the sound of the voice behind me. Standing on the top of the stone parapet was a balding man of medium height and build in his late forties. Wearing a light-blue T-shirt, russet sailcloth trousers and a pair of sandals, he was evidently trying to quiz the fuel pump attendant. And so far he wasn't doing very well. It was clear from the attendant's sullen scowl, his repeated shrugs, that he didn't know a word of English. But at least he knew that his name wasn't Pedro.

'What-time-you-shut?' said the man more loudly, pointing repeatedly at his watch. This time the attendant took the easy way out. Turning his back on his inquisitor, he headed, muttering darkly, for the sanctuary of his kiosk. 'Rude so-and-sos, aren't they?' complained the man, placing both hands on his hips.

'I don't think he understood you,' I said. 'And you'll find the times are on the board over there, I think.' I looked back quickly at the fuel filler pipe. It had suddenly started to make a gurgling noise, suggesting that the tank was nearly full. At the same moment came Richard's warning shout from below. I slowed the delivery to a trickle.

'Ah, yes . . . there we are,' replied the man. He consulted the board. 'Five thirty. No, I think I'll leave it until tomorrow morning. Anyway,' he continued, turning towards me once more, 'I thought I'd just walk over to have a look at your boat.' He was still sweating from his exertion. 'That was us that passed you coming up the river earlier on,' he added, the satisfaction evident in his voice.

I remembered. In the light breeze to which we had become accustomed over the past week, the 40-foot light displacement sloop had glided easily past us soon after we had entered the Tagus river. He had been standing up in the cockpit, regally waving his arm as the boat had headed on towards the enormous span of the Salazar bridge. 'Ah yes,' I replied, most of my attention still directed at the filling operation. 'You were going well, I must say.'

'You can say that again,' he rejoined immediately. 'She may be a bit light but she'll go, all right. No, the broker tried to palm me off with another one, as a matter of fact, but I'm no fool. I saw through that one straight away.'

'That's it, Ron,' called out Richard from below. I removed the nozzle and screwed the cap back.

'Your boat's a fair size, isn't she?' persisted the man, studying her critically as I carried the hose back to the pump. I started to tell him that it wasn't my boat, but he cut me short. 'Really, you would think she'd do better under sail, but I suppose it's all that weight.' I let him suppose. 'Anyway, I know one thing,' he added, perhaps reacting to my silence, 'I decided long ago not to go anywhere near a wooden boat myself. They may look very nice and all that, but you never stop working on 'em. No, I certainly wasn't going to get caught that way. Like I said, I'm no fool where boats are concerned.' He ended with a short laugh, then paused. 'Are you going on down to the Med?'

'I'm going as far as Gibraltar myself,' I replied, 'but not for a couple of days.' The Adcocks had wanted two days of sightseeing in the Portuguese capital and in view of our frustrations so far, I had decided to bend one of my rules.

'Yes, well, I expect you'll quite like Lisbon,' said the man, blandly assuming that it was my first visit. 'Not like it used to be, mind, but not many places are these days, are they? Anyway, we're heading on south tomorrow, round the corner, probably pop in to Cadiz and then straight on to Gib'.' He looked at his watch. 'Well, I'd better go and see the blokes in the office, I suppose. So long.' He clambered heavily over the stone parapet and set off in the direction of the marine buildings, wiping his brow with a large handkerchief as he did so. I returned to *Thunderer*.

'Has he gone?' enquired Richard cautiously from below.

'Yes, all clear now,' I said.

'What an unpleasant man,' said another voice from the cabin, this time a female one. A moment later Janine's small, neat figure was following her husband's up the companionway steps. Collapsing onto the cockpit seat, she looked at me, the distaste still apparent in her hazel-brown eyes. 'I had an awful feeling he was going to hang around,' she said. 'But obviously, all he really wanted to do was to tell us how much faster his boat was than ours.' She shuddered, starting her auburn hair shaking in sympathy.

'I wouldn't bother about it, love,' said Richard, gently placating her. 'Anyway, you know what they say: the man who keeps saying he's no fool usually has his suspicions.'

There was a sudden thump of feet on the pontoon behind me. I turned to see 'Roo trotting towards me. Tall, lean, heavily sun-tanned, wearing shorts and gym shoes, he jumped lightly up onto the starboard toe-rail amidships, grabbed hold of the lower shroud and swung easily over the lifelines.

'Welcome back, Casanova,' I said. 'Just in time to scrub the diesel off the deck.'

'Roo stopped dramatically, spreading his arms out in a gesture of mock appeal. 'There he goes again, Richard. Like I told you, he's got a very ugly side to his nature, this Skipper of ours. Pity, really – especially in a man of his age.'

'He's absolutely right, you Aussie lead-swinger,' said Richard. 'It's high time you got down to something useful.' He was smiling as he said it, knowing full well that the energetic 'Roo had done far more than his share of the work on the way down from Falmouth. 'Anyway, what luck with the berth?'

'There's a nice one just behind the cruiser,' said 'Roo. Then, noting the look on our faces, he added quickly, 'Now come on, you blokes, it's nothing like that. It's the only space big enough for *Thunderer* in the whole marina. Have a look for yourself, if you don't believe me. That's why I was talking to the sheila, as a matter of fact. She's going to save it for us.'

'Of course we believe you,' said Janine, still laughing. 'Don't we, Ron?'

'Yes, I suppose so,' I said. 'Tell you what, 'Roo, if you'd like to nip back over there, we'll join you in a minute. You can see us in with the boat.'

'What about the diesel?' asked 'Roo.

'What diesel?' I asked. 'We're not all messy like you, you know.'

In the softness of the late evening I strolled quietly around the perimeter pontoon towards the floodlit monument to Prince Henry the Navigator that marks the marina seaward entrance so dramatically. Earlier I had politely declined an invitation to join the Pursers for a meal ashore, feeling that it was time we all had a break from each other's company. Nor had they tried too hard to change my mind. As for 'Roo, I decided I would rather not know where he was.

Even by day the monument is quite striking, showing Henry standing at the head of a group of people crowding somewhat fearfully up the broad prow of a ship. Now, thrusting as bright as day up and outwards over the darkness of the mighty river, it seemed to have taken on an almost magical quality. I bet he had his problems with light winds too, I thought. But he would also have known, as I did now, that sometime it just had to change.

★ ★ ★

'I don't know, I suppose I was expecting it to be up higher, on top of a cliff or something.'

Janine was staring out across the water at the Cape Trafalgar lighthouse, some two miles ahead of us on our port bow. About 60 feet high, the tower rose up from the end of a low promontory sticking out about 200 yards from the flat coastal plain behind it.

I knew what she meant. 'Well, that's it, anyway,' I said from my seated position at the wheel. 'Just out to our right, folks, was where, arguably, the greatest naval battle of all time was fought. And you do realize that it was only a week later than today's date, don't you?'

'Twenty-first of October, 1805,' said 'Roo. 'Thirty-three British against 40 French and Spanish.'

'Spot on, 'Roo,' I said, half in surprise, half in admiration. 'I didn't know you were such an authority.'

'Oh, he's a man of hidden depths, our 'Roo,' said Richard. He was climbing up into the cockpit from the cabin, a bottle of port and four plastic tumblers in his hands. 'Here, grab hold of this lot,' he said. Moments later we were standing together in the cockpit, tumblers charged.

'I think the Skipper should do the honours,' said Richard.

Feeling decidedly self-conscious, I raised my glass. 'To the immortal memory,' I said. The others repeated the toast, took a sip of port, then settled down onto the cockpit seats in silence. I took up position again behind the wheel.

Having attended more than one Trafalgar night in my time as a guest of the senior service, I knew something of what this place meant to them, to the whole British nation, in fact. It wasn't simply that this crushing victory had guaranteed Britain unchallenged supremacy of the seas for a hundred years afterwards. It had much more to do with the character of the small, slight man who had master-minded it. His loss of an arm and an eye telling, with ultimate eloquence, of a lifelong insistence on leading from the front, Nelson had by this time evoked such love and devotion from his thousands of hard-bitten sailors that they had literally been ready to die for him. Yet he had died instead, leaving not only a fleet but a nation to their overwhelming grief.

As though sensible of the solemnity of the occasion, there came a long rumble of thunder from over the southern horizon.

It was enough to bring me back to the present, to the rueful acknowledgement of our fate since leaving Lisbon three days ago. Yet again, and almost incredibly, we had been plagued with light winds all the way down to Cape St Vincent, along the lush coastline of the Portuguese Algarve and even as far as here, not 40 miles from our final destination. The first of the thunder had made itself heard last night from the direction of Tangier, on the southern threshold of the Straits of Gibraltar. Gradually, as the night wore on, it had moved slowly eastwards, eventually showing up on the distant horizon in fitful glimmerings of light as we came closer. Now it seemed to have come to a halt right in the mouth of the straits themselves. For some time past now we had actually been able to see the huge mass, black and forbidding, on the horizon ahead.

By now the lack of wind had become, by common consent, a taboo subject. The jokes about sticking a knife into *Thunderer*'s substantial wooden mast, about taking turns to whistle, had long ceased to be funny. Not that we had given in easily. For a whole day on our way down to Cape St Vincent we had steadfastly refused to use the engine, coaxing instead every last bit of impetus from the giant spinnaker. But even this had yielded barely 3 knots for most of the day and none at all by dusk. Now, we were finally resigned to our fate. It looked as though *Thunderer* would be denied any chance to show us what she could really do before we reached Gibraltar.

'There's a yacht overhauling us from the north,' said Richard suddenly. 'Looks a little bit familiar, too.'

I looked astern. There, about two miles behind us, was what certainly seemed to be a light displacement yacht, about 40 feet long. Can't be her, I thought. The odds against it being the same boat were simply enormous. All the same, there was something about her that rang an unwelcome bell. And the man had talked about 'popping in' to Cadiz, I remembered. Cadiz lay almost due north of our present position. I preferred to change the subject.

'If you're happy, Richard, we'll pass pretty close to the lighthouse, no more than about 100 metres off, in fact. There's 14 feet of water in there even at dead low tide, whereas further out there's a patch of rock just below the surface. Just thought I'd mention it in case you started to wonder.'

'Whatever you say, Skipper,' said Richard. 'It'll cut the corner off a bit too, won't it? Anything that gets us more quickly into Gibraltar now suits me fine. When do you think that will be, by the way?'

I tried to gauge the strength and direction of the wind. It was blowing at about 8 knots or so – Force 3 – from a shade north of east, allowing *Thunderer* to make a little over 4½ knots through the water. 'Well, from here to Tarifa at the western end of the Straits is about 27 miles,' I said, thinking aloud. 'Under sail in this breeze that will take us just under five hours with the tide in our favour. Then, for the last 12 miles through the Straits and across Algeciras bay to the Rock, we'll have the wind more or less on the nose. So we'll have to switch the engine on for that leg. Say another two hours.' I looked at my watch. 'It's just gone 1200 hours now – call it an ETA of 1900 hours, God willing.'

'Hello yacht *Thunderer*, hello yacht *Thunderer*, this is yacht *Cordic*, request working channel, over.'

I recognized the voice immediately, faint though it was in the cockpit. So did the Pursers. 'Leave it?' asked Richard, looking at me.

I sighed. 'Don't think we can, Richard, really. We're obliged to return his call, at least until we know what he wants. Offer him Channel 67.'

By the time Richard had replied, then flicked the VHF radio on to the new channel the voice was already speaking. ' . . . *Cordic*, over.'

'This is yacht *Thunderer*, over,' said Richard.

'Ah, good morning, *Thunderer*,' came the reply, 'we thought it had to be you up front. You may remember we met briefly in Lisbon, in the marina at Belem, over?'

'Yes, good afternoon, over,' said Richard, his voice quite expressionless.

'I take it you are heading straight for Gibraltar, over?'

'Correct, over,' said Richard.

'We were just wondering if you would like to make a race of it?' said the voice. 'Handicaps as we stand, first one to the Rock, over?'

Richard looked quickly up at me through the hatchway. I shrugged my shoulders, deciding to leave the choice to him.

'Well,' said Richard after a pause, 'we were just enjoying the sunshine, really. Thanks all the same, over.'

'Quite understand, old chap,' came the reply. 'Perhaps another time.' I was waiting for him to say 'over' or 'out', but he did not oblige. The way he had said 'quite understand' clearly demonstrated that he did not. Stung more than I cared to admit by his words, I watched Richard come back out into the cockpit.

'Who was that bloke anyway?' asked 'Roo, mystified. Janine told him. 'Well, it sounds to me as though he needs taking down a peg,' said 'Roo. 'Why don't we take him up on his offer?'

Richard and I looked at each other. 'Well,' I said slowly, 'I suppose we could at that. He's still some way behind, it's just possible that he's bitten off more than he can chew this time. And there could be a change in the weather before long.' I couldn't be sure, but the black mass ahead of us seemed to have advanced very slightly in our direction. 'One thing, though,' I added as Richard started for the companionway. 'Only as far as Tarifa. The only way we could sail through the Straits with the wind where it is would be by tacking from one side to the other, right across the shipping lanes. Oh sure, we could put in shorter tacks, but that boat's a lot handier than this one when it comes to going about. One thing is certain: you can easily get as many as 20 big ships in the Straits at one time, all doing about 15 knots. In the circumstances it would be downright irresponsible to start playing games there.'

The reply to Richard's call was brief, the voice no longer heavy with the innuendo of a few moments before. 'This is *Cordic*. Right, Tarifa it is. Out.'

'OK, 'Roo,' I said, 'come on, let's have you on the wheel. As of now I want you to steer better than you've ever steered in your life. Keep her up to the wind but, at all costs, keep her going.'

Despite Janine's rather surprised look at my decision, there were two reasons for it. First, I wanted to spend as much time as it needed to tune the sails properly. But second, I knew – as I suspected Richard did – that in 'Roo we had one of those very rare creatures indeed: a completely instinctive helmsman. Nor had it taken me long to discover the fact once we had left Falmouth. At the risk of sounding immodest, I have always considered myself to be a reasonably good helm, the years of experience having, not surprisingly, reinforced and refined whatever natural ability I may have. But 'Roo was something else again. Far from having gradually to learn the art, he always managed to give me the feeling that he was merely expressing through the wheel something that had always been there inside him. Again, I knew he had been sailing for little more than three years before this trip. Yet even the matter of reading the wave pattern up ahead, divining the one right path to choose among a number of perceived alternatives, seemed for him much less a matter of experience than of sheer intuition. No, I thought, if we don't get to Tarifa first, it certainly won't be 'Roo's fault.

It was just after 1400 hours that I saw the floats. The Spanish fishing dory had been visible on our starboard bow for some time, but we were less than a mile away before I suddenly realized that, drifting in a long line from her stern, was a seemingly endless line of fishing floats. Noticing the look on my face, Richard turned to follow my gaze. 'My God!' he said, looking further and further to our left. 'It's some sort of net. It just goes on for ever!'

I groaned. Stretching for at least a mile right across our path, the floats represented an impenetrable barrier. 'Right, helmsman, change course to leave that dory 100 yards on our port side,' I instructed, moving quickly to ease the sheets. In the last two hours, while the wind had stubbornly refused to increase even a little, the tiny tell-tales at the front of the big genoa and on the leech of the mainsail had hardly fluttered once under the spell of a gifted helmsman. But despite that, *Cordic* had been gaining remorselessly on us in the light breeze. Now, she was little more than a quarter of a mile behind. Nor, I knew, would she fail to profit from our sudden 25 degree change of course. Cursing my stupidity for not seeing the floats earlier, I looked anxiously astern. Sure enough, *Cordic* was already changing course to avoid the hazard to which we had alerted her. The trouble was that, in her case, the course change would be much less acute, allowing her to make up even more ground. Clutching at straws, I turned again to look at the black cloud-mass up ahead. By now it was closer still, the occasional rumble of thunder louder, the flashes of lightning more brilliant.

Yet so far we were still bathed in sunshine and likely to remain so for some time to come. No, I decided, we can't expect any help from that department, not yet, anyway.

Cordic passed us just before 1500 hours. She was no more than 100 yards away on our port beam, quite close enough for us to make out the triumphant expressions on the faces of the three men aboard. Once again, our wave of acknowledgment was answered by the owner's imperious sweep of the arm.

'Damn!' said Richard. 'I'd give anything to have beaten him. He's so bloody cocky about it, isn't he?'

'We've not lost yet, Richard,' I replied, trying to cheer him with an optimism I was far from feeling myself. It really was beyond belief, I lamented. All this time, all these miles from Falmouth, and *Thunderer* still hadn't had one decent chance to show us what she could do. Give us a break, I pleaded silently, looking up at the heavens. And with that gesture came the first glimmer of hope. The storm clouds were a lot closer all of a sudden. Looking ahead, I could see a distinct line across the water, about three miles away; black on the far side, with little flecks of white, azure blue on ours. 'Just keep her going as well as you can, 'Roo,' I said, trying to keep the excitement out of my voice. 'I think we may be about to get a little help.'

'Good God! Have you seen this wreck over on the starboard side?' asked Richard suddenly. He was pointing, awe-struck, at the skeletal remains of a ship's bow sticking up out of the water about half a mile away.

'Yes, it's called "Los Cabezos": that's "the heads" in Spanish,' I replied, most of my attention still fixed on the squall line ahead. 'Mind you, the heads themselves are some way under the water, the wreck is relatively new. I saw it when I came through last time, about three months ago, but it certainly wasn't there last year. You'll see more of the same along the northern shore of the Straits, I'm afraid. Even the big ships get it wrong sometimes.' Things were happening up ahead. 'Anyway, never mind that now, time for oilskins, I think.'

'Oilskins?' echoed Richard incredulously.

'That's what I said, chum. Where are yours, 'Roo?'

We had just finished putting them on when 'Roo suddenly pointed ahead. 'Look, they're reefing the mainsail,' he said.

Five hundred yards ahead of us, two of *Cordic*'s crew were standing up at the mast, frantically trying to shorten sail. Nor was it hard to see why. Even as we watched, the ominous line of black and white suddenly hit the boat, the squall sending it staggering violently over to starboard. Slowly, *Cordic* started to right herself as she came up into the wind. Even from this distance the sound of her madly flogging sails reached us clearly across the water.

Now we too entered the gloom as the clouds raced over our heads to obscure the sun. 'Shouldn't we be reefing, Ron?' asked Richard anxiously. He was starting to shout.

I had already considered the matter, then rejected it. 'Not if you want to win this race, Richard,' I replied. 'Anyway, I'm hoping it won't be necessary. I'm betting that this boat will stand up to her full canvas even in that lot. Either way, we shall soon know, folks. Hang on to something down below, Janine! Stand by, everyone!'

The sudden, savage blast of wind hit *Thunderer* full on her port bow. Reeling under the impact, she heeled steeply over, I judged about 35 degrees or so. Even as I heard Janine's startled cry from below, I saw 'Roo scramble to maintain his position at the wheel, propping his right foot up against the top of the starboard cockpit seat to maintain balance. Yet despite the confusion, it was already beginning to look as though *Thunderer* would cope with the onslaught. Nor, I suddenly realized, had there been any thunder and lightning for some time now. Things were looking up.

Then came the hailstorm. Never before or since have I known anything like it. Suddenly we were being bombarded by hailstones the size of marbles, deafened by the ear-splitting drumming noise they were making on the deck. And they were hurting too. Even through my oilskin hood the ice marbles were stinging my ears, drilling into the crown of my head. I didn't even try to look up; against the machine-gun force of the hail it would have been a physical impossibility. Instead, keeping my head lowered, I turned to look back at the man on the helm. As I had expected, he was now steering by feel alone, gauging his angle off the wind by the degree of heel as he kept his head pointing downwards at the cockpit sole. 'Alright, 'Roo?' I yelled at the top of my voice.

'Yeah. Can't see a bloody thing but, other than that, I'm fine,' he shouted back.

Janine was sheltering just under the companionway hatch. 'Saucepan,' I yelled at her. 'We need a saucepan.' She disappeared, returning a moment later with a large one in her hand. 'Lovely, can you find a couple more?' I shouted. I handed my way back to 'Roo and stuck the saucepan on his head, handle at the back. Instantly a new noise was added to the cacophony of sound as the hailstones struck up a high-pitched tattoo on the inverted bottom. 'Sorry I can't put two holes in the front for your eyes, 'Roo,' I yelled into his ear, 'otherwise you could pretend you were one of your famous forbears!'

'Oh, funneee, Skipper!' shouted 'Roo, smiling broadly. 'I owe you one for that! Stone the crows, this noise is just unbelievable.'

Even so, it seemed to have done the trick. Now 'Roo was able to see just enough from under the edge of his improvised armour to be able to hold his course properly. In no time at all, Richard and I were similarly protected in saucepans of different sizes, turning the three of us into an involuntary xylophone as each saucepan rang out to its own individual pitch.

In all the pandemonium I am ashamed to say that I had rather lost sight of our main objective for a moment or two. But *Thunderer* hadn't. In the space of a few moments she had undergone an awesome transformation. At long last, after all her petty trials and tribulations, she had suddenly come alive, suddenly become the true embodiment of her name. As though contemptuous of everything that had gone before, now she was simply tearing through the seas, throwing great sheets of spray off her bows as she did so. Somehow it seemed to be a time for mere mortals to be silent in the face of such irresistible, majestic impulsion. Nor was the sheer power of her progress lost on Richard. Beneath his ridiculously incongruous headgear he was just staring in front of him without speaking, as though in a trance.

'At last she's showing you what she can do, Richard!' I shouted at him, no longer able to contain my excitement.

'I just can't believe it,' he said, slowly shaking his head. 'Just look at her. How could I ever have doubted?'

It was high time to see how the competition was getting on.

Crouching low down on the leeward cockpit seat, I craned my neck round the edge of the straining genoa. Dimly through the cloud of spray I saw that *Cordic* was now little more than 400 yards ahead. Even double-reefed as she now was, she was finding it hard to hold her course, I realized, noting how her skipper had scandalized the mainsail quite drastically in order to relieve the pressure.

The hailstorm lasted for another ten minutes, eventually giving way to rain. But it was still blowing hard. Janine climbed up into the cockpit in her oilskins. 'Good gracious!' she gasped, 'Just look at the hailstones.' The floor of the cockpit had been buried in a bed of white marbles, ankle deep on one side, nearly knee deep on the other. There was another trough between the coachroof and the windward side deck, yet another in the crook of the starboard cockpit seat. 'Right: camera,' she said, about to hurry down below again.

'Hang on, Janine, can you take these please?' said Richard. As he and I handed over our saucepans, Janine looked enquiringly at 'Roo.

'No, I think I'll hang on to mine for a bit,' he said with a grin. 'No sense in tempting fate.'

Two minutes later, with Janine back in the cockpit, I surveyed the scene that she had just photographed. It was one that has stayed sharp and clear in my mind to this day. *Cordic* was now only some 50 yards ahead, close on our starboard bow, while on the horizon beyond her the southern, Moroccan side of the Straits of Gibraltar appeared dark and forbidding in their shadow. Dark too were the northern cliffs over on the port side, yet in this case they were providing a perfect backdrop for the sunlit lighthouse and little town of Tarifa, barely two miles ahead. And capping it all, with true Wagnerian grandeur, was the ragged trailing edge of the storm.

'We're going to do it, Skipper, aren't we?' said 'Roo, the excitement obvious in his voice.

'Well, we won't tempt fate,' I replied, 'but it's beginning to look like it.'

'Roo was looking across at *Cordic* at the moment that we actually passed her. 'Funny,' he said drily, 'they seem to have found something fascinating down in the cabin all of a sudden. What about calling them up?'

'Nothing to say, really,' replied Richard. '*Thunderer*'s said it all for us.'

In fact, we were a good 300 yards ahead of *Cordic* when the Tarifa lighthouse finally shot by, a mere 400 yards away on our port beam. By then it had stopped raining; by then too, Richard had taken over the wheel. In the circumstances it had seemed wholly appropriate to let the owner enjoy the pleasure of taking his boat past the post, and I could sense that 'Roo thought so too.

'OK, one and all,' said Richard as our celebratory cheer died away, 'you may not know it yet, but tonight you are going to enjoy the very best meal that Gibraltar can provide – on us!' Janine was nodding vigorously as he said it.

'Well, that sounds like an offer we can't refuse,' I said. 'What do you reckon, 'Roo?'

For once he came out with a typical Australian mannerism as he stretched his arms blissfully upwards towards the warm sunlight. 'Better'n a poke in the eye.'

Poole Harbour, Dorset

N

POOLE
Parkstone
Amphibious Training Unit
Hamworthy Lake Yard
Poole Yacht Club
Wych Channel
Brownsea Island
Sandbanks
Car Ferry
Studland
Parachute Dropping Zone
Wareham Channel
Landing Craft
Arne
River Frome (to Wareham)

Miles
0   ½   1

Brady '88

Chapter Eleven

FALMOUTH TO POOLE
(WITH MEMORIES)

It was going to be a scorcher.

The early morning mist that had kept us hugging the channel markers all the way in from Poole Bar buoy was still very much in evidence. But now it was thinning, lifting off the surface of the water. Now, instead of just hearing the splash of the school bass as they drove the sand-eels to the surface, we could actually see the tell-tale swirls in the smooth water all around us. And now, with every minute that passed, the diffused light from above grew brighter, warming the back of our necks.

Like us, the bass had come in with the flood tide. We had entered Poole Harbour ten minutes ago, dodging past the car ferry as it clanked laboriously across the narrow entrance between Studland and Sandbanks. Now it was 0930 hours: three bells in the forenoon watch. And all was well. Around and above us gulls were wheeling and turning as they waited for the next shoal of sand-eels to spatter the surface.

Whenever I deliver a yacht in United Kingdom waters I try to arrive during the morning. That gives me a fighting chance of getting back to Cornwall by rail or coach the same day. This time it had worked out perfectly. My crew, Lance-Bombardier David Steer, and I had set off in the Sadler 26 from Falmouth the day before. Now all that remained were another seven miles to our destination: Wareham, lying up the River Frome at the head of Poole Harbour. Actually, in David's case there was hardly any return journey to make. He was based here in Poole with the naval gunfire support battery and had come down to Falmouth by train to join me for what had proved to be a memorable trip. We had enjoyed perfect sailing all the way up Channel with a brisk north-westerly breeze just abaft the port beam. True, the previous night had been clear and decidedly cold for late May as we reached across Lyme Bay. But now it was warming up again as we beat smoothly up the harbour. Leaning gently on the tiller, I was feeling drowsy, lethargic. . . .

'Here you are, Skipper.'

I opened my eyes with a guilty start. David was standing in the companionway smiling, holding out a steaming cup of coffee. I looked quickly around to check that we were still in the middle of the channel. It was all right. Fifty yards away to port, a thin pole with a can on top marked the left-hand side of the Wych Channel. The next one was just materializing through the mist ahead. Reassured, I reached out for the coffee.

'Thanks a lot.' I took a gulp. 'My word, that's good, David. Well, you're nearly home. We've made pretty good time.'

'I was just thinking the same thing,' he replied. 'Pity in a way. At this rate I'll be back in camp by lunchtime. Just in time for Sergeant-Major Bradwell to collar me for something or other.' He grinned ruefully.

I smiled back, thinking as I did so of the young Bombardier Bradwell I had known some ten years ago. It was difficult to think of him now as a warrant officer. But he had been an intelligent and motivated young NCO, and I concluded that David's present forebodings were probably justified. Not that he would mind, I judged, looking at him. In the last 24 hours this slim, fresh-faced youngster had impressed me with his zest for life, his appetite for work and responsibility.

'Still, I've really enjoyed it,' said David, confirming my thoughts. 'Bit nippy last night, but that was nothing. Anytime you want another crew, Skipper. . . .'

I laughed. 'Fine by me, David, but, as I said earlier, I always leave the choice to the Regiment. If you can persuade them to pick you I shall certainly be happy to have you aboard again.' I drained my mug. 'Right, if you'd like to take her for a bit, I'll get below and tackle the washing-up.'

By the time I emerged once more into the fresh air the sun was burning off the last remnants of mist where they clung to the foreshore of Brownsea Island. David knew these waters well and was obviously enjoying his spell on the tiller. So I left him to it and made my way forward to carry out my morning rounds. This involved checking the security of all load-bearing items such as shackles and bottle-screws, examining the sails for chafe and generally seeing that all was shipshape. This has become a strict daily routine with me in all winds and weather, and long experience has convinced me that it pays off.

Duty done, I subsided gently onto the foredeck, my back to the mast. This part of Poole Harbour was especially familiar to me, and I wanted a moment alone to savour the nostalgia. By now we were almost abeam of the western end of Brownsea Island. It was just ahead of this very spot, I reflected, that we used to practise our parachute water-jumps from the Wessex helicopter. Such memories were more vivid than any others, evoking as they did moments of real stress. Particularly the jump that we did in the late spring of 1972. That too had been a day in May, just like this one. And even now, as I recalled it, the pin-pricks of sweat started to break out on the palms of my hands. . . .

Climbing into the back of a Wessex helicopter is quite easy. Unless, that is, you are encumbered by one heavy parachute on your back and another – the reserve – on your chest. Never mind, I thought, as I joined the others on the canvas seating flanking either side of the cabin. At least it would be easier getting out.

Secured by a long safety line, Flight Sergeant Allen chattered into his throat microphone as he took up position near the open door. The subsequent crescendo of engine noise and vibration indicated that he had just given the standard despatcher's instruction to the pilot:

'Up 800 feet, eight men jumping.'

The Wessex came unstuck from the parade ground with a lurch, swayed, then rose into the hazy sunshine of a May morning. Gradually the wide waters of Poole Harbour emerged beyond the roofs of the Amphibious Training Unit, Royal Marines. It was here that my commando battery was based, and today we were due to complete, to use army jargon, 'a routine continuation training jump'. As we spiralled slowly upwards, I reflected how grotesquely out of place the word 'routine' seemed in this particular context. Granted there may have been one or two in the battery for whom parachuting held no fears. For me, however, each jump was a self-examination, an ordeal in which a morbid fear of death or mutilation would be ultimately subdued more by the sheer enormity of any public refusal to jump than by any effort of will.

With practised ease Flight Sergeant Allen strode across the cabin to shout into my ear. I couldn't catch his words, but his broad grin told me that he didn't really need an answer anyway. One of his jokes, no doubt. Nodding my head, I managed a vacuous smile before resuming my private battle. Water-jumps could be tricky. Admittedly, the landing was softer than with a ground-jump but in winds above 10 miles per hour – like today – the parachute could drag you face downwards across the surface of the water for quite a distance. One or two people had almost drowned that way. So the drill was to undo your harness on the way down and then slip out of it about ten feet above the water. That done, the parachute would just drift harmlessly away downwind. Fine, I reflected grimly, so long as you could judge when you were ten feet above the water. As I said, water-jumps could be tricky.

The spiralling stopped, the engine note dropping as the helicopter finished climbing. We had reached jumping height. Now the nose of the Wessex dipped slightly as we started slowly forwards over the dropping zone. Once again I checked that my strop, like all the others, was securely hooked to the strong point: the metal bar running above and behind me all the way down the side of the cabin. Satisfied, I slumped back in the seat and tried to relax. Through the open door I could see, far below, the white 'V' of a speedboat's wake as it weaved its way between the tiny triangles of sailing boats. That's the place for any normal person to be, I told myself, sitting in the cockpit of one of those boats, tiller in one hand, gin and tonic in the other. Instead of which you are about to fling yourself bodily into the sea from a height of 800 feet. You need certifying.

I caught a sudden movement out of the corner of my eye. Flight Sergeant Allen had raised both hands to his earphones, evidently listening to a message from the pilot. The next moment he was beckoning me to come forward, his smile almost obscene behind his crooked finger.

My mouth had gone dry. With ridiculous care I edged slowly

towards the open door, sank to the floor then swung my legs out over the sill. I knew exactly what would happen now. First, the red warning light would go on over the door, the signal for me to shuffle still further forward on my bottom into the doorway. Then would come the green: the order to go. The idea was to push yourself out and away from the sill as far as possible to avoid hitting it with the back of the parachute. What happened after that didn't bear thinking about.

Heart thumping, I waited for those last, climactic seconds. The trouble was that you had to sit so far forward that you couldn't actually see the lights at all. That was where Flight Sergeant Allen came in. He would be watching the lights and at the appropriate moment would yell 'Red on!' into my left ear. Then, after a final, heart-stopping pause, there would come the thump of his hand between my shoulder blades. That would be the signal to go.

Time passed. It seemed that I had been waiting for ever. I was just starting to entertain the wild hope that something had happened to cancel the jump when the yell hit my left ear. I tensed my arms ready to push off and stared, unseeing, straight ahead. Anywhere but down.

The thump on my back acted like a trigger. I was out of the helicopter and falling like a stone into space. The old remembered feeling of helpless panic washed over me as my stomach tried to force its way up into my throat. Then at last came the violent jerk in the centre of my back. That was the strop coming taut, breaking the ties on the pack and allowing the parachute to stream out above me. For a moment or two longer I continued to fall sickeningly, the air rushing past. Then, blessedly, the brakes came on as the parachute canopy developed. The worst was over.

In a moment everything was transformed. The deafening noise of the helicopter was now little more than a faint drone somewhere above me. All tension gone, I was floating, dream-like, in my own private world. I looked lazily around. Below and before me, Brownsea Island lay shaded and mysterious under its dense canopy of trees, while out to my left the factory chimneys beyond Poole Town pierced the last shreds of morning mist. It was all quite beautiful. Far below, someone called out across the water.

Reluctantly, I forced myself back into the present. Time to think about the landing. The adrenalin still coursing through my system made it easy. First pushing the seat strap well under my buttocks, I rotated the quick-release box on my chest and banged it with closed fist. The leg and shoulder straps fell away. Now the surface of the water was coming up fast, reminding me suddenly of what could yet go badly wrong. Holding on with both hands, I eased gingerly out of the seat strap and allowed myself to slip, little by little, out of the harness. Finally, letting go with my hands, I fell the last few feet to the water, bracing myself for the sudden shock of cold.

It was more than a few feet. It's never easy to gauge one's height above a smooth, featureless expanse of water. In this case it was nearer 30 feet than ten. I hit the water hard and plunged downward until, surprisingly, my feet actually touched the bottom. Then I was surging upward again, my lungs fighting against the squeezing effect of the cold for a first, coughing breath of air.

I had noticed the Royal Marines pick-up boat on the way down, lying idle in the water about 200 yards away. Now it was planing towards me, its outboard engine whining away like an angry bee. Treading water as I waited, I looked up. By now the second man out, a strapping six-foot subaltern in the Special Boat Section, should have been well on his way. What I saw took my breath away for the second time in less than a minute. He was certainly out of the helicopter, but something had gone very badly wrong. Even from this distance I could see, silhouetted against the sky, a small dot suspended about 30 feet below the helicopter as it circled slowly above. My God, I thought, he's stuck on the end of his strop. The ties haven't broken on his parachute.

The pick-up crew had evidently seen him too. They came alongside and dragged me into the boat. One of them pointed upwards.

'Looks like Mr Dyke's in trouble, sir.'

Trouble indeed. On the one hand, it would be next to impossible to haul John Dyke's 14-stone frame some 30 feet up into the aircraft. On the other, any attempt to land the helicopter ran the obvious risk that the ties might break during the last stage of the descent, allowing the parachute no time to open.

Right now, I guessed, Flight Sergeant Allen would be jerking frantically on the other end of the strop. As it turned out, I didn't know the half of it. It was not until later that morning that I learnt the full extent of the drama being enacted above our heads.

As soon as I left the aircraft John Dyke had moved forward into the door to take my place. He had been sitting on the starboard side next to me, leaving just two others on that side and four on the other. All had gone well until John actually left the aircraft. Then everything had happened at once. The inexplicable failure of the parachute ties to break under John's very substantial weight had put a sudden, savage snatch load on the metal bar strong point. In an instant the whole thing tore away from the side of the cabin to come hurtling towards the door.

Had the bar carried on through the doorway, there is little doubt that it would have taken with it the other two men still attached to it. That would have put all three into a macabre free fall. Nor would it have helped much if they had activated their reserve parachutes. One parachute on its own would not have been enough to break their fall, while two or three would inevitably have become hopelessly entangled during development. The result would have been the streaming, useless aberration known as the 'Roman Candle' – and certain death.

It was Flight Sergeant Allen who averted disaster. He might not have been very big, but he was wiry and tough – both physically and mentally. With many hundreds of jumps to his name, he was not only an expert despatcher but also an active member of the RAF Falcons free-fall display team. It was just as well. In the split second before the bar shot out of the aircraft he flung himself across the doorway to block it.

For the next few moments it was touch and go as he struggled to prevent the bar from dragging him out of the opening. Mercifully, he was soon joined by the others. Eventually their combined strength sufficed to pull the bar back into the centre of the cabin. Two men then joined Flight Sergeant Allen on the strop to try to break the ties 30 feet below. At last, after repeated attempts, they managed to time their efforts perfectly in one desperate heave. The next moment the strop was flapping loosely in the helicopter downdraught.

Down below we had been waiting in an agony of suspense.

Suddenly, to our immense relief we saw the dot fall away from underneath the helicopter. Moments later the parachute developed. Even now, though, John Dyke's troubles were not over. The Wessex had been flying in quite a wide circle, and it happened that John had broken free above a closely-packed flotilla of moored sailing boats lying off Poole Quay. We held our breath as he descended closer and closer to the forest of masts. He missed them by the skin of his teeth. A moment later we saw the parachute collapse as he let go of the harness. He plummeted gracefully into the water just alongside one of the yachts.

Not surprisingly, that was the end of parachuting for that day and, indeed, for some weeks afterwards – at least from the Wessex helicopter. The subsequent court of inquiry noted that this was the first time that such a structural failure had occurred with the Wessex. It also made two main recommendations. The first, predictably, concerned certain modifications to the metal bar and its fixings. The second urged strongly that Flight Sergeant Allen's conduct be suitably and formally recognized. It was. A few weeks later it was announced that he had been awarded the Air Force Medal for his courage and resource in a moment of extreme danger.

'Skipper!'

I turned to see David standing up in the cockpit. He pointed ahead of us.

'Which side of the landing craft do you want me to go?'

I turned back again to follow his pointing finger. Almost half a mile dead ahead the first of a long line of landing craft lay moored in mid-channel. Painted smartly in battleship grey, they looked for all the world as though they were waiting patiently for another D-day. In fact, they had been waiting a long time, I knew. They had certainly been there on the day of the fateful water-jump. If my memory served me correctly, Lake's shipyard over there at Hamworthy had a contract to keep them in a state of care and preservation. A bit like painting the Forth Bridge, I reflected.

'Keep them on your starboard hand please, David,' I called. 'And you'd better switch the engine on. We're almost headed as it is. I'll drop the genny.'

There was no point in trying to sail any more. With the wind gradually dying on us, tacking up-river would take forever.

Five minutes later I was back in the cockpit, the steady note of the Volvo diesel engine reflecting back off the hull of the first landing craft as we creamed past it.

'Any water-jumps coming up in the near future?' I asked David.

'Next week,' he replied. 'We're sharing it with the SBS, weather permitting.'

'Looking forward to it?'

David shot a quick glance at me, then looked away again as though he knew what I was thinking. 'Well, yes and no,' he replied at last, the smile on his face a little rueful. 'If you know what I mean?'

Yes. I knew what he meant.

Chapter Twelve

FALMOUTH TO CORK

It's always nice when a new customer contacts me on the recommendation of an old one. Only last week I received an exploratory call from a man about to buy a second-hand Rival 34. He had wanted to know about having it delivered 250 miles to his home port.

'Actually, I was given your name by an old client of yours,' he said.

'Oh, that's nice,' I replied, my interest quickening. 'Who was it?'

'Ben Oakley. He says you sailed with him from Falmouth to Cork last year. Reckons you got his boat to go faster than it's ever gone before or since.'

'Oh, I'm not sure about that,' I protested, laughing. Nor was I; if my memory served me correctly, Ben's boat was one of the slowest I had ever come across.

The phone call concluded, I soon found my thoughts drifting away from the immediate business at hand and back to those frustrating three days in the western approaches, little more than a year ago. In some ways it had, indeed, been a trying time. All the same, I reflected, as the deeper memories gradually surfaced, there had been compensations. . . .

★   ★   ★

I didn't have to go up into the cockpit to realize that Tuesday, 18 August 1987, had started quietly. For the past few minutes running up to 0800 hours, my navigational work before going

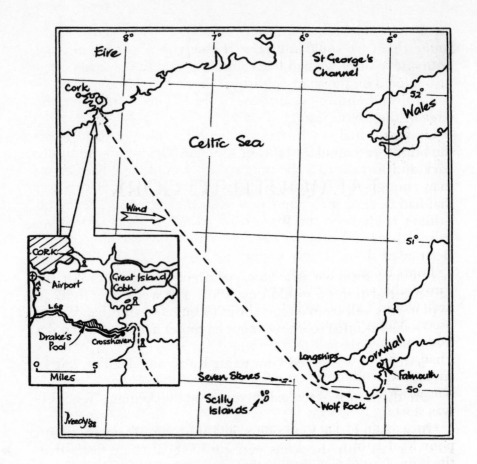

Falmouth To Cork With Cork Harbour Inset

on watch had been completed in conditions so sedate as to suggest that we could still be in harbour. Yet it was nearly 24 hours now since we had left Falmouth, and the position I had just entered on the chart confirmed that we were now some 30 nautical miles north-west of the Scilly Islands and nearing the edge of the Celtic Sea.

Under normal circumstances the quiet sea, not to mention the bright, rectangular beams of sunlight tracking rhythmically back and forth across the port settee, would have been more than enough to gladden my heart. Yet the vague depression that had dogged me yesterday was still there, I conceded. And I didn't really need the Walker log to tell me why. For some reason that I still couldn't pin down, this six-year-old, 28-foot Bermudan sloop simply would not sail. So far she had taken 22 hours to cover just 88 nautical miles from Falmouth marina, a miserable average of 4 knots in conditions that my own Super Seal would have revelled in. Admittedly, the south-westerly breeze had rarely exceeded Force 3 at any stage, while between midnight and 0400 hours it had fallen so light that, in the end, I had resorted to the engine. Even so, in a breeze often steady enough to send most boats along at something close to 6 knots, *Sahaaba* had so far blankly refused to do more than 4½. And it was starting to get me down.

Once again I tried to divine where the problem lay. It wasn't poor load-trimming – she wasn't more than a touch light in the bow. Nor was it overloading; that too I had checked before leaving. As for sail-trimming, I had by now tried and re-tried every combination and set of sail known to man. No, I decided gloomily, rather than stemming from a single source, it's probably a whole combination of things. If you begin with an indifferent hull design, add to that poorly-setting sails, then compound the whole thing with a weeded hull for good measure, you can't really be too surprised at the result. Nor, in the strictly narrow sense in which I was thinking, did it help my frame of mind to have the owner on board. In other circumstances I could at least have vented my frustration on my surroundings with a few well-chosen words. It wouldn't have been the first time. But nothing is more guaranteed to depress an owner than the sober realization that his boat does not perform well in comparison with others, especially if the

verdict comes in fairly uncompromising language from someone in a position to know. At all costs I had to avoid imparting
that knowledge, at least too brutally, to Ben.

I climbed up into the cockpit. 'Top o' the mornin', Ron,' he
said with one of his rare Irishisms, the warmth of his greeting
reflecting in his grey eyes. His long, spare frame was sprawled
out on the port cockpit seat. One hand resting gently on the
tiller, he had already opened his oilskin jacket to the warmth
of the morning sunshine. 'Sleep well?'

'Like a top,' I replied, stretching my arms and yawning as I
looked around me. Apart from the white flecks of tiny wavelets
here and there, the sea was a glorious blue-green colour in the
sunlight. Far off on the port bow a big tanker was ploughing
her way across our path from left to right, heading for the Irish
Sea. Other than that, nothing disturbed the horizon ahead. I
turned to look astern. 'Still a few pots around, I see.'

'Yes, they seem to come in patches,' he said, scratching his
head through his thin brown hair. 'How are we doing?' He had
seen me crouching over the chart table.

'Just under 100 miles to Cork,' I replied. 'At this rate we'll
arrive this time tomorrow morning. Then again, if we intend
going on round the corner to Limerick, that will be quite a bit
longer; another day at least, probably more.'

'Yes, you know, I was thinkin',' he said, the musical Irish
accent just apparent, 'with conditions being as quiet as they are,
I really think Cork will do me fine. I can always take her round
to Limerick later. The important thing is to get her across the
open sea. If we can do that I'll be more than happy.'

'Up to you, Ben,' I said, conscious of a feeling of relief at his
words. 'I really don't mind plugging on round the corner if
you'd like to. The trouble is that, the lack of wind apart, it
would mean altering course about 20 degrees to port, and that
would bring the breeze much more on our nose. I doubt if we
could hold our course without tacking, in fact.'

'I know,' replied Ben. 'No, Cork will do me fine. Anyway,
let's get down to the serious stuff. What about a little breakfast?'

As I watched him step stiffly down into the cabin I once again
acknowledged my good fortune at having such a congenial
companion. Yet, at the risk of being outrageously subjective,
I have found that boat owners are invariably good company.

For one thing, the varied and interesting lives that most of them lead ashore are, for me, a welcome source of diversion, especially on the longer trips. For another, though, I am persuaded that the constant vicissitudes of seafaring seem often to bring out the better side of human behaviour. Whatever the case, most owners that I have met have conducted themselves in a way that has undoubtedly made my task easier to accomplish.

Ben was certainly no exception. In the short time before leaving, and particularly over the past 24 hours, I had become aware of an essentially gentle Irishman blessed with an equable, sunny temperament. Certainly, whatever knocks life had dealt him, they seemed to have left him with an outlook that was trusting, refreshingly free of cynicism and serenely content with its surroundings. And here again, I had soon discovered, was someone with a story to tell. As his somewhat muted Irish accent testified, for most of his professional life Ben had worked for a big multinational oil company in different parts of the world. But it was the account of his last eight years in Libya that I found most fascinating. Gifted not so much with blarney, but with the ability of so many of his countrymen to tell a story simply and well, I had been treated to an insight of life in General Gaddafi's Libya that was always interesting and often quite arresting in its imagery. Fortunately for him, he had left Tripoli on retirement just three weeks before it had been bombed. Now, having returned some months before to his boyhood home in Limerick, he had asked me to accompany him as he brought his boat across from England.

With Ben busy below I applied my mind yet again to item one on the agenda. Although I had certainly heard of this class of boat before, had frequently seen it advertised in yachting magazines, this was the first time that I had actually sailed one. And I didn't much care if I never sailed another. Mindful that the 0555 hours forecast had promised little change in the light conditions, and recalling Ben's almost pathetic admiration of the small gains I had so far been able to make to the boat's speed, I felt a sudden surge of anger at the sheer meanness of its response. Grimly determined, I set about trying to shake her out of her sloth.

It was five o'clock in the evening before I finally gave up. Until then my efforts had been sustained, if rather spasmodically, either by the formulation and trial of some new theoretical remedy or, more promisingly, by an occasional freshening of the breeze. Yet both had repeatedly flattered only to deceive, until now I simply refused to be drawn any more. Instead, I contented myself with drawing up a damning mental indictment of the boat's other shortcomings. Her poor performance apart, the list included under-sized blocks and shackles, cleats far too narrow to allow sheets to be properly secured, a poorly-balanced rudder and, most obvious of all, a number of instances of poor laying-up of the glass-fibre skin. Without even moving from the tiller, I could count at least five places in and around the cockpit where gaping voids under the gelcoat had caused quite sizeable craters to appear on the surface. Admittedly, Ben had not exactly helped matters by his failure to attend to these defects in their early stages, so that frost had quickly seized its opportunity. Even so, I could readily sympathize with the apathy he must have felt at the prospect of labouring over a lady so grudging with her favours.

Happily, however, three things combined to restore my sense of proportion as we ambled onwards at 4 knots into the early evening. The first was the iridescent green sheen on the neck of a cormorant as it jack-knifed with consummate suppleness under the water. Second, my simple decision finally to abandon the unequal struggle with *Sahaaba* was effectively dismantling, stone by stone, the prison I had so foolishly built for myself. But third, and more potent still, Ben, no doubt sensing my mood, had once again set himself to divert me, employing all the skill of a born raconteur. Whether on the subject of cruising, overseas oil operations or even – during one entrancing interlude – social and intellectual life in Dublin, his fascinating insights carried me, spellbound, right through supper and beyond. Indeed, it was only the need once again to fix our position before coming on watch at 2000 hours that brought things to an end.

'Not the best time for reception but I managed to get two acceptable bearings,' I said as I took over the tiller, two minutes late for my watch. 'One on Mizen Head, the other on the Old Head of Kinsale. Can't pick up Ballycotton light yet but that ought to come through before long. Anyway, I make it just under 50 miles to go. Allowing for a short tack to starboard after first light, it still looks like 0800 hours tomorrow.'

'Oh well, that won't be so bad,' said Ben, moving across to the opposite seat. He paused for a moment, sighed, then looked me straight in the eye. 'This one's never going to win any races, is she?' he said with a rueful grin.

There was no point in dissembling; he would see through it straight away. 'No, I'm afraid not, Ben,' I said as gently as possible, glad to be able to speak at last. 'Quite honestly, she ought to be doing a lot better. It beats me, it does really. She's not badly fouled up underneath, is she?'

'She shouldn't be,' he replied. 'I mean, she was properly anti-fouled at the beginning of the season and that usually lasts pretty well. And it's only mid-August now.'

I relapsed into silence, trying yet again to fathom the unfathomable.

'To be honest, it's been a bit of a love-hate relationship from the start,' said Ben. 'You wouldn't believe the trouble I had getting her built in the first place. First of all, I couldn't get hold of anyone in the firm to talk to me. Then, when one of them finally did, all he could say was that it really wasn't their time of year for building boats anyway, and did I really want one?'

I blinked, hardly able to believe my ears. In a market so fiercely competitive as to have sunk many of its contestants without trace over the past few years, the idea of anyone actually having to persuade a firm to build a new boat for him seemed totally unreal.

'Anyway, they built her in the end,' said Ben. 'But she was months late being finished, and even then there were bits and pieces of equipment missing or badly fitted. Then these holes started to appear in the gelcoat.'

'When did that happen?' I asked.

'About 18 months or so after I bought her,' he replied. He must have read in my face the question that was burning inside me. 'Why did I stick with her?' He thought for a long moment. 'Well,' he said with a wry smile, 'if the truth be told, I suppose I'm a bit of a sucker for lame ducks. With all those problems I couldn't really desert her, could I?'

★   ★   ★

A sleek white cruise liner was passing majestically about two miles astern of us, heading north-eastwards up the coast, as the outer fairway marker passed close down our starboard side. It was 0815 hours on yet another quiet, if misty, morning and before us the steep green headlands either side of the dramatically narrow entrance to Cork harbour seemed to be receding with every minute before our advance. Dead ahead, and some way beyond the entrance itself, the gaunt outline of Great Island reared up, stark and uncompromising, across the back of the harbour. Up the channel leading around to port of the island, and still completely hidden from view, lay the city of Cork. But we were aiming closer. Just inside the left-hand headland lay the Owenboy river and there, not far up the port-hand bank, we would find Crosshaven marina.

'No question, it's a truly impressive natural harbour, Ben,' I said, looking around me appreciatively. 'And I can finally say that I've visited the home of the first yacht club in the world.'

'Right enough,' said Ben. 'The Cork Water Club, founded in 1720 and now the Royal Cork Yacht Club. I don't belong to it myself, as a matter of fact, living over in Limerick. Still, maybe I'll make a few enquiries.'

An hour later, having said my goodbyes to Ben, I was walking the country mile from the marina to the little village of Crosshaven itself. Notwithstanding my heavy grip and briefcase, I was enjoying the chance to stretch my legs and to inspect the local countryside. Still heavily diffused by mist, the morning light was filtering softly through the dripping trees either side of the road. I was distinctly aware of things growing all around me in the warm moist air, a feeling accentuated by the contrast of my last two days afloat.

The teenage boy in the marina office had given me directions to the house of Mickey O'Halloran, the local taxi driver. Finding it on the outskirts of the village, and noting the black, hearse-like car in the yard, I knocked on the door. It was opened by an attractive young brunette.

'You'd better come on in,' she said, smiling, once I'd explained my needs. 'Father's up with the chickens, but he shouldn't be many minutes.' I was led into a small, dark living room.

Ten minutes later I was finishing my coffee when her father, a man of at least 70 years of age, entered the room. Wearing a flat cap on his head, he was still holding an empty bucket in his hand. 'Good mornin', sorr,' he said, trying to find me through thick pebble glasses. 'Was it the airport you were wantin'?'

'Yes please,' I replied, suddenly nervous. Obviously, visiting yachtsmen had sought his help before. Ten minutes later I was sitting bolt upright, like an undertaker's assistant, in the front of the taxi as it whined its way out of the village. My driver was pressed right up against the wheel, squinting through his glasses and wiping the windscreen with a rag as we meandered crazily from one side of the road to the other. Consoling myself with the thought that we were hardly likely to break our necks at 20 miles an hour, I tried to listen to what Mr O'Halloran was saying. So far he hadn't stopped talking from the moment that we had got in.

Throwing the rag on the floor between his feet, my elderly companion settled back into his seat. 'Didja say it was your furst time here, sorr?' he asked, starting at last to favour the left-hand side of the road.

'That's right,' I said, relaxing. 'It's a beautiful part of the world, I must say.'

'It is that, roight enough,' he agreed. For the next two or three minutes he delivered a non-stop travelogue of the local beauty spots. Then he paused for a split second. 'You'll have heard about Drake's Pool, now?'

'Drake's Pool?' I echoed.

'That's it,' he said. 'Sure, and we're just coming up to it now, over on the roight here.' Separated only by the continuous belt of trees, the road had so far followed the River Owenboy around every one of its twists and turns as it threaded its way up the valley. Now, though, I saw that the river was starting to widen out. The next moment, as we turned yet another corner, an unexpectedly wide expanse of water opened out before us. 'There it is, sorr: Drake's Pool,' said Mr O'Halloran proudly.

'Why is it called that?' I asked.

'Well, now, and didn't Sorr Francis Drake himself come in here once upon a toime,' he said. 'Chased into Cork by the Spanish, so he was. Brought his great ship roight up the Owenboy and roight into the pool here.'

'Good Lord, I didn't know that,' I said. Through the moving tracery of branches I looked again at the wide sweep of water, placid, dark, mysterious in its veil of mist. 'It doesn't look deep enough – or wide enough, come to that. Not back in the neck of the entrance, anyway.'

'Ha, ha,' he cackled, thumping the palms of his hands delightedly on the wheel. 'That's what the Spanish t'ought too, so it was. Went all the way up to Cork, they did, lookin' for 'im. But he'd just disappeared into thin air. No, it's deep, all roight. Squeezed through here with the lead goin', so they say.'

The image of the pool stayed sharp in my mind all the way to the airport. Romantic as the story was, its impact had been all the greater for being unexpected, for the fact that I, too, had just come into Cork harbour under sail from the open sea. For a few tingling, luminous moments I had seemed to be in direct contact with the people, places and events of 400 years ago.

Cork airport is relatively small, perched on the high ground above the city. Yet if the planners had chosen this site to avoid the local mists they had evidently miscalculated. The dank air had swallowed up Mr O'Halloran and his taxi long before they had rounded the corner of the terminal building, while the crush of passengers inside told its own story. At intervals throughout a long morning, apologetic loudspeaker announcements sent batches of dispirited people trooping out to the coaches that were waiting to take them to Shannon or Dublin. Virtually certain of the same fate as my flight time of 1340 hours approached with no sign of the fog lifting, I was pleasantly surprised when it was suddenly announced that the Brymon light aircraft was, even at that moment, circling above the airfield, looking for a hole in the clouds. Ten minutes later, I had joined a dozen other people walking out across the concrete apron towards the Dash 7 that would take us to Plymouth.

One of the pilots was stretching his legs just beyond the end of the wing as I waited at the tail of the queue to board. 'Well done,' I said. 'I didn't think you had a hope.'

'Nor did we,' he replied, grinning. 'We were just about to give it up, as a matter of fact. Then a window suddenly appeared in the fog.' He nodded upwards. 'Somebody up there must like us,' he said, just as two nuns came hurrying past me. 'Well,' he added in a low voice, 'they like somebody, anyway!'

As we levelled out in the bright sunshine at our cruising height, two business men across the aisle from me were exchanging notes, their voices unnaturally loud above the engine noise. 'Yes, we're pretty heavily involved with this big festival in Plymouth next year,' said one. 'You know, "Drake 400".'

The other man was silent for a moment. Then he said, 'Oh, I get it – the link with Drake's Pool and so on?'

'That's it,' said the other. 'Not that many people bother about all that sort of thing these days. From our point of view it's more a way in to another market. The rest is just history.'

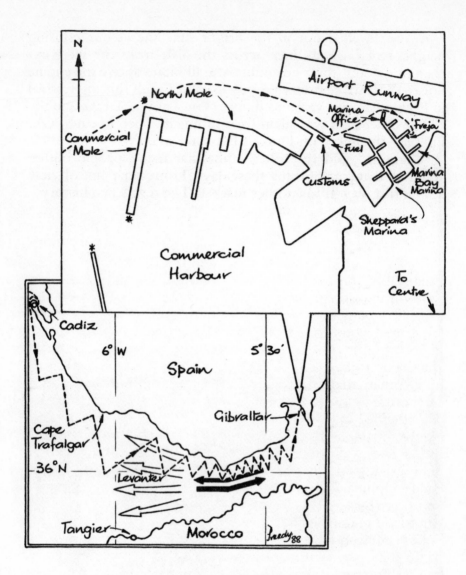

Straits Of Gibraltar With Gibraltar Marina
Complex Inset

Chapter Thirteen

NEWHAVEN TO GIBRALTAR

Predictably, most of the boats I deliver belong to men who work in industry or commerce. Once in a while, though, the exception comes along to prove the rule. Such was the tall, fair-haired young man that I saw striding towards us across Paddington station one early Saturday evening in mid-June 1987. For Robert Clark enjoyed a no-less celebrated station in life than that of First Violin to the London Symphony Orchestra.

I extended my hand to him as he reached us. 'Bob, I would like to introduce John Adcock who's come along to crew for me,' I said, gesturing towards the tall, slim, dark-haired man in his early forties standing beside me. The two of them shook hands. 'John lives right opposite me in St Agnes, and he's a very keen sailor. He's certainly been looking forward to this trip to Gibraltar for quite some time.'

Explaining briefly that he had only just escaped from a full day of rehearsal with the LSO in preparation for an imminent concert tour in Russia, Bob led us quickly back to his car. Moments later we were on our way to his home in Shepperton. 'Jane's been on duty today, but she should be home by the time we get there,' he said, his long fingers drumming out a rhythm on the steering wheel as he waited his chance to filter into the traffic passing the station. Aware as I was that his wife was a senior supervising stewardess with British Airways, it was clear that, for them, life was lived very much in the fast lane. This was a Saturday, after all. 'Anyway, we'll try to make you comfortable tonight and then go down to Lymington first thing tomorrow morning,' he continued. 'Barring any snags you ought to be able to get away by lunchtime at the latest.'

'That's fine,' I replied. 'As long as we catch the tide starting down channel at about 1300 hours, I shall be quite happy. What about the return flights, by the way?'

'All fixed up. Two seats booked for a fortnight tomorrow from Malaga. OK?'

'Yes, right,' I replied, trying to keep the mild dismay from registering in my voice. Originally, I had rather weakly acceded to Bob's wish to book two return flights in advance, realizing that from his point of view it would work out cheaper that way. Yet by so doing I had broken one of my principal delivery rules: never to be bound by a deadline. Really, it had been a self-inflicted injury on my part. For in the course of our subsequent contacts by letter and telephone it had become abundantly clear that Bob would not have baulked for a second had I pointed my rule out to him and my reasons for it. Indeed, I soon discovered that in a previous existence he had actually delivered a number of boats himself, in the USA. So he would have understood my reservation better than anyone. As it was, however, I had once more allowed my over-willingness to co-operate to take me well beyond the limits of prudence.

Still, there it was. To be honest, I admitted, a fortnight should be more than enough for a trip of 1300 nautical miles or so. Yet I had spent quite long enough at this game to know that the writ of Murphy's Law ran no less surely afloat as ashore. All things considered, I should have known better.

*　　*　　*

Take one boisterous easterly wind and stoke it up over two or three days to gale force. Then squeeze it through the Straits of Gibraltar so that it spurts out of the other end like a shot from a gun. The result is an aggravated form of something called the Levanter.

It was Friday lunchtime, nearly a fortnight later. After a pleasant and uneventful voyage down from Lymington aboard *Freja*, Bob and Jane's 36-foot Sweden yacht, John and I had already spent half of Thursday trying to fight our way through the Straits to our destination. But in the teeth of the easterly gale it had proved impossible even to reach our secondary objective, the tiny anchorage immediately in the lee of Tarifa Point. Battered and bruised after seven hours of beating across the outer threshold of the straits, I had finally deferred to our accumulated tiredness and run back to Cadiz. And now, today, we were trying again in conditions that were almost a carbon copy of yesterday.

That the Levanter was well established had been abundantly clear from the crush of sailing and motor boats that greeted us in the cramped yacht harbour in Cadiz. Nor had there been any lack of jaundiced skippers to confirm the fact. Apparently it had been roaring away nicely for a full three days before our arrival, while the local weather forecast was still giving no hint of any let-up. Sometimes, I knew, these winds lasted for a week or more at a time.

Small wonder that the misgivings I had tried to ignore during the car journey to Shepperton had now returned to haunt me. Despairing, as we passed Cape Trafalgar for the second time in as many days, that I would ever learn to stick to the rules, I realized that John and I might well not reach Malaga airport by 1100 hours on Sunday morning. And that would be awkward, to say the least. It wasn't just the additional expense that would be involved in buying more seats, nor even the fact that I was due to start another delivery from Falmouth in five days' time. What troubled me more still was the possibility – faint but tangible, nonetheless – that a prolonged delay might ultimately interfere with Bob's and Jane's holiday. For I knew from my own experience in the army that, given the sort of hectic lives both of them led, it is often only the prospect of a fortnight's holiday in the sun that makes bearable the more frenetic moments of one's career. No, one way and another, the consequences of not getting through to Gibraltar by sometime tomorrow just didn't bear thinking about.

Exactly as had happened yesterday, the wind and sea started to pick up with a vengeance as soon as we lost the lee of Cape Trafalgar. Once again it was time to batten everything down, grit our teeth and just get on with it. Notwithstanding the bright sunshine of early afternoon, the scene that I contemplated was already a grim one. Under a brassy-looking sky streaked from east to west with wispy streamers of cloud, the waves were becoming higher and steeper by the minute, their ragged crests stacking ever tighter one behind the other. And I knew that the closer we got to Tarifa, the worse it would get. For to say that the Levanter causes the cliffs either side of the Straits to act like a venturi is nothing less than the literal truth. Spreading out like a fan into the outer approaches, the continuous blast of wind manages somehow to issue in a straight line from the mouth of the entrance directly towards the boat, regardless of the direction of attack. Today, admittedly, there did seem to be a very slight advantage to be gained on the starboard tack, allowing us to make reasonable progress whenever we angled back towards the Spanish coast. But heading across the eight miles or so in the other direction, toward the shipping lanes, it was as much as we could do just to hold on to what we had gained.

Bracing myself as *Freja* slammed hard into one wave after another, I decided it was time to take stock of boat and crew. So far as the former was concerned, I had no qualms whatsoever. Of all the boats I had seen waiting in Cadiz, I think I would have voted *Freja* as easily the best-fitted to tackle what lay before us. One of the latest examples of the well-tried and highly efficient Bermudan sloop rig – at least to windward – the Sweden 36 was, even now, amazingly light on the helm under her reduced sail area, a tribute to the overall balance which her designer had achieved. Equally important, though, was her substantial displacement, a decided advantage in these conditions. For in short, steep seas of the kind we were meeting now, a heavier boat will usually carry her momentum through waves that will often stop a lighter one in her tracks. Like all generalizations, however, there was one important proviso: the boat's load had to be correctly trimmed. Far too often I have found my charges to be trimmed quite markedly by the stern under the combined weight of engine, fuel, crew and stores. In such circumstances the relatively light bow tends to rise above the waves, causing the boat to lose momentum, rather than driving through them as it should. Certainly, right at this moment I was glad that I had used the opportunity that Cadiz had afforded me to confirm that the load trimming was correct.

Now to my crew. Here again, I had little to worry about. No less keen a sailor than myself, John had done quite a bit of local sailing prior to the trip, including one longer passage down the Irish Sea. All the same, a deep-sea voyage of some 1300 miles was a different matter; certainly different enough for me to wonder, as we had left Lymington, how things would work out. But I needn't have worried. John had manifestly enjoyed every aspect of the voyage so far, good or bad, with the possible exception of the drubbing we had taken yesterday. Even last night, though, he had been quite philosophical about it, entertaining no serious apprehension that I could detect about repeating the experience today. As for his competence as a crew, the only failing that I was still conscious of from time to time was his tendency to react too slowly to the unexpected. Yet this was a somewhat harsh judgment, I knew, one that reflected inexperience more than anything else. And he was improving with every day.

'Well, you did say you were looking forward to the heat of southern Spain!' I called out to him. From his hunched position under the spray hood John threw a wry smile in my direction.

'Late June, too,' he said, slowly shaking his head. Then he put into words the question exercising both our minds. 'Do you think we'll get through this time?'

An extra large wave suddenly slammed hard against the port bow, causing *Freja*, almost for the first time, to stop in her tracks. 'Still too early to say,' I replied, watching the boat pick up speed once more. 'We're doing all right so far, but it's gradually getting worse as we get closer to Tarifa. Still, we can but hope.'

'One of the others seems to have turned back for Cadiz again,' remarked John, looking astern. I glanced back quickly. Originally, three other boats had followed us out of Cadiz at 0800 hours this morning, all of them Bermudan rigged. Now only two remained: the nearest about two miles astern, the other half a mile beyond again. Of the third yacht there was now no sign at all, even in the far distance. Nor was that surprising. Once he had taken the decision to give up and turn back, he would have shot away downwind in no time.

I looked at my watch, hardly believing what I saw. 'Good God, it's two o'clock already,' I said. 'Fancy something to eat?'

'No, not for me,' said John, the quickness of his response suggesting repulsion at the thought.

'No, you're probably right,' I concurred. 'Best let well alone for the time being. Never mind, at least we can look forward to a good meal once we get in.'

It was just before dusk when I looked astern again for signs of our two companions. But now they too had gone. We were on our own.

In his book *Sailing to the Reefs*, the famous French single-hander Bernard Moitessier tells how he ruthlessly suppressed all feelings and emotions for days on end as he battled westward across the Indian Ocean into the north-west monsoon. Only by descending to the level of an unthinking animal, he maintains, was he able to come to terms with the pitifully slow progress. And now, whilst not in a situation remotely comparable with his, I felt a little of what he must have meant. Dismissing all thoughts about when we might arrive, all hope that the wind might magically moderate below its present 35 knots, I concentrated solely on the task of sailing *Freja* to the best of my ability.

Earlier, we had conserved our strength by employing the automatic steering system. But as the evening progressed and we came gradually closer to Tarifa, the wind had started to gust under the influence of the approaching cliffs. In such circumstances few steering systems perform as well as a conscientious helmsman, since steering systems tend to fall away off the course momentarily with each slight lull. One or two such lapses would not have mattered a jot, involving as they did a loss of about ten yards or so to leeward. But multiplied by thousands, the distance wasted would amount to miles. So John and I had taken the wheel over, two hours at a time.

It was just before midnight when we finally came abeam of the Tarifa light. If anything, the wind had become even stronger by now, gusting on occasions close to 40 knots.

'By the way, have you noticed the phosphorescence in the water?' said John, looking at the luminous wake streaming out behind us.

'Yes, it's quite something, isn't it?' I replied. Then, while I had his attention, I continued, 'Well, at least there's one thing. If we do have to run for shelter, we won't have to go all the back to Cadiz any more. With the echo-sounder going we should be able to get close in under the lee of Tarifa and drop anchor there.'

In the darkness and against the roar of wind and sea, I didn't know if he had heard me. Then he spoke. 'How much longer now?' There was something in his voice that told me that he had just about had enough of our habitual 30 degrees of heel.

'Can't say, John, I'm afraid. It all depends on how bad things are from now on. We've just got to keep plugging away, I'm afraid. By the way, now that we're actually inside the Straits we'll be putting in much shorter tacks.' I pointed at the long, irregular line of lights out in the middle of the channel. 'The west-going shipping lane is only about two miles now, and I'd just as soon keep clear of it.'

In the event we were twice caught out by the big ships. In each case I had been tempted by a convenient gap in the convoy to cross over the near lane, so extending the port tack to a really useful distance. But on both occasions I lost any advantage we had gained on the way back, having to give way first to a container ship, then to an enormous tanker. From now on, I decided, we would stay north, no matter what. In retrospect I can see that it was always the sensible thing to do anyway, given that the seas were undoubtedly wilder out in the middle of the channel.

In all this time *Freja* had withstood her severe pounding magnificently, betraying only one abnormal sign of the stress she was under. Due to take over the watch at midnight, I first went below to complete the log. It was then that I saw the two wooden wedges sliding about on the floor of the cabin. Until now, in company with two others still in place, they had been wedged around the mast at the point where it passes down through the deck. Clearly, though, the constant battering had shaken them out. Alarmed, I reset them as firmly as I could before dashing outside again to see how much the mast was moving. Thankfully, all seemed well; mainly, I suspected, because of the high tension applied to the rigging. Even so, after that I checked the wedges every ten minutes or so.

It was just before 0200 hours that John emerged from the cabin where he had been trying to sleep. Without knowing it, he had timed things perfectly. At long last we had reached the point that, despite all my attempts to avoid pleasurable anticipation, I had visualized so often over the past few hours. Going about to begin yet another starboard tack, I realized with a sudden lift of the heart that, this time, we were actually going to clear the north-eastern corner of the Straits. That would take us straight into the blissfully quiet waters of the Bay of Algeciras. I was just about to break the glad tidings to John, still rubbing the sleep out of his eyes, when he forestalled me.

'Ah, there it is at last!' he cried, suddenly wide awake. 'The Rock of Gibraltar!'

In fact, I knew that he had seen it not long before, when he and his family had holidayed in Morocco the previous winter. But not, I suspected, as it was looking right now. Visible intermittently over the past hour each time that I had reached the southern extremity of my port tacks, now it was fully revealed at last. Rising majestically like the great fortress it was, high into the night sky, it was studded with thousands of lights. Quite honestly, it wouldn't look out of place in a Disney fairytale, I reflected, so magically ethereal did it seem after the harsh reality of the Straits.

Half an hour later we were close-reaching across the bay towards it in a Force 4 breeze, luxuriating in the relative smoothness of the water. Quietly euphoric, I was just thinking how utterly impossible it would be to better our situation when I happened to glance back over the port quarter.

'John, quick, look at this! Porpoises!' The sheer excitement of the moment almost stopped the words in my throat. Coming towards us at something like 30 miles an hour were four thin trails of phosphorescence, weaving and criss-crossing under the water as they approached like so many rockets on Guy Fawkes night. Spellbound, we held our breath as they continued without the slightest slackening of speed right underneath the boat and out the other side. We swivelled round, anxious not to lose sight of them. We needn't have worried. Each describing its own wide semicircle, now they were on their way back again to repeat the performance. Once again we felt the momentary thrill of alarm as they seemed about to collide with *Freja*. Once again, they shot harmlessly underneath.

So it went on for the next ten minutes. Sometimes describing figures of eight, sometimes streaking up from far astern, once or twice content just to escort us either side of the bow, they put on a show of phosphorescent fireworks that was quite unforgettable. Then, suddenly, they were gone.

It was just after 0300 hours by the time we had tied up alongside the arrival quay, satisfied the friendly customs officials and moved across to the Marina Bay marina. There a sleepy berthing attendant guided us into a finger berth. Twenty minutes later we were asleep.

Of all the places to choose for a lie-in, I can think of better ones than 50 yards from a busy airstrip. In fact it was seven o'clock in the morning when the screaming engines of the first departing aircraft caused me to sit bolt upright in terror in my sleeping bag. After that, sleep was impossible. Never mind, I thought, at least we've finally made it. And for the first time in a fortnight we've got a nice quiet day ahead of us. It was just as well. The pounding we had taken over the past two days had left me feeling as though I had just gone ten rounds with Mike Tyson. Nor, judging by the way he eased himself gingerly out of his bunk, was John feeling much better.

By lunchtime we had almost finished paying our debt to *Freja*. Scrubbed down outside, cleaned and tidied up inside, shipshape and Bristol-fashion, she was looking as immaculate as ever in the bright sunshine. I was just standing on the pontoon admiring her when I heard a voice behind me.

'Good mornink. I thought I must come to say hello to a fellow Sweden owner. My name is Elvers Singsen.'

A short, stocky man was standing right behind me in shorts and sandals, smiling broadly as he extended his hand towards me. Introducing myself in turn, I quickly explained that I was not *Freja*'s owner, just the delivery skipper. 'So you have a Sweden too?' I asked him.

'Yes, a Sweden 36 just like this one,' he said, pointing. About five yachts further up the pontoon was what appeared to be an exact replica of *Freja*. And she, too, was white. An attractive blonde was, even at that moment, standing on the coachroof in a two-piece swimsuit and high-heeled shoes, spreading out clothes on the boom to dry. 'Please, what is the sail number of this one?' asked Elvers. I told him. 'Yes,' he said, 'I thought so. She is quite a bit newer than mine. I wonder if you will mind if I have a look inside? I would very much like to see what changes she may haf.'

I hesitated for a moment. It was not my boat, after all. Still, I had little doubt what Bob's reaction would have been. Ten minutes later, the tour complete, we were back on the pontoon again.

'Thank you very much,' said Elvers. 'That was very interesting. You say that the owners will not be arriving for a few days yet?'

'That's right.' The gap between our departure and their arrival was something that I had always been a trifle uneasy about.

'Well, if you will be goink tomorrow perhaps I can repay your kindness by keepink an eye on the boat until they arrive. Of course, you will wish to leave the keys with the marina authorities, but I shall be more than happy to check her warps, her fenders and what haf you from time to time. We are going to be here for a week at least, I think.'

I gladly accepted his offer. Admittedly, the marina staff would be carrying out their routine patrols, but there was no substitute for a watchful neighbour.

Elvers started to move away up the pontoon. 'You are sure you will not come aboard for a drink?' he asked. He had asked me once already.

'No thanks, Elvers. It's very kind of you but, as I explained, I'd like to finish up our chores and then catch up on some sleep if you don't mind.'

'Yes, I quite understand,' he replied. 'Perhaps we'll see you later.'

As it turned out, I would have been better off accepting his offer. As so often happens when one is over-tired, sleep managed to elude me completely during the long, hot afternoon, although John was luckier. Even so, the rest was enough to recharge my batteries sufficiently to allow the two of us to enjoy our evening meal in the centre of the town. By ten thirty we had walked back to the marina, passing as we did so the undistinguished-looking filling station that, less than a year later, would be flashed across the television screens of the world. It wasn't long before we were in our bunks and fast asleep.

This time it wasn't an aircraft that woke me at three o'clock in the morning. It was too much wine with the meal, I decided.

Picking up the key to the marina ablutions from the chart table, I crept as softly and quietly as I could up into the cockpit, along the starboard side deck and then down on to the finger pontoon.

The night was still, the sky clear in the moonlight. The early evening forecast might well have been right about the Levanter still blowing out in the Straits, but here we seemed to be in perfect shelter. Listening to the occasional groan of the pontoon joints as they rubbed arthritically together, I made my way down the branch pontoon, turned right along the main trunk pontoon and so to the marina office and ablutions complex at the seaward end. Looking in through the lighted window of the office as I passed, I saw no sign of the night berthing attendant.

I was nearly back at the boat once more when I heard the low throb of an engine. There, coming round the side of the marina, was the silhouette of a large ketch, her navigation lights flickering through the forest of masts. Now she was turning in towards me, coming up the opposite side of the pontoon from *Freja*. Two of the crew were standing up in the bow, looking anxiously ahead for a spare berth. In the absence of the attendant, and remembering that I had just passed an empty space, I walked quickly back towards it, holding up my arms as I did so. Moments later the helmsman was turning smoothly into the berth towards me.

One of the crew stepped quietly down on to the end of the finger pontoon with the stern rope, the other passed me a line from the bow. Almost at the same moment the helmsman went quietly and briefly astern, then cut the engine. That was just how it ought to be done, I thought admiringly. The whole evolution had been completed in little more than 30 seconds and with the absolute minimum of noise. Now the man at the bow stepped down to join me. I handed him the line.

'Thanks very much for your help,' he said in a low voice. 'We can manage nicely now.'

'OK, I'll leave you to it,' I whispered. Turning, I walked across towards *Freja*. With any luck, I thought, John will still be fast asleep. Now it was up to me to see that he stayed that way as I climbed back aboard.

So careful was I not to make a noise or rock the boat that it was all of a minute before I was once more down in the cabin, listening to John's steady breathing. For a moment I stood motionless at the foot of the companionway as I tried to accustom my eyes to the darkness. Then, just as I moved slowly forward once more, my foot kicked something on the cabin floor, sending it rattling against the side of the starboard bunk. Damn, I thought, that was clumsy. Anxious not to do the same thing again, I reached down in the darkness to locate the object and remove it from harm's way. Suddenly, my fingers encountered a tiny buckle on the end of a long, thin strap. It was then that, following the strap the other way, I came to something that froze the very blood in my veins. It was the high heel of a lady's shoe.

Looking back now, I can only conclude that I might have made a reasonably competent cat burglar, had the need ever arisen. Somehow I managed to resist the almost overwhelming temptation to bolt. Heart pounding, I turned in agonized slow motion towards the companionway steps, the steady breathing continuing uninterrupted behind me. Little by little, I climbed up and out into the cockpit. Altogether it was a full two minutes before I regained the safety of the pontoon.

Still quaking with the thought of what might have been, I was making for the sanctuary of the real *Freja* when I noticed one of the crew studying me intently from the bow of the ketch. And judging by the mystified expression on his face, he had been there some time. What he had thought of my slow-motion antics I couldn't imagine, still less what he would make of my next trick as I boarded another boat. Too bad, I thought, getting colder by the moment in the cool night air. This was no time for explanations. 'Good night,' I said in a loud whisper. He raised a limp arm in wondering acknowledgment. What he did after that I simply don't know – because I certainly didn't look back.

*   *   *

'Superb!'
Breaking at last the silence that followed the final, stunning chords of the 'Rhapsody in Blue', I looked across at Mary. Like me, she had sat spellbound in our living room throughout the entire piece as the London Symphony Orchestra had breathed vibrant life into Gershwin's most famous score. Even now the

emotions the music had evoked were still plain to see on her face.

It was the evening of 12 July, and the LSO had been reliving the story of the 'Gershwin Years' on BBC2 in their own, inimitable way.

'He's very young-looking, isn't he?' said Mary. I had pointed Bob out to her early on in the performance.

'You'd make his day if he could hear that,' I replied, smiling at her. 'Yes, they both are.' Once more I picked up the letter that had been lying in my lap throughout the performance. It was from Bob – and he seemed satisfied.

'Jane and I are extremely pleased with the way you have completed the delivery of our yacht. We both felt from the outset that *Freja* was in very good hands.'

In fact, my motive in re-reading the letter was not simply a wish to bolster my ego, much less to bask in the reflected glory

of a gifted musician. It was more like the feeling one has when depositing a sum of money. For I knew that the moment would come all too soon when, wet, cold and drained of energy, I would once again be hanging on for dear life on some storm-tossed sea or other, kicking myself for some new tactical blunder. And it was then that, in my mind, I would draw this letter from the bank.

Chapter Fourteen

PALM BEACH TO NORFOLK, VIRGINIA

'Right, so next time we go through it we'll be recording, OK?'

'Right,' I replied, gulping hard.

'And don't forget,' said Colin Hamilton, 'try and keep your answers fairly short each time, won't you?'

'Yes, will do.' Not much problem about that.

'The engineers are nearly ready,' he said comfortingly. He tried to put me at my ease. 'What's the weather like in North Carolina?'

I didn't have to look outside the telephone box to tell him. 'It's raining cats and dogs,' I said. 'Can't you hear it on the roof?'

'Oh, that's rain, is it? I thought it was a bad line. Still, if it's any consolation the weather here in London is . . . hang on, here we go.'

Five minutes later I escaped from the telephone box and ran through the rain towards the nearby cluster of buildings, my mind wrung out like a wet towel. For once I was glad to find the main reception room of the Morehead City Yacht Basin crowded with people. Right now all I wanted was the chance to sit down and recover.

It was early May 1985, and I had reached another landmark in my double transatlantic voyage for the RNLI in my 26-foot Bermudan sloop *Miss Fidget*. Hence the recording I had just made for the 'Outlook' programme of the BBC World Service. By now *Miss Fidget* and I had covered about two-thirds of the trip. Indeed, in just three weeks' time or so we would be

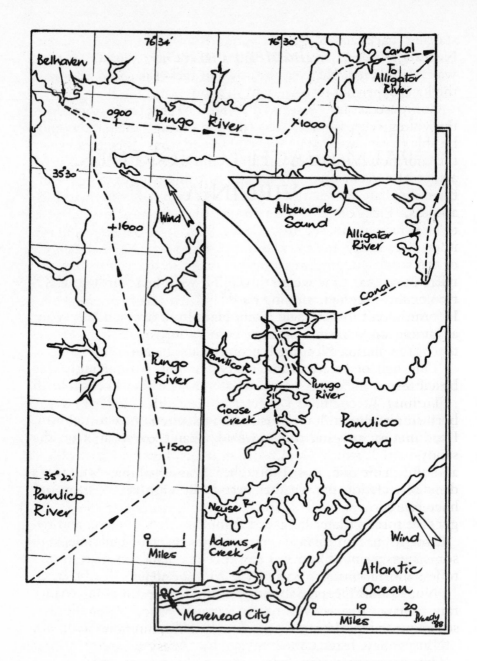

The North Carolina Sounds With Pungo River
Inset

starting back across the Atlantic. But first I had to reach Norfolk, Virginia, some 180 miles up the intra-coastal water-way. And before that – right now, in fact – I needed a bus to the local supermarket to buy fresh food.

Composed at last, I joined the huddle of people surrounding the young receptionist at the counter, hoping that she would be able to give me a local timetable. And it was then that I saw the enormous aerial photograph on the wall behind her. It was a shot of a yacht marina – though not this one, I realized – in the immediate aftermath of a hurricane. Entitled, with macabre aptness, 'Pick-a-Stick', the photograph seemed at first glance to be a crazy muddle of masts, hulls, buildings and other sundry items. Gradually, my blood turning cold, I began to make sense of the scene. Judging many of the boats to be 50 feet long or more I saw that, in some cases, they were stacked on their sides two or three high on top of each other, their masts interlocked. In others, yachts had been thrown a good 50 yards into the adjoining car park. Two had even been deposited straight on top of the marina office, crushing its roof into matchwood.

'One hell of a picture, huh?' said a quiet American voice beside me.

Turning, I recognized Ty Vincent. He and his girlfriend were berthed just down the pilings from me in their Vancouver 27. I had met them yesterday afternoon when I arrived. Ty was a sandy-haired, athletic-looking man in his thirties; a little older and quite a bit taller than Nancy, his diminutive, pig-tailed and decidedly volatile partner. 'It certainly is,' I agreed. 'That must have been down south somewhere, though, surely? You don't get that sort of thing up here, do you?'

'Not as bad as that, I guess. But you can get a twister sometimes; they can be real bad too.' He changed the subject to less morbid matters. 'Still fixin' to leave today?'

'No, I think I'll leave it until tomorrow morning. Give this rain a chance to move away. As a matter of fact, I came in to see about the local buses. I've got some shopping to do.'

'Buses? Say, listen, why not use the courtesy wagon?'

'The courtesy wagon?'

'Sure,' he nodded. 'It belongs to the marina. You just take the wagon free of charge, use it for what you want, then put some gas in it and bring it back.'

'Gosh! That sounds marvellous – what a nice idea.'

Five minutes later I wasn't so sure. The square-fronted Dodge pick-up looked enormous, especially from side to side. Nor was that all. Having climbed up into the driving seat I soon discovered, apart from a hand-operated gear shift on the steering column, that there were only two pedals. She's an automatic, I realized in dismay. Suddenly, what had seemed so simple in the office had become alarmingly complicated. Not only did I have to remember to drive this small tank down the wrong side of the road but, for the first time in my life, I had an automatic gearbox to contend with. I paused for a moment. Come on, I thought, let's not get carried away. Automatics are supposed to make life easier, not more difficult. And at least the rain's stopped. I clipped the loosely fitting seat belt into its socket and started the engine.

It was difficult to see behind me as I pulled out into the traffic, but I managed it at last. The adrenalin salty in my mouth, I concentrated hard as I changed up through the gearbox. It was simplicity itself. One after another the gears cut in, the engine note dropping slightly each time. My confidence starting to seep back, I settled into a comfortable space in the slow right-hand lane and sat back to await the second set of traffic lights. 'Just turn right there, off the freeway,' the young lady had said, 'and, why, you'll be right slap bang in the shopping mall.'

It was just as well that the traffic was well spaced out. Suddenly realizing that it was slowing as we approached the first set of lights, I changed down without thinking, my foot pressing on what it thought was the clutch. The next moment I was catapulted forward in my seat, straining at the end of my seat belt as the pick-up screeched to a sudden, shuddering standstill.

That was the brake, you idiot, I scolded myself. I was still trying to piece my shattered nerves together when the driver behind me pulled out to overtake. Thankfully, I had been some way ahead of him, but it didn't seem to have made much difference where he was concerned. ' . . . learn to drive a friggin' car, buddy!' he yelled, jerking his right forearm upwards through his open window as he accelerated past.

Quite right too, I acknowledged. Next time you won't be so lucky.

Concentrating fiercely thereafter on every single manoeuvre, I was thoroughly relieved when I reached my destination without further mishap. Yet if I had seen my shopping as a means of gentle recuperation, I soon realized my mistake. Altogether, my tour of the supermarket took a full hour, despite the fact that I only needed about ten items. It wasn't so much the problem of finding them amongst the maze of shelving, though that was certainly not easy in a store half the size of Wembley Stadium. It was more the difficulty of choosing between the seemingly endless variety of each particular foodstuff, of deciphering the peculiarly American descriptions. For instance, I soon discovered that there was no such thing as an ordinary pint of milk. Altogether, there were a least a dozen different cartons on display, their labels taunting me with a whole new vocabulary of descriptions. Nor were things any better in a huge bread bay stacked high with every conceivable type, shape and cut of bread except, apparently, a medium-sliced white. Mercifully, a helpful assistant came to my rescue in the end. Fifteen minutes later I had passed through the check-out and was on my way back to the marina.

In the light drizzle that had replaced the earlier downpour Ty Vincent was just backing his Vancouver 27 out of its berth as I carried my shopping down the pontoon towards *Miss Fidget*. Nancy was standing up in the bow, a fender in her hand. 'Get your shopping done?' she called, her black pig-tails bobbing as she waved.

'Yes thanks, no problem,' I replied, lying through my teeth.

'We're headed up north,' called out Ty as the boat started to turn. 'Gonna look up some friends in Belhaven.' I nodded.

'Why don't you call in there yourself?' added Nancy. 'We aim to stay on there for a day or two. And it's a nice day's run from here – if you leave early tomorrow morning you should be in by late afternoon.'

'I might just do that,' I called back. 'Have a good trip.'

For a brief moment as I watched them I felt a sudden impulse to leave too. So far today my contacts with civilization had left me feeling distinctly fragile, so that now the peace and quiet of the inland waterway were calling strongly to me. But I resisted the temptation. The need to keep going over the past few weeks had taken its toll, and I knew that what I really needed now was a little rest. Besides, I thought, maybe the weather will have improved by tomorrow.

*　　*　　*

It was just after 1500 hours the following afternoon. And for once my optimism had not been misplaced. The sun was just peeping above a clear horizon when I left Morehead City at 0500 hours that morning. Now, as I turned left up into the wide River Pungo, it was simply beating down.

About 200 yards ahead of me to port, a glittering 'V' of silver showed up on the dark surface of the water under the trees. Otter, I decided, watching it continue unhurriedly up river towards a half-submerged log. Had the wake been bigger, it might have been a deer; that really would have been something. Once more I felt the thrill of pleasure inside me. I had seen the first one about a week ago, striking out strongly from the edge of a wide lake I had just entered towards the lush green vegetation of a little island in the middle. A little concerned that he might overreach his strength, I had slowed right down, waiting to see if he would need rescuing. But moments later he had splashed up onto the island, tail wagging furiously, to disappear without a pause under the trees. It was just as well, I discovered later. Apparently, more than one well-meaning rescuer had finished up with hands and arms badly bruised by a powerful kick or, worse, lacerated by their knife-edged hooves. Nor could it have helped when they discovered, as I had in subsequent conversation with others, that they can actually swim like fish.

Under the white billow of the poled-out genoa, the western bank of the Pungo River weaved its intricate, heavily indented way into the blue haze ahead. Here, giant oaks, heavy with leaf, draped their branches low over the water; there, the twisted limbs of a fallen tree showed white through a green lattice-work of reeds; all were mirrored, dark and mysterious, in the still water beneath. By contrast, and seen from the other side of the cockpit, the surface of the middle of the river was ruffled and opaque under the light south-easterly wind. Yet, running as we were before it, the breeze itself was making not a sound.

Only the delicious tinkling sound of *Miss Fidget*'s bow-wave disturbed the profound peace and quiet all around me.

Once again, I found myself wondering at the sheer variety of this marvellous inland waterway. Stretching 1500 miles up the eastern seaboard of the USA from Key West in Florida even as far as New York, it was a quite entrancing mixture of river, estuary and canal. Never dull, often breathtakingly beautiful, I still couldn't make up my mind whether it was the scenery or the wildlife that impressed me more. Certainly, I had watched at my leisure – not once, but time and time again – a number of wild creatures that I had never seen before in my life, except, of course, in the artificial environment of a zoo. Thus, there had been the flocks of pelicans skimming improbably, like squadrons of World War II bombers, low over the limpid waters of Florida. Then there had been the menacing, splay-legged alligators and the bland, inoffensive manatees. The occasional otter, raccoon and deer had started to appear as I continued north. Not surprisingly, in competition with these the more familiar grey herons, hawks and kingfishers had seemed rather less exciting, if no less delightful to watch.

The other wonderful thing about the waterway, I had dis-covered, was how much of it one could sail; so far well over half, I estimated. Granted, there were some stretches of canal where the wind, if it encroached at all between the high banks, did so far too fitfully to permit sailing. But this was more than compensated for by the many wide rivers and, most of all, by the huge inland lakes and sounds that abounded. Particularly here in North Carolina, such conditions provided sailing of the highest quality as the low-lying land bordering the waterway permitted freely of wind but only rarely of waves. Time and again *Miss Fidget* had been able to cut through the water like a knife, the speedometer needle unmoving for long periods of time at nearly 7 knots.

It was just as well, I reflected, returning suddenly to sober reality as I remembered the outboard engine. It had started to play up just before I reached the northern end of Adams Creek earlier in the day, the growing harshness of its note punctuated now and then by the occasional misfire. Then I was able to switch it off for a while as I first close-reached, then ran, across Pamlico Sound under full main, cruising chute and self-steering gear, cleaning the spark plugs as I went. But ten minutes after entering the mouth of Goose Creek the misfiring had started again, this time so badly that I had considered whether to stop there and then to attempt a repair. Yet I knew that if I could once get clear of the creek I stood a good chance of sailing all the way to Belhaven, where I planned to stop for the night. There I could attend to it properly.

It was nearly 1700 hours before I realized that my plan had succeeded. For it was then that I entered a long channel between two rows of buoys that marked the entrance to Belhaven. Expecting, from the name, some sort of harbour, I was a little surprised to find that the 20 or 30 yachts ahead of me were anchored in what amounted to an open roadstead.

Spotting the Vancouver 27 early on in my approach, I made a pass about 50 yards astern of her before selecting a suitable anchorage. Nancy was standing up in the cockpit wearing a black bikini, looking away from me towards the wooden landing stage inshore. Of Ty there was no sign.

'Hello Nancy,' I called out as *Miss Fidget* glided quietly through the water under genoa alone.

Startled for a moment, she turned, then raised both arms in welcome as she recognized me. 'Hi there, you made it!' she replied, waving. 'Good trip?'

'Yes, a bit of engine trouble but otherwise marvellous. Where's Ty?'

She turned again to point at a small inflatable dinghy close in under the landing stage. 'That's him in there,' she cried. 'He's just taking John and Paulette ashore. They came aboard for brunch this morning and just stayed over. Wanna come aboard for a drink?'

'No, I'll take a rain-check, Nancy, if I may. Once I drop the hook, I think I'd better try and sort this engine out. It would be nice to come over later, though.'

'Sure, that'll be fine,' she shouted. 'Tell you what, I'll have Ty come across to you. Maybe he can help fix the engine.'

She was almost out of earshot by now. Acknowledging with a wave of my arm, I returned to the business at hand. Two minutes later *Miss Fidget* was drifting back on her anchor, about 100 yards astern and to port of the Vancouver 27.

Attributing the source of the engine trouble to fuel, rather than ignition, I was soon starting to dismantle the carburettor. Thankfully, I had put aboard a complete set of engine spares before leaving England, so that I was reasonably hopeful of completing my own repair. From then onwards time ceased to register. Indeed, so absorbed was I in my work that it was gone six o'clock before I remembered Nancy's words about Ty coming over in the dinghy. Standing up in the cockpit to stretch, I looked across at the other boat. Nancy was still standing up in the bow, one hand on the forestay, the other shading her eyes as she looked shorewards into the setting sun. Manifestly, Ty was still ashore. Anxious both to get a meal going and finish the repair before dark, I returned to my work. Perhaps he's gone for a quick drink, I conjectured; or maybe he's met up with some more friends. Whatever the case, he shouldn't be long now.

It was nearly dark by the time I finished the repair. I squeezed the rubber bulb on the fuel tank a few times, then waited to let the mixture reach the carburettor. Moments later I had the engine running. I looked at my watch: seven thirty. Ty must be back by now, I thought, glancing round at the Vancouver. The dinghy was nowhere to be seen. Nor was there any sign of Nancy; evidently she had given up her vigil and gone below. It was when I switched the engine off again that I heard the crash of a saucepan, followed by a few short Anglo-Saxon words. It looked as though Ty was in trouble.

It was just then that, looking back towards the landing stage, I saw him gradually materializing through the curtain of twilight. Paddling in short, quick strokes, Ty was forcing the dinghy through the water as fast as he could go, the pulsing surge of foam bubbling at the bow. Ah well, I thought in relief, at least nothing's happened to him. Not yet, anyhow. I decided it was time to retreat below.

The row started almost immediately. After a brief and rather ominous pause the two voices started to rise by stages, soon reaching the level of a full-scale shouting match. Moments later there came, once again, the sound of flying metal objects. Then there was silence.

I stood the suspense for about two minutes. They've made it up, I kept telling myself. Like the two adults they are, they've put things firmly back into proportion with an abject apology on the one hand, a forgiving kiss on the other. Yet if so, it had all happened a bit quickly, I reflected. One moment fireworks, the next silence. What if . . . I was unable to bear it any longer. What I saw when I peered anxiously over the top of the hatchway almost took my breath away. The inflatable was bobbing up and down a good ten yards behind the boat at the full extent of its painter. And in it, still wearing her bikini, her arms folded in hunched defiance, sat Nancy.

Even as I watched, Ty appeared from the cabin. And it was immediately clear what his tactics were. Composed and silent, he slid gradually along the cockpit seat to the stern, sitting there for a moment as he contemplated his partner. Then, in words honeyed with conciliation yet thankfully too low for me to hear, he began his attempt to coax her back aboard. Deciding that I had already seen far more than I should, I crept back into the cabin. But it wasn't long before I realized that Ty's efforts had failed. Even from below I heard the explosion of anger clearly.

'OK, that does it! I just don't give a good goddam, you can sit there and freeze your ass off if you want to!' Peeping out through the cabin window, I was just in time to see him storm below once more. As for Nancy, she was still sitting unmoving in the dinghy, her head averted pointedly to one side.

Conscious though I was of the comic side of the drama being enacted, I suppose none of us can be unaffected when those we know and like are seriously at odds with each other. For me, at least, the quarrel was quite enough to spoil my enjoyment of the beef risotto I had prepared. Yet in the end, perhaps resentful of the indigestion that I knew was on its way, I decided to leave them to it. After all, right now I could do without the more turbulent side of human relationships. In a little over three weeks' time I was going to be setting out single-handed across the Atlantic with a spinal disc that, even now, I had to regard as suspect. And already I could feel the pressure mounting inside me.

Over the next hour there were two more violent altercations. Determined to ignore them, I was halfway through the washing-up when curiosity and concern finally overcame my best intentions. By now it had long since become completely dark outside, yet the lights ashore were more than enough to silhouette the figure of the young woman still sitting there in the dinghy. This is starting to become quite ridiculous, I decided. Apart from anything else, she must be freezing cold by now. Then, as my eyes became accustomed to the darkness, I saw something that, for the first time, gave me reason to hope. There was something draped around Nancy's shoulders; it looked like a cardigan. Well, at least it's a start, I thought with a sigh of relief. Much more than mere protection against the chill night air, the garment represented the first material evidence of reconciliation. I decided to finish the washing-up.

It was ten o'clock when I looked out for the last time. By then the Vancouver 27 was in complete darkness. And there, close up behind the stern, was the empty dinghy.

In the tall reeds off to my left a single, upright stick suddenly moved. Slowly, the grey heron raised his long neck once more then shook it three times as, beak pointed skywards, he swallowed his breakfast alive.

No, can't be breakfast, I corrected myself, not for him. He would have been up and fishing with the first of the light. Now, with the time just coming up to 0945 hours, that little morsel would have been more like a mid-morning snack. I looked around me. Once again, I had been lucky with the breeze. Still coming from the south-east, it was a little gentler than yesterday, now hardly disturbing the champagne-coloured surface of the water. Yet it was still enough to allow me to dispense with the engine, to send me close-reaching deliciously up-river under full sail, at one with the tranquillity of my surroundings. Ideal conditions for observing wildlife, in fact.

I looked astern. Far off on the river horizon I could still just make out the tiny clump of masts lying off Belhaven. Really, I had meant to be on my way earlier, but there had been no sign of movement aboard the Vancouver 27 by the time I had been ready to weigh anchor at 0800 hours. And I hadn't liked the idea of just leaving without saying goodbye, particularly after last night. Ty and Nancy might have interpreted it as a sign of disapproval. So I had waited. Eventually, though, a different thought had struck me as I hung around doing odd chores. Perhaps, ashamed of what had happened, they were lying low until I departed. Already half an hour late, that was enough to decide me. Moments later I had weighed anchor and was motoring gently through the wind shadow towards the double row of buoys. The engine seemed to be enjoying it.

I was already past the Vancouver when I heard the shout. Still clad in his striped pyjamas, Ty was leaning over the cockpit gunwhale, looking after me. I slowed the engine to tick-over speed, then pushed the gear lever into neutral.

'Morning, Ty,' I called, 'I didn't want to disturb you.' By now, Nancy had appeared in the hatchway in a nightgown, her black hair, free for once of its pig-tails, almost hiding her blinking eyes.

'Ron,' started Ty, looking distinctly embarrassed, 'I hope we didn't. . . .'

'Everything's absolutely fine,' I interrupted him quickly. 'Really. I just have to keep pushing on if I'm going to get up to Norfolk in good time, that's all. Maybe we'll meet up again there.'

'Have a good trip,' called out Nancy wistfully, waving.

It was just after 1000 hours that I saw it. Having eased the sheets a few minutes earlier to follow the river's bend north-eastwards, now a whole new stretch of river had opened out before me. The Pungo was narrowing, I saw, as it approached the canal cutting through to the Alligator River, the navigational markers either side of me drawing ever closer together. And there, perched improbably on one of the triangular port markers some way ahead, I saw the bird's nest. Really, it would have been impossible to miss, so large was it, so conspicuously sited. In fact, I had already seen two others during my journey north, but one had been situated tantalisingly out of reach down a disused tributary, while the other, precarious and disintegrating, had clearly been abandoned. By contrast, there was something about this one that told me that it was still very much in business. Although ragged at the edges, the freshness of the twigs, together with their tight interlacing in the centre of the nest, were both already obvious, even from 200 yards away.

What happened next will always send a shiver of pleasure

through me whenever I recall it. Appearing as from nowhere, a bird of prey was coming directly up the line of the river from the direction of the canal, flying low over the water. And it was holding a fish in its talons. Unable to drag my eyes away, at least I had the presence of mind to pull the tiller over to port so as not to approach too closely and frighten the bird.

It had to be an osprey, I decided, my whole body tingling with excitement. And judging by the size, it was a female. She was certainly too small to be an eagle, particularly if there were young in the nest; although by no means an expert, I knew of no other land bird of prey, except an osprey, that went fishing. Despite my evasion tactic she was obviously disturbed by my presence, circling above the nest as though undecided whether to land. Now I could see that the fish she was carrying was quite large. No wonder her wings are beating so fast, I thought. Then, almost as though she had read my thought, she started slowly to descend. The next moment she was down in a flurry of wings, balancing, with quick flicks of her tail, on the rim of the nest.

Although blissfully ignorant of the fact, from my standpoint it wasn't a moment too soon. Turning at last to look where I was going, I was horrified to discover that we were already well beyond the starboard margin of the channel, heading straight for a half-submerged tree barely 20 yards away. Holding my breath, I pushed the tiller sharply over to starboard. A few moments later we were out in the middle once more. Heart still thumping, I looked back at the nest. By now the osprey was tearing lumps of flesh off the fish with her short, powerful beak, each time dipping her head down into the nest to feed her young.

The glow of pleasure stayed warm inside me long after I downed the sails and entered the canal. Yet gradually the more prosaic promptings of prudence were starting to remonstrate with me, reminding me how close I had come to hitting the sunken tree. Not that there had been any real risk of going aground – I would only have needed to winch the keel up in order to float off again. But I might easily have torn the sails, or even damaged the rudder, and that would have been serious.

Silly really, I thought, taking a chance like that. Quite apart from the isolation of my present surroundings, I was only three weeks away from a transatlantic voyage back to Cornwall. Anyone could have told me that it simply hadn't been worth it. But they might have had a little trouble convincing me.

Chapter Fifteen

VILAMOURA TO FALMOUTH

On Thursday, 15 October 1987, the 36-foot Biscay ketch *Nandisa* lay some 40 miles off the north-west coast of Spain, heading north-north-east towards Bayona, when it encountered the hurricane that was to devastate south-east England later that night. This is the story of what happened. . . .

On the face of it, bringing *Nandisa* from Vilamoura in Portugal to Falmouth looked like just another delivery job. Admittedly, it was mid-October, a little late for crossing the Bay of Biscay, but *Nandisa* was immensely seaworthy. She was a traditional deep-keel boat built by Falmouth Boat Construction to Lloyds 100 A1 standard and meticulously maintained by her owner. So in the bright morning sunshine it was hard to account for my uneasiness as I turned to starboard outside the Vilamoura fairway into a light breeze at 1000 hours on Tuesday, 13 October. Nor was there anything particularly sinister about the impressive 20-foot swell from the west-north-west that met us as we rounded Cape St Vincent early that evening. After all, the last ten days had seen a succession of vigorous Atlantic lows; with the barometer steady at 1021 millibars, it seemed reasonable to assume that this swell was more a legacy than a portent.

As so often happens in those latitudes, the light breeze died away with the onset of dusk. Long before the magnificent Cape St Vincent lighthouse faded astern, I had to resort to the Perkins diesel engine, and thereafter it stayed on right through the night. The pronounced oily swell that remained did nothing to dispel my strange uneasiness. For a fleeting, fanciful moment I recalled

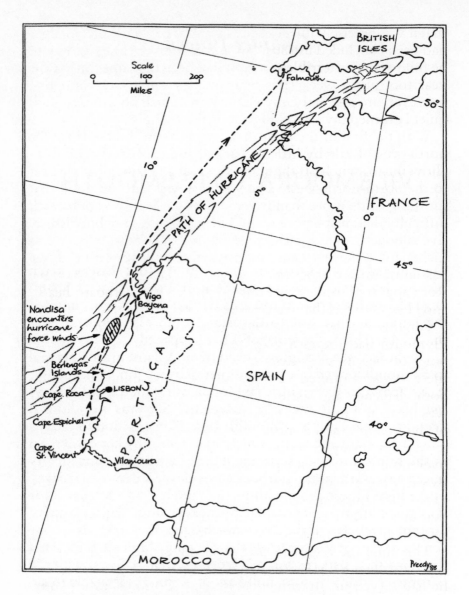

In The Path Of The Hurricane – Thursday, 15
October 1987

that it was precisely this sea state in which the battle of Trafalgar had been concluded in 1805, some 200 miles to the east, only to be followed by a terrible storm. It had been the same time of the year too, just a week later than today's date. Such thoughts, however, are distinctly unwelcome on a small boat at sea, and I quickly turned my attention to something else.

With the first of the light there came a faint breeze from the north-west. Little by little, it backed and freshened enough to allow me to switch off the engine and set all plain sail as we beat to the north-north-west. The visibility was not too good that morning, little more than five miles or so. So it was only with difficulty that, just before noon, I identified the faint but distinctive silhouette of Cape Espichel. As for the Tagus estuary and Lisbon itself, they remained hidden in their industrial murk as we passed them. By 1500 hours, however, the grey bulk of Cape Roca appeared some seven miles away on the starboard beam, and I began to feel that we were starting to make progress.

For this voyage, as for many others, my old army unit in Plymouth had found a volunteer to crew for me. From the point of view of 29th Commando Regiment, Royal Artillery, these voyages offered valuable adventure training, providing both challenge and variety. As for me, such an arrangement was ideal, and I counted myself very fortunate. Not that many of the volunteers had more than basic sailing experience. But it was reassuring to know that each of them had faced and overcome the daunting physical and mental demands of the Royal Marines Commando course at Lympstone. Having survived that course myself some years ago, I knew exactly what that meant. Suffice it to say that I was never once disappointed with their performance.

This time the regiment had done me proud. John Rencher was actually a REME warrant officer specializing in radar, but he had served on attachment with 29th Commando for some years. Although I never found out, I judged him at the time to be about 40 years old. Of medium height and build with a sandy moustache and an open, agreeable manner, John soon proved himself to be good company. More than that, I became quickly and increasingly aware of an inner self-confidence in his make-up born of natural resourcefulness and considerable mental toughness. Little did I realize then how important those qualities would prove to be. Granted a period of leave to accompany me, John's previous experience amounted to some dinghy sailing and a flotilla cruising holiday in the Greek islands. This was his first deep-sea voyage, and the quiet start had allowed him an ideal opportunity to re-discover his sea legs. So I kept to myself the fact that the barometer had fallen slowly to 1016 millibars.

At 1630 hours, as we headed north in a fresh breeze to weather the Berlingas Islands, my morbid uneasiness at last found something to bite on. The wind backed to the south-west, rising as it did so to Force 6. Meanwhile the barometer had dropped 3 millibars in one and a half hours: nothing by UK weather standards but a little ominous down in these latitudes. It would take a better meteorologist than me to explain why it is that, in this part of the world, even quite small variations in pressure cause quite marked changes in the weather. But I have always found it to be so.

Once more I tried, and failed, to pick up a forecast from Radio Lisbon or Radio Cascais, but eventually I obtained one from Montedor, a little further up the coast. Because I couldn't contact them direct, a passing tanker kindly relayed it for me. Commercial ships can be very helpful in this way, provided, that is, someone on the bridge can speak English. I, alas, speak little more than elementary French and German and even less Spanish. Apparently, the south-westerly 5 or 6 would increase during the next 24 hours to a 7 or 8. No problem, I decided, somewhat relieved. With the wind dead astern as we made for Bayona – our only scheduled staging point – even a Force 8 would hardly tax a boat like *Nandisa*. On the contrary, it would push us nicely on our way in an area where one normally expects head winds. Moreover, I knew the Vigo estuary and Bayona very well by now. I was confident of entering in any weather conditions, particularly with radar – let alone a radar expert – on board. Perhaps now, I told myself, you'll stop worrying and relax.

By 2100 hours that evening the lights marking the Berlingas had disappeared astern in the driving rain. It was blowing Force 7, and we were running before a building sea at about 7½ knots. Down came the reefed mainsail, leaving only the genoa up front. Yet as time went on even this sail proved too much as

Nandisa yawed more and more despite the best efforts of the Hydrovane self-steering gear to prevent it. Accordingly, at 2300 hours we replaced the genoa with the storm jib, restoring full control with little loss of speed.

John, I think, had expected the sail change to be more difficult than it actually was. True, there was plenty of movement up front as the bow yawed and pitched steeply in the following sea. But with the powerful deck lights to lighten our darkness, we soon had the big genoa down and the tiny storm jib hoisted in its place. Even so, we wasted no time in getting back to the cockpit.

It had been John's watch – we were on three-hour watches at this stage – but I stayed up for a minute or two after the sail change to try and judge what the weather was doing. I also wanted quietly to gauge John's reaction to the worsening conditions.

'It's getting a bit lively, Skipper, isn't it?' said John. He was standing behind the wheel, his eyes fixed on the binnacle-mounted compass immediately in front of him. I had deliberately disengaged the Hydrovane once more after the sail change because it was important that he should get as much practice on the wheel as possible.

'Yes, I think we're in for a gale all right,' I replied. 'Still, it will be coming from right behind us, so it shouldn't be too much of a problem. How are you coping?'

He looked briefly up at me, his face lit just sufficiently by the compass light to disclose a wide grin.

'Oh, this is great fun!' he exclaimed. 'It beats sitting on my backside behind a desk, I can tell you.' So saying, he looked down again, totally absorbed in his task.

When I came on watch at midnight the barometer was down to 1008 millibars. It was still raining hard and now blowing a full gale. From then on things got steadily worse through a dirty night, the barometer dropping to 1001 by first light at 0615 hours. It had fallen 20 millibars since leaving Vilamoura, I realized with a gulp.

The murky dawn that Thursday morning revealed a decidedly angry and confused sea. The original west-north-west swell was still very much in evidence, but by now the wind had reached Force 9 and was stoking up real trouble from the south-west. The resulting cross-seas were starting to form peaks here and there as they came together. Ah well, I thought, at least the gale has finally arrived. From here on it would just be a question of sticking the incessant rolling and lurching, consoling ourselves meanwhile with our excellent progress. At 1000 hours we recorded a second day's run of over 130 nautical miles, all in the right direction. Thankfully, the Walker Satnav was working beautifully. It showed that our present course, with the wind on our port quarter and the storm jib comfortably out to starboard, would bring us directly to Bayona, and in about 24 hours at our present rate. This was duly confirmed by dead reckoning off the chart and by the Lokata radio direction finder that accompanies me on every voyage I make.

Astern the seas were becoming yet steeper as they queued up to assault us. To guard against pooping we had already resorted to watertight drills: one man on the wheel, the other battened down below with washboards in place and hatch closed. Now, as the morning progressed, the need for this became more and more obvious. By 1100 hours it was occasionally blowing Storm Force 10, and I was getting worried about the storm jib. The Hydrovane was still working well but occasionally it allowed *Nandisa* to yaw up to 30 degrees off course, twice causing the storm jib to slam viciously aback. Small and tough as it was, if the wind got any stronger it would either rip the sail or cause a failure somewhere in the running rigging. And anyway, we were once again going too fast. So down it came. Under bare poles *Nandisa*'s speed decreased from 7 to 3½ knots, and for a time control was restored.

It was soon after this that *Aldesan*, a large cargo ship, approached us and remained for some 15 minutes on our starboard quarter at about 3 cables' range. Eventually, worried that she might be trying to contact us, I asked John to come up on deck and went down to check the radio. It was still on Channel 16 at low power and appeared to be working perfectly, in which case John should have heard had she tried to call us up. I called her twice anyway, but there was no reply.

When I went up on deck again to take over the watch, the ship was already dropping astern of us.

'I'm not too sure what that was about,' I said. 'I tried calling her, but for some reason she didn't answer. Language problem, I expect. I suppose she just wanted to make sure that we weren't in any immediate difficulty. Or perhaps she was just curious.'

John was certainly no fool, and I am sure that the implication of my remarks was not lost on him. If the ship had actually followed us at close quarters for 15 minutes, then, whatever the reason, it suggested that things were starting to get a little serious. But there was no point in my hiding this from him – even supposing I could. Perhaps it was time to sound him out again, I thought, studying him as he turned to go below. For the first time I was seeing the signs of stress in his face.

'You're OK, John, are you?' I asked. 'I realize you've not met up with this sort of weather at sea before.'

'No, I'm fine, Skipper,' he replied, managing a smile. 'It's like they say, if you can't take a joke. . . .'

I laughed, heartened by his determined cheerfulness. 'Just remember that *Nandisa* is very strong and very seaworthy. She'll look after us all right.'

I realized that I was shouting to make myself heard, even though John was barely six feet away from me. As he disappeared below once more I decided that it was time to take stock. Even now, I concluded, I was still not seriously concerned at our situation, so well had *Nandisa* behaved. But I sensed that John, despite his calm exterior and exemplary performance, was understandably becoming a little frightened. This in itself was remarkable. Here was a man experiencing all the savagery of a storm on his first deep-sea voyage in a small boat. Yet he was still managing to fulfil all his duties, let alone govern his emotions, in a way that I could only admire. For with every minute the seas were getting bigger, whiter in appearance. And now, once in a while, a huge roller would break with a great roar to one side or other of the boat. That was the danger, I realized. It seemed only a matter of time before we were pooped, before one of the huge waves broke right on our stern. As against this, we were now stripped for action: battened down, sea cocks closed, under bare poles and doing what we should be doing, running before the storm. As for *Nandisa*, she still seemed quite unaffected by it all. So far everything was still intact with no damage whatsoever, while regular operation of the pump demonstrated that she had taken remarkably little water into the bilges.

It was at about 1300 hours, with the barometer down to 997

millibars, that I decided it was my turn to become frightened. The wind increased over a ten-minute period to a convincing Force 11, sometimes gusting higher still. Smoking trails of spume snaked whip-like over the surface of the water, while the air itself seemed to be getting whiter as spray in suspension rapidly reduced visibility to less than half a mile. But it wasn't only this that I found frightening; I had, after all, met similar conditions once or twice before. It was more that I was becoming genuinely worried about our ability to cope with these very bad cross-seas. For somehow it seemed as though the original swell from the west-north-west, far from subsiding, was actually becoming steeper. Whatever the case, it was obvious that I would have to disengage the Hydrovane. It simply couldn't react quickly enough to deal with two waves in quick succession and some 70 degrees apart in direction.

Yet I soon found that my own strenuous efforts on the wheel weren't much better. Once in a while a big swell from the west-north-west would nearly break, so steep had they become, pushing *Nandisa*'s bow irresistibly to starboard. And when this happened only the most vigorous action on the wheel sufficed to bring her back quickly enough to meet the next big wave rearing up from the south-west. It was for this reason, incidentally, that I didn't even consider towing warps. They would only have reduced *Nandisa*'s ability to manoeuvre in this cross-sea – and that was crucial. Feeling a little desperate, I switched the Perkins on at 1500 rpm to gain a little more steerage way. Thankfully, this seemed to help, and although we were now doing 5 knots, it was less of a struggle to bring the stern into line when needed.

The first pooping came at about 1430 hours. The wave hit us square on the stern, sending cascades of water into the cockpit and half filling it. I watched with curiously detached interest. There were four drain plugs of the 'bathtub' variety, and I doubted their ability to work quickly enough. In the event the water drained away in about 30 seconds, not bad, but not good either. A few moments later I saw the cabin hatch slide back. John poked his head out.

'Everything all right, Skipper?' he yelled.

'Yes,' I shouted back at him. 'We were pooped. Any water below?'

I didn't hear his reply but saw him shake his head. For a few moments he watched me battling with the wheel. Then he clambered up into the cockpit, closed the hatch and made his way towards me, holding on to anything he could reach.

'Steering's becoming a bit of a handful, John,' I shouted. 'It's this cross-sea that's causing the trouble. Whatever we do, we've got to keep the stern square on to these waves as they come through.'

John didn't reply immediately. Instead he was looking astern, a distinctly worried expression on his face. Yet, as so often happens, the wave eventually passed under the stern without breaking.

'Do you think you could cope with this, John?' I yelled. Wheel steering in these conditions is far from easy, and there was really no room for error. The greatest danger of all, of course, was that a really big wave, instead of hitting square on the stern, might catch *Nandisa* on the quarter and swing her round to lie across the seas. Should she broach in that way, there was then every chance that the next wave would just roll her completely over, leaving her awash and easy prey to the waves that followed. All the same, my question to John had been a stupid one. How could he know if he could cope until he tried it?

'Don't know,' replied John, almost into my ear. 'I can certainly try.'

'Don't worry,' I said. 'We'll see what conditions are like at the end of my watch.'

John nodded and made his way down below again.

The second pooping occurred just before the end of my watch – we were down to one-hour watches by now – and hit even harder. By now it was gusting Force 12. Three o'clock came, and John poked his head out of the hatchway, about to climb out to take over the wheel. But after asking him to read the barometer – it was now down to 993 millibars – I decided to send him below again. Conditions had become even worse, and I knew that, right now, we couldn't afford a broach. The only trouble was that I was getting tired and feeling every one of my 52 years.

By 1530 hours the realization that I just had to have a break from the wheel coincided with a slight easing of the wind. I called John up on deck and, having emphasized that he was to hand over to me the instant I laid my hand on the wheel, stayed beside him as he took over. To my intense relief he coped marvellously well. After the first few minutes he came to see exactly what was required, and soon I was able to get below for a breather. Once in the cabin I checked the barometer. It was still registering 993 – 28 millibars below its reading at Vilamoura. We were pooped again quite badly at about 1615 hours, but John managed to keep *Nandisa* straight. When I took over the wheel again at 1630 hours, it was once more blowing very hard indeed.

The crisis came just before 1700 hours. Just when it seemed to me that the wind could not possibly get any stronger, it did precisely that and by at least another 10 miles an hour. To the screaming in the rigging was now added a kind of low, unnerving moaning noise. I looked around me, awe-struck. Visibility was little more than 400 yards, so filled was the air with spray, while secondary waves of about Force 4 size were actually climbing up the backs of the huge breakers and peaks that surrounded us. And now *Nandisa* was really surfing with a vengeance. She had started this earlier, now and then careering 30 or 40 yards down the face of the waves. Yet that was nothing out of the ordinary when running before a big sea. Now we were surfing for 100 yards or more at a time. How fast we were actually going on these occasions I cannot say because the speedometer would just shoot up to the 10 knots mark at the top of the dial and stay there. But right then I simply didn't care. All I knew was that, at all costs, I had to keep *Nandisa* straight. If I once let her sheer even a little off line, we would be bound to broach.

Suddenly, to my surprise, the blurred but enormous bulk of a super-tanker materialized very close on the port bow. Presumably she had come to check on our situation, not that there was much that she could have done. She was pitching, rolling and yawing through the mountain peaks like a rowing boat in slow motion; even now I can distinctly recollect looking, at one point, straight up the centre-line of her enormous deck from bow to stern as she yawed and dipped steeply towards us. She wallowed slowly past like an enormous whale, then gradually faded astern.

For the next 20 minutes the scene around me resembled something out of a nightmare. The total noise of wind and sea had become almost unbearable, the waves simply enormous. Mindful of how easy it is to exaggerate when under stress, I remember at one point taking particular care to gauge their height. I can therefore say with absolute certainty that one or two waves were at least half again as high as *Nandisa*'s masthead when she was in a trough and momentarily on an even keel. That would make them some 65 feet from trough to crest. Suddenly, my calculations were rudely interrupted as another wave came crashing over me, nearly filling the cockpit. This time I only just managed to keep *Nandisa* from broaching – and thus, quite certainly now, from rolling over.

I began to feel really desperate. For the first time that I could ever remember in my years at sea, I was suddenly and starkly aware that from now on I was absolutely powerless to affect our situation in any way. Even taking for granted that I could go on steering the boat indefinitely to the very best of my ability, even that might just not be enough. For at this final, climactic stage in events there seemed to be a careless, random savagery about the wind and sea, a raw brute strength in the waves as they hit us, that caused me suddenly to feel very afraid, very mortal. So it was that in those moments of real peril I found myself asking, very quietly, for a little help.

At last, just after 1720 hours, the miraculous happened. The moaning and shrieking in the rigging suddenly died down and stayed that way for one or two minutes. It rose again briefly, then dropped back once more. I could hardly believe it. Yet ten minutes later the relative lull was still persisting. By then the wind had veered to the north-west and was down to a Force 7 or so. After what we had just come through, it felt no more than a light breeze.

John's head appeared in the hatchway. He looked very tired, but the lines of strain around his eyes had almost disappeared.

'Barometer's up to 994, Skipper,' he called, giving me a thumbs-up sign. His voice sounded unnaturally loud in the relative quiet that surrounded us.

'That's fine, John,' I replied, feeling myself relax for the first time. 'Looks like we've made it.'

Although the seas became, if anything, even more confused over the next hour or so, they no longer struck with the same brute force as before, and it was clear that, bar the shouting, it was all over. It was then that we discovered our only significant damage. Re-engaging the Hydrovane, we found that it wouldn't keep *Nandisa* on course; one look over the stern explained why. Despite its truly massive construction, the steering paddle had been bent through about 20 degrees at the point where it emerged from the stainless steel tubing above.

At 0530 hours next morning, with the barometer back to 1006 millibars, we lay off the Vigo estuary waiting for daylight and just before 0700 hours came alongside the fuelling pontoon at the Monte Real Yacht Club, Bayona. There, in between fending off a great deal of close questioning about our experiences, we discovered that Bayona had taken a real beating the day before. Part of the marina pontoon had been carried away, and boats had been driven ashore or badly damaged. A number of houses had suffered structural damage, losing roofs and even walls. Trees had been uprooted and flung carelessly aside. Gusts of wind up to 86 knots had been recorded at several places along the coast, while Northern Spain had been put temporarily on an emergency footing.

Next day we left again for Falmouth, reluctant to waste a Force 7 wind that had once more backed towards the south. Six days and two more, comparatively minor, gales later, we finally reached Mylor Yacht Harbour in Falmouth.

Looking back now, I cannot help but reflect how lucky we were, particularly in terms of timing. The last 12 hours of the storm had occurred almost precisely between dawn and dusk.

Had the final hurricane-force winds hit us in pitch darkness, I seriously doubt whether we could have prevented a broach, and thus a roll-over. For at times it had been vital to be able to see a good hundred yards astern of us in order to decide how best to present the boat to what was coming. We were also very fortunate in having such a boat under us. I can think of others that I have delivered over the years to or from the Portuguese Algarve which, while sound enough for all normal purposes, would hardly have had the strength or seaworthiness to survive. *Nandisa*, bless her, had both.

Finally, I still can't work out the reason for my genuine uneasiness on leaving Vilamoura. I suppose it was due to my awareness that it was getting a little late in the season and that this would probably be my last delivery for 1987, the sting in the tail, perhaps. Odd, though.

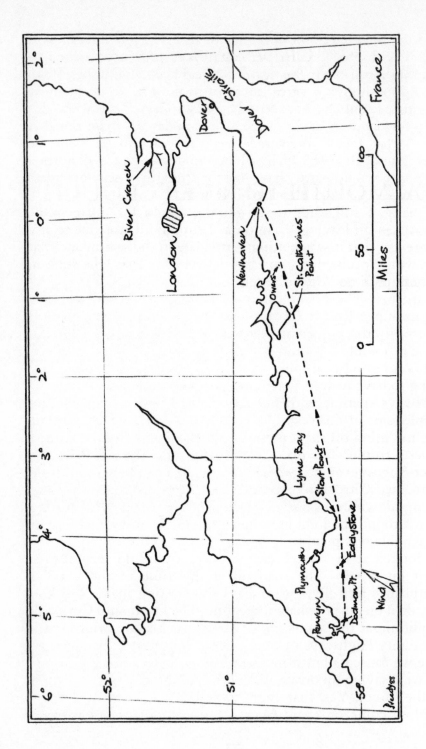

Penryn To Newhaven

Chapter Sixteen

FALMOUTH TO RIVER CROUCH

Sometimes I no sooner hear about a boat than I want to be aboard her. The Nicholson 55 belonging to the Pursers was one example; Robert Clark's Sweden 36 another. Yet it is not necessarily the bigger or newer boat that whets my appetite. Once in a while it is quite the opposite. . . .

'It's no good champing at the bit,' said Mary. 'You're just going to have to wait your turn like everybody else.'

Always sparing with her strictures, I had to concede the simple logic of this one. I let go of the steering wheel, tried to take my mind off the long line of traffic in front of us. After a hitherto trouble-free drive from St Agnes in the soft light of a quiet August evening, we had coasted to a halt behind the little corrugated Citroen five minutes ago, at the bottom of the hill leading down into Penryn. Since then we had crawled fitfully after it round the long left-hand bend until, now, the cause of the trouble was plain to see before us.

I looked at my watch: seven thirty. 'Why do they always insist on digging the road up at this time of the year?' I complained fretfully, aware that I was starting again. 'I reckon they do it on purpose half of the time. They wait until Cornwall is splitting at the seams with tourists, then some bright spark in County Highways or South-West Water says, "Right lads, time we caused a bit of mayhem. Now then, where's that one we were saving up down at Penryn? Ah, here we are . . . right on the corner. Yes, that ought to do it." '

'Now come on,' said Mary, laughing, 'that's not fair and

you know it. What if it's a leak in the mains? They can't forecast that. Anyway, I know what all this fuss is about. It's the boat, isn't it? So near and yet so far.'

Touché. I had been itching to see *Beatrice* for over a fortnight now. Indeed, I had spent the last delivery thinking of little else. After all, it wasn't every day that I had the chance to sail a sixty-year-old boat. And quite apart from that, I was looking forward to meeting John Thornton.

In his late twenties, John was a Yorkshireman, born and bred. A London bus driver, he had telephoned me three weeks ago to ask if I would accompany him and *Beatrice* up the English Channel and across the Thames estuary to the river Crouch, in Essex. I remembered the crux of our conversation clearly. . . .

'The thing is,' John had explained hurriedly, 'I've only got the fortnight's holiday, so one way and another I've just got to get her up to the Crouch by the end of it. If I don't manage it then, I'll. . . .'

'You've just bought her, you say?' I broke in, aware that he was in a public call box. 'And she's a 24-foot gaff-rigged wooden ketch built in . . . you did say 1924, didn't you?'

'Ay, that's it.' There were only three words but the pride in his voice was obvious. 'She's a real old-timer.'

'And have you actually seen her yet?'

'Well no, I 'aven't, to be honest.' His accent only surfaced once in a while, I was beginning to notice, suggesting that his exile from Yorkshire was of fairly long standing. 'See, I just haven't had the chance to get down there. But I know a lot about her – I've just had her surveyed.'

Thank goodness for that, I thought. 'And the survey was OK?'

'More or less. Mind, the report's not arrived yet. But the surveyor told me over the phone that she's pretty good, considering her age. Nothing disastrous, anyway. And I'm planning to come down a few days early to sort out the smaller bits and pieces before we leave.'

All in all, it didn't sound too bad, I decided. And the prospect of a 1924 gaff-rigged ketch was . . . suddenly I heard the pips go at the other end, followed by the sound of more coins dropping into the box. Then John spoke again.

'That's the last of the money,' he said. 'Look, the real thing

I wanted to ask – apart from whether you'll do it, of course, – was how much would you want?'

There was something about the last question, something in the breathless pause that followed, that told me how crucial my answer would be to him. Nor, remembering how I was at his age, was that surprising. Although I suspected that London bus drivers earned reasonably good wages, the purchase of a boat is a costly business at the best of times. And on top of that there had been the additional expense of the survey. I quoted him a price.

'Oh, right.' The relief came flooding down the line. 'I think I can manage that. Anyway, look, I'll write to you with a few more details about the boat and then. . . .'

'Come on, love, we're off!'

Mary's voice jolted me back into the present. Moments later we were skirting the traffic lights, bumping over the rubber hose-pipes laid across the road. It was a burst main all right. Anyway, never mind all that, I thought. Only a few moments more now, and I would see the boat. Not that I really needed to, of course. In my mind I could see her already: her varnished topsides, gleaming and unblemished, mirrored in the still waters of the Penryn river; her tan-coloured mainsail sandwiched in neat folds between boom and gaff; her oiled rigging bedecked with baggywrinkle, shod lovingly with canvas gaiters at the deck fastenings. Almost drooling with anticipation, I turned into the alleyway leading down the side of David Carne's 'Boathouse' chandlery to the river.

I was still pulling my grip out of the back of the car when I heard the shout from across the water. I turned to see a short, stocky, sandy-haired young man standing on the end of a bowsprit on the other side of the river. Holding on to the forestay with one hand, he was waving with the other. Then, even as I responded, my heart sank like a stone into the river. Wiped in an instant from my mind was the ageless, cosseted old lady I had so fondly imagined. In her place, shocking me with all the impact of a bucketful of cold water, was what appeared to be a miniature coal-barge. Black and somehow menacing behind her long bowsprit, she was lying low, squat and seemingly immovable in the water. And it was obvious, even from here, that she had seen better days.

227

Hurrying back to the stern, the young man quickly untied a painter from the taffrail before dropping down out of sight. Moments later he had reappeared round the starboard quarter, rowing the largest inflatable dinghy I had ever seen in my life. Mary must have seen my jaw drop. 'It really is a bit big, isn't it?' she said, awe-struck.

'A bit big?' I echoed. 'Don't look now, but I wouldn't mind betting it's nearly as long as *Beatrice* herself. Where on earth did he find that one?'

The next moment the dinghy was alongside the jetty immediately below us. 'Hi, I'm John Thornton,' squeezed out the youngster, breathless and red-faced as he scrambled forward to hand me the painter. Making it fast, I introduced Mary, then myself.

'That's quite a dinghy,' I observed as I handed down my grip and briefcase.

His face suddenly went redder still. 'Yes, it's a bit big, I must admit. But it were the only one the boatyard had – going cheap, anyway.'

Immediately regretting my words, I realized I might have to go carefully over the next two or three days if I was not to trample on his feelings. 'Oh, don't worry, it's fine,' I said casually. 'I'm sure we can fold it up pretty small if we try.' I turned towards Mary. 'OK, love, I'll give you a ring when I can but don't worry about us, will you? With the weather as quiet as it is, it's bound to take time to get to the other end.' I kissed her good-bye, then watched as she started up and drove away.

The closer we came to *Beatrice* in the dinghy, the more it came home to me that I had already seen her best side. Thus, viewed from a distance it had been possible to overlook the dull roughness of her topsides, the tell-tale signs of wear in her sails, the ragged, rusted appearance of her wire rigging, the grime ingrained into her planked deck. But not now. Seen at close hand she looked every one of her sixty years, bearing all the signs of a boat long neglected, long exposed to the wind and weather of the four seasons. Never mind, I thought, trying to head off my growing sense of doom; maybe she's better than she looks. Wait till you've inspected her properly.

It took less than ten minutes to realize the worst of my fears.

Shadowed anxiously round the boat by John – until I hit on the expedient of asking him to collapse the dinghy – I had been confronted by one defect after another. Admittedly, many of them were fairly minor, ranging from seized-up blocks to tired splicing. But others were not. There was the bilge-pump, for instance. Positioned immediately inside the companionway entrance, I was appalled to find that, of the four bolts that should have anchored it firmly to the bulkhead, only two remained. The result was that, when I tried to operate the handle, the whole pump clattered uselessly back and forth on the bulkhead.

Then there were the sails. Dirty, crumpled, patched, stiff with dried salt, the majority were barely adequate for their purpose. But the mizzen sail was in a class of its own. Lacking any protective cover, its decidedly faded exterior warning me of what was to come, my suspicion only deepened when I finished unravelling the knotted piece of rope spiralling around it. No longer held in place by anything, the sail just sat there on top of the boom, the depth and solidity of the grooves left by the rope telling their own story. This sail had not been even shaken out, much less hoisted, for a year at the very least, I realized, probably longer. At last, in response to my repeated tugs, it fell apart to disclose a gaping, tattered hole, at least a yard in diameter, right in the middle of the sail.

There was one bright spot to relieve the gloom. Despite its venerable appearance, at least the diesel engine sounded sweet enough. And I had to admit that there was a certain Heath Robinson charm to the gear lever. Consisting of a two-foot metal rod with a large black knob on the end, it protruded horizontally into the cockpit from the middle of the port-hand cabin bulkhead.

Lastly, there was the rigging. Surprisingly, and notwithstanding the rusting in those places where the galvanizing had failed, I was gratified to find that the standing rigging was reasonably sound. But I was much less happy with the running rigging. Both jib sheets had been badly chafed in several places, while the main sheet, though better, had clearly suffered from prolonged exposure to the light. Nor were the rope-tailed wire runners much better.

Wondering how to break the news to John, I faced him at

last across the narrow cockpit. But first I wanted to know something. 'Is the survey report on board by any chance, John?' I asked.

'No, it's back at t'flat,' he replied, his subdued manner a deeper reflection of mine. 'I meant to bring it, but in all the rush I forgot.'

'Can you remember what it said about the state of the sails and rigging?'

He shook his head. 'No, I don't think it really covered that side of things, as a matter of fact.' His answer didn't surprise me as much as it should have done. Some surveyors seem to exclude so many things in their reports that I sometimes wonder why they bother at all.

'And what about the bilge pump – anything about that?' Again, another miserable shake of the head.

'Well look, John,' I began, wishing devoutly that I had the surveyor standing in front of me now and not the poor unfortunate owner, 'the plain truth is that this boat isn't fit to go anywhere in her present state, and certainly not 350 miles up the Channel and round the corner. Sorry, but there it is.' I watched his reaction. Despite the fact that he must have been half-expecting this verdict, it was just as though I had hit him with a twelve-pound sledge-hammer. He sank slowly down to the cockpit seat, his hands splayed out on his knees for support, his eyes dropping to the cockpit sole.

'Couldn't you see what she was like when you came aboard yesterday?' I asked him as gently as possible.

He shifted his position uncomfortably. 'Well yes, I suppose I did, really,' he admitted, his voice suddenly flat. 'But I thought I might be able to sort it out – enough to get by, anyway. Like I said in my letter, I hadn't really planned to leave for another two or three days yet.'

'I'm sorry, John, but two or three days wouldn't have made much difference to this boat in her present condition. What she really needs is a six-month refit. And anyway, you'll remember me saying over the phone that I've got another delivery coming up straight after this one. I just couldn't accept a two or three-day delay right now, I'm afraid.'

A thin whistle sounded from below, reminding me that John had put the kettle on a few minutes earlier. Following him down into the cabin, I pulled my notebook out of my briefcase to read again the general weather synopsis that I had copied down in my living room back at St Agnes. 'High, one thousand and thirty, lying northern France, moving slowly north-eastwards with little change. Expected German Bight. . . .' I went on to the detail for sea areas Dover, Wight, Portland and Plymouth; it was much the same thing. 'Variable, becoming south or south-westerly 3 or 4, moderate to poor with occasional fog patches.' That tied in. The winds would be coming clockwise round the centre of the high pressure, crossing the channel from the south.

Nothing to worry about there, I concluded. By the look of it, we could probably have counted on two or three more days of quiet weather, two anyway. Yet that was all quite academic now. This boat's sails and rigging were patently unfit for sea in their present state; unfit, at least, for anything other than the quietest conditions. Nor did I have an experienced crew to count on if things went suddenly sour. All the ingredients for a disaster at sea, in fact.

Yet the counter-arguments were even now refusing to lie down. Thus, there was no denying that the engine sounded happy enough, while I had already seen enough of John to realize that, however slim his experience, he was quick on the uptake. Certainly, I wouldn't have to tell him the same thing twice. As for the bilge pump, that was really just a matter of replacing the two missing bolts. Finally, there were neap tides running at the moment, so things would be pretty quiet round the headlands.

Somewhat alarmed at the direction my thoughts were taking, I looked across at John once more, at the order and neatness all around him. Not once had he tried to twist my arm, I acknowledged, despite the consequences that he knew would follow my rejection of the boat. Now, in all probability, it would take him two or three days to find another skipper, assuming he could find a responsible one at all – and by then it would all be too late. Obliged to return to work in another week, he would be left with a boat 300 miles away on the other side of the country, far beyond the reach of any attempt at maintenance and repair. That decided me.

'I'll tell you what I'm prepared to do, John,' I began, trying to ignore the sudden light of hope in his eyes. 'So long as the weather stays quiet we'll have a go at getting as far as Salcombe. After that we'll just have to wait and see. But you must understand that if the weather even shows a sign of changing for the worse, we shall have to put in to the nearest port we can find and call it a day. How about that?'

'That's grand,' he said, almost jumping down my throat. 'Even if we only get part of the way, at least it'll make it easier for me to reach her later.'

'Right, well in that case we've got a great deal of work to do before we see our bunks tonight. As soon as we drink this tea, we'll make a start.'

There's one thing, I thought, noting the mass of rubber fabric spilling out from the forecastle into the cabin. If we ever have to take to the dinghy, we certainly won't be cramped for room.

★   ★   ★

At 0730 hours next morning it looked as though our voyage was over almost before it had started. We were still inside the harbour nearly a mile from St Anthony's light, motor-sailing in the light breeze, when the engine note suddenly climbed in pitch. At the same time *Beatrice* started to fall away off the wind, most of her impulsion gone. It took me five minutes to discover what had gone wrong. Expecting some hideously complicated gearbox problem, I was relieved – at least in terms of our immediate aim – to find that it was nothing more than wear in the gear teeth. It was a matter of two or three minutes to secure the gear lever in the upper, 'ahead' position with a piece of rope so that it didn't jump out again. Heady with the success of my repair – if not with its sophistication – and heartened by the absence of water in the bilges, I decided to press on.

Once clear of the harbour I gave all my attention to the goal of achieving the highest sustainable speed in the prevailing light conditions of wind and sea. The result was much as I expected. Even with the engine to help her, it was clear that *Beatrice* took a dim view of anything over 5 knots. Without it, she barely touched 3. Our tactics were therefore clear. Given the over-riding need to get as far as we could in the shortest possible time, I decided I would leave the engine on, allowing just ten minutes every four hours for engine checks and cooling. It was just as well. As the land gradually receded northwards into the thick haze on the far side of the Dodman, so the wind dropped further. Never more than a light breeze from the south-west, now it became fitful, fluky in direction. Indeed, during the two hours that it took either side of lunchtime for the Eddystone lighthouse to materialize, harden into solidity, then fade away again astern, the wind disappeared completely. Gradually, though, it picked up again, doing just enough to keep the sails quiet as they hung broad out on the port beam.

It was just after 1800 hours when we came abeam of the Salcombe entrance, placid and inviting under the lee of Bolt Head. Until now I had deliberately said nothing about our next move, preferring to leave my options open until after the 1750 hours forecast. Warning only of a shallow depression still some 200 miles west of sea area Shannon, it was pedestrian enough to remove any remaining doubts from my mind.

'OK, John, so far, so good,' I announced. 'But now we come to the serious bit. Once we clear Start Point – that should be around 2000 hours when you come on watch – we shall have the whole of Lyme Bay to cross. And once committed, it won't be easy to turn back, particularly if a wind pipes up from the west. Still, in view of the forecast I'm prepared to have a go. I take it you have no objections?' John had no objections.

The increase in shipping off Start Point kept me in the cockpit well beyond the end of my watch. But I had already decided to linger anyway, at least until I had re-checked the compass deviation on this heading. I also wanted to delay my sight-taking for our departure from Start Point for as long as possible. After all, in this visibility the next land we would be likely to see would be St Catherine's Point, on the southern tip of the Isle of Wight. And that was 110 miles away.

It was nearly dark by the time I went below. Aware that the light on the chart table was not working, I reached up to switch on the central cabin light in order to rummage in my briefcase for my small torch. The next moment the whole light assembly had come away in my hands. Having found the torch I turned back to the hatchway, holding up the light assembly for John to see. 'Sorry,' I said. 'I hardly touched it, I promise.'

Totally inured by now to the sorry condition of his mistress,

John just smiled. 'Ay, I can see I've got a bit of work to do when I get her back home.'

'Right, I'm for bed,' I announced, handing him the torch. 'Don't forget; fishing boats, fishing floats – if you can see them coming – and call me if anything bigger comes near. You've got my watchkeeper's card there, haven't you?' He nodded.

Silly question, I thought as I climbed into my sleeping bag. After all, it was my home-made card of instructions for watchkeepers that had provided the framework for the inquisition to which I had been subjected ever since leaving Falmouth. Not a Yorkshireman for nothing, John's native hard-headedness had asserted itself with a vengeance. Sniffing a bargain in the shape of a captive tutor, his barrage of questions had been unceasing all day, running the whole gamut of seamanship, navigation, rule of the road and much, much more. At least, though, there had been something to show for my strained vocal cords, I admitted. For the subtlety of his questions had reassured me that John had done his homework, at least in theoretical terms. And that was now going to make it easier for me to sleep.

That night, and the day that followed it, passed almost without incident. Contained within a hazy cocoon never more than a mile in radius, often much less as we encountered the occasional fog patch, it was rarely indeed that anything other than fishing floats invaded our world. Now and then we saw the dim outline of a fishing smack, sometimes the distant sound of a fog-horn, once a Leander-class frigate exercising off Portland Bill; these diversions apart, we were left to ourselves. Then, to break the monotony, the wind picked up to a brisk Force 4 soon after midday, still from the south-west. Glad of the chance to give both the engine and our ears a rest, we watched the speed climb steadily to a dizzy 5½ knots.

It was almost exactly 24 hours after leaving Start Point when I realized that, if nothing else, at least *Beatrice*'s log and compass could be relied on. Having noted from my log entry at 2000 hours that there were now just four miles to go to St Catherine's Point, suddenly I heard John call out from his position at the tiller. 'There it is, Skipper!' he yelled excitedly. 'Dead ahead!'

I went up on deck. The lighthouse was just visible through the haze, fine on the port bow. 'Well, I'll be blowed!' continued

John, the relief apparent in his voice. 'Nothing at all since last night and now there it is, right on the button! Bloody marvellous, I call it!'

Not for the first time on this trip I could hear myself talking, 20 years ago. 'Not really, John,' I protested. 'I think you'll find Lady Luck had quite a bit to do with it, especially in view of the fact that we haven't been able to pick up St Catherine's Point on the radio direction finder for some reason. But at least it ought to give you confidence in dead reckoning. Provided you take the trouble to calculate leeway, work out the effect of the tidal streams properly – and pay attention to the steering, of course – it's amazing how accurate it can be, particularly with a reliable log. Anyway, this is just what we wanted, no time wasted in getting back on course.'

'What now?' he asked. I tried not to smile at his attempt to make the question sound casual.

'Well, we'll go on as we are past the Owers light and then close in towards the coast a bit, somewhere around Newhaven. After that it's all in the hands of the weather.'

The blinding strobe of the Outer Owers light was passing down our port side about a mile away as I went below for the 0033 hours forecast. Having noted the way that the barometer had been slowly falling since lunchtime, I wasn't too surprised at what I heard. Moments later I came out into the cockpit once more, wondering how best to break the news. Just tell it like it is, I decided.

'Sorry John, but we've come to the end of the road, I'm afraid. There's a south-westerly 5 or 6 on its way. Too much for us, I fear. We'll have to put into Newhaven.'

With the tide against us, it was well after dawn by the time we tied up in the little marina on the left of the main channel leading into Newhaven. I switched off the engine. 'Right John,' I said, lowering my voice in deference to the sudden quiet all around us. 'Let's have a cup of tea down below before we do anything else. It's time we had a little chat.'

Down in the cabin I opened the chart to its fullest extent, then started to explain the proposal that had been forming in my mind all the way from the Owers light. 'OK, let's start with the facts. On the one hand, the weather is likely to keep you here for two days at least, possibly three. But that will still leave you five or six days of holiday. Yes?' He nodded. 'On the other, as I explained before, I can't afford to wait that long myself. So what I propose is this. Because the delivery is not completed I am prepared to accept a reduced fee.' I named a sum. 'Use the money left over to do the following over the next three days. Got a pencil?' He started writing to my dictation. 'Right,' I said as he scribbled down the last one, 'once you've managed that lot – and three days should be quite enough provided you get your skates on – you have one of two choices. Either leave the boat here until you find someone to accompany you the rest of the way or, if the weather has really settled down again, day-sail it on your own in short hops from port to port. Now, what do you feel about that?'

John paused, shot a quick glance at me. 'Yes, I had already considered doing that, I must admit. You think I could manage it all right?'

'I'm sure you can. For one thing, you've picked up a great deal over the last 48 hours; for another, you've already told me you've done a bit of sailing in other boats in the Thames estuary. If I brief you in detail about the route and the timings that I recommend, I don't think you'll have any problem. Always provided, of course, that you don't take any chances with the weather; that's crucial.' I thought for a moment. 'Oh, and one other thing.'

'What's that?' asked John nervously, perhaps afraid that I was about to introduce some new complication at the last moment.

'When you finally get home – get rid of that flaming dinghy!'

★　　★　　★

A letter was waiting for me when I returned in late September from my last delivery of the season. I opened it.

'It's from John Thornton,' I said, conscious of a distinct feeling of relief as I started to read. After thanking me in equal measure for my help and for the refund, it proceeded to a triumphant, blow-by-blow account of his day-sailing adventures from Newhaven to Burnham, on the river Crouch. Nor was that all. At the end there was enough emphasis on maintenance matters to persuade me that the formidable *Beatrice* was, even then, having her face lifted. I showed the letter to Mary.

'That's nice,' she said. 'I'm glad you did what you did over the refund.' She paused. 'Mind, I know why.'

'Why?' I asked.

'Because that wasn't a young man called John Thornton at all. That was you, 25 years ago.'

Trust her to make it 25, I thought.

Chapter Seventeen

CONCLUSION

It was a cold day in March. Impatient to begin the first delivery of a new season, my crew and I had been frustrated by two days of equinoctial gale. At last, though, the centre of the depression had moved away in the night, pulling in behind it a vigorous bluster of heavy showers from the north-west. Buoyed up with the prospect of better things to come, we had decided to make a start.

In the grey gloom of morning we were still less than a mile from the harbour, pitching into a short, steep sea, when a black squall came racing up on the starboard bow. As we turned our backs to the first patter of rain, we were just in time to catch a sheet of spray full in the face. Recovering my balance, I looked in shocked silence at my crew as he stood there by the hatchway. Head lowered, shoulders hunched, arms hanging down, his body bent forwards slightly from the waist, he was doing his best to offer the least obstruction to the water as it ran off him. Then he shook himself, turning slightly towards me as he did so.

'What a life!' he said at last, darting an eloquent glance at me from beneath the dripping hood of his oilskins.

It was ten minutes before the rain stopped, and just two more before the sun came out. Quietly grateful for the first hint of warmth on the top of my head, and suddenly aware of the new world all about us, I twisted my body at the tiller to savour the scene. It was one of sharp contrasts. In front there was the broken confusion of the head sea, stretching in a carpet of green marble chippings towards the horizon. Then, as I turned slowly to starboard and my perspective changed, the sea seemed gradually to be subsiding, as though soothed by the first signs of more settled weather in the blue distance. Again a contrast close astern, where the rain had set the roofs in the town gleaming and glistening in the brilliant sunlight. And so, finally, to port;

to where, even now, the black raincloud was emptying itself in a ragged curtain onto the land below.

The sails were slatting. We had entered yet another back-eddy of wind coming off the land. Grudgingly aware that the last one had persisted for two or three minutes, I laid the boat over on to the port tack. Then, as my crew adjusted the sheets, I settled down at the tiller once more. Now there was a trickle of water running down the back of my neck. I sighed. Life at sea was rarely simple and straightforward, I decided. There was always something to attend to, something else to try your patience.

I thought about what the coming season would bring. As always, of course, it would be a balance; a mixture of good and bad. For every period of fine weather there would be a corresponding gale. For every exciting greyhound of a boat there would be a stubborn, heart-breaking sluggard. For every flying fish there would be a flying plate. Yet it was the people, whether owners or crew, who would once again tip the scales overwhelmingly in my favour. The people – and the sheer exhilaration of sailing.

All in all, I decided, my crew had summed it up very well. What a life!